LOUIS

PHILIP CALLOW

Louis

A LIFE OF
ROBERT LOUIS STEVENSON

CHICAGO   Ivan R. Dee

Library of Congress Cataloging-in-Publication Data:
Callow, Philip.
    Louis : a life of Robert Louis Stevenson / Philip Callow.
      p.   cm.
    Includes bibliographical references (p.) and index.
    ISBN 1-56663-343-5 (alk. paper)
     1. Stevenson, Robert Louis, 1850–1894.   2. Scots—Travel—Foreign countries—History—19th century.   3. Authors, Scottish—19th century—Biography. 4. Travelers—Scotland—Biography. I. Title.

PR5493 .C28 2001
828'.809—dc21
[B]   00-063916

To Bruce Mawdesley,
who ransacked his library for me

Whenever I find myself growing grim about
the mouth; whenever it is damp, drizzly
November in my soul; whenever I find myself
involuntarily pausing before coffin
warehouses, and bringing up the rear of every
funeral I meet; and especially whenever my
hypos get such an upper hand of me that it
requires a strong moral principle to prevent
me from deliberately stepping into the street,
and methodically knocking people's hats off—
then, I account it high time to get to sea
as soon as I can. This is my substitute for
pistol and ball. With a philosophical flourish
Cato throws himself upon his word;
I quietly take to the ship.

—Herman Melville, *Moby Dick*

Foreword

THERE HAS BEEN no shortage of books about Stevenson, and they keep coming. What is the fascination? Most people agree that there is something very attractive about him. Exhumations continue to appear as biographers take on the challenge of trying to make his bones live. Meanwhile his spirit goes marching on. "That man must be a poet," someone said of Tennyson, seeing him for the first time. Stevenson decided to look like a bohemian poet before he was twenty, when he was less interested in art than in the artistic life, which meant for him the freedom to live as one pleased. But what started out as adolescent rebellion remained with him as the role he felt happiest in. His temperament was romantic, lyrical. In *Catriona* he wrote, like the poet he felt himself to be, of "the romance of destiny."

What he called his "old gypsy nature" was his explanation for his vagabondage, but in fact—like Chekhov, like Lawrence—it was his illness that drove him to find better places for his fragile health. All the same, he was in flight from more than disease. I like to think of his spirit fretting to be set free, wanting to roam, to fly, away from that Presbyterian upbringing, out of the dreary, smug commercialism and blight of his century altogether. He propelled himself across Europe, over to New York, to North America's Pacific Coast, and then

to the South Seas, a road to the isles starting in Edinburgh and ending with him "head of a household of five whites and twelve
Samoans," a mama's boy burdened with heavy responsibilities.

He has been called too noble, too vain, outspoken but disin-
genuous, strict-principled but self-indulgent. *Treasure Island*, that
"treasure-hunt daydream," is, it seems, the masterpiece of a man who
preferred not to grow up, the inspiration for Barrie's *Peter Pan*. And it
is true that Stevenson became father to another man's children and
played with his stepson's toy soldiers on the floor.

When traveling becomes tangled with literature, journeys turn
into stories, odysseys, exoduses, pilgrimages, infernos. Yet paradoxically a journey is the opposite of a story. It is shapeless, often a chaotic
muddle, subject to accident and at the mercy of chance, especially if
you are in a small boat being driven by the wind. Its very unpre-
dictability is its attraction for the person Thoreau called the true
Traveler.

Stevenson was happiest at sea, when he felt astonishingly well
even in the worst squalls. His hired schooner, a mere speck in the
landless waste, felt more ark than boat—a God-given thing. Aboard
it he halted the cruel flooding of his lungs, and saw his rainbow. His
boyish delight in a voyage as an adventure that might lead anywhere,
maybe into a lagoon of the Hesperides itself, was what kept his soul
alive and sprang him from time to time out of the cage of a Calvinism
he would carry deep inside him to the end of his days.

Most of all he loved being afloat, adrift, on that huge expanse of
water the Pacific, largest of oceans, letting everything go hang, his
cramped, nagging past, the misery of hemmed-in modern life, the
grind of fiction-writing which kept his ménage fed. Even with his
wife ill with seasickness below deck, even with his Victorian mother
aboard, he felt rapture, like Melville and Jack London, those other
South Sea escapees, and his heart beat joyfully as the boat rose and fell
under his feet. He was free at last. On this enormous ocean that had
no end he wanted his voyage to go on forever, forever free. "They are a
romantic lot," wrote Henry James of the Stevensons, "and I delight in
them."

Blocking the way to any appreciation of the man and his work looms the legendary figure enshrined by his devotees, called by Isherwood, one of his debunkers, the Dying Wanderer. As a seafarer he was far from dying. Legends survive, along with the harsh reactions they produce, and I have sought to steer a path between these extremes. Studying Stevenson I have become acquainted with his various personae and been made aware of occasional sententiousness, yet I admire him now as greatly as I did at the beginning. In setting out to show a man dedicated to his craft I have avoided textual analysis of the work, painting a portrait for the intelligent reader with no specialized knowledge. I have dispensed with notes and an overlong bibliography—the full Stevenson bibliography is enormous—and have leaned heavily on the work of scholars.

Fundamentally honest, Stevenson owned up to his shortcomings as a novelist, though the unfinished novel he left at his death encourages us to see him as a great writer in the making, of greater stature than the man whose flair and energy delighted his contemporaries. Chesterton appreciated, as few did, the fastidiousness of his style, which had, he thought, a kind of swordsmanship about it, and he praised the courage of his sane levity and pugnacious optimism. Stevenson's whole position was expressed for Chesterton by that sentence in one of his letters: "Our civilization is a dingy ungentlemanly business; it drops so much out of a man."

For all his love of company he was restless, sometimes lonely. He died suddenly, in mid-flight, melancholy in the remote island kingdom he had made for himself, missing his friends, an exile longing for Scotland, still burning with passionate life in the sick body that tormented him.

Contents

LOUIS

PART I

CHAPTER ONE

Why Has God Got a Hell?

S TEVENSON WAS BORN Robert Lewis Balfour Stevenson on November 13, 1850, at 8 Howard Place, Edinburgh. After a spoiled and sickly childhood, educated at home or left to his own devices, he entered Edinburgh University at seventeen to read for a degree in science.

In most of the recollections of the young man, soon to be called Louis because it made him sound French, one has the impression of a person readily accessible, open to all and sundry, happy to spill all his secrets, fears, and troubles. This, together with his great charm, has been called Stevenson's lovableness. By all accounts he was a marvelous talker, a teller of tales, a nonstop monologuist. So it is remarkable to read that he could really listen, making himself wholly receptive as he concentrated intently.

One could say that to sit looking for the real Stevenson is to risk losing sight of him altogether. He was forever on the move, "by native instinct and temperament a rover," as he confessed, and if we want to know him truly we have to travel with him, be his shadow, follow in his footsteps. Everything would be stored in his interior baggage, as it is with all of us—in his case the peculiar isolation of his childhood, Cummy his nurse, his "unwholesome" background, a complex father who opposed as he loved him, an ailing mother, Edinburgh with its rigid streets and vile weather which "weighs on me like a curse," his rebellious friends and his cousin Bob, and that other city of the night, Old Town, with its proletarian taverns, dank alleys where the Middle Ages still lingered, its rabbit-warren slums and brothels where he became a pet of prostitutes and known as Velvet Coat.

When he was twenty-five he sat one evening in the family house in Heriot Row listening to William Seed, a New Zealander who had come to consult his father Thomas Stevenson on the subject of lighthouse engineering. Louis listened to Seed talking about his travels, explaining that he had been to Samoa to compile a report on trade in the islands for the New Zealand government. The young Stevenson couldn't hear enough about the South Seas, native customs, sights and sounds, plying their guest with questions late into the night. "Awfully nice man here tonight. Public servant—New Zealand," he wrote to his new friend Mrs. Sitwell. "Telling us all about the South Sea Islands till I was sick with desire to go there. . . ."

Bruce Chatwin, a recent denigrator of Stevenson who was at the same time uncomfortably aware of resemblances to himself, derided the Scot for being an aesthete who yearned for adventure, for, in Stevenson's own words, "a pure dispassionate adventure such as befell the great explorers." Considering other literary vagabonds such as Whitman, Rimbaud, and Hart Crane, Chatwin saw Rimbaud's marathon walks as a way of walking away from sickness and back to health. It is a startling idea.

Can Stevenson's wanderlust ever be emphasized enough? Was it perhaps lodged in his blood? His father, a seemingly staid and conscientious engineer, had a taste for adventure stories and traveled around the coasts and islands of Scotland as part of his profession: he built harbors and lighthouses. Robert, Louis's grandfather, built the Bell Rock lighthouse, and like his son traveled around the Scottish coast inspecting sites and supervising lighthouse and beacon construction. On his annual tour of the Northern Lights in 1814 he had Sir Walter Scott as a traveling companion. Before this, the Stevensons of the past belonged to a tradition of settlement and husbandry, modest farmers and millers in the Lowlands outside Glasgow. Margaret Balfour, Louis's mother, came like her husband from a large family. The Balfours were as eminent in their fields as was the Stevenson dynasty of engineers, and their line could be traced much farther back. Generations of doctors, philosophers, and clerics bring us to the Reverend Dr. Balfour, Margaret's father, minister of the Church of Scotland. She had brothers who became doctors: John saw service as a doctor to the East India Company and was the last man to leave Delhi in 1857 when the Indian Mutiny began. Another brother, James, emigrated to New Zealand and became a government engineer there.

When G. K. Chesterton set out to write his book on Stevenson, he said cunningly that he was interested in the story of his life, "but not exactly the story in his biography." What really interested him was the internal story. For him the clue lay in Edinburgh, or more precisely in Louis's childhood and youth. Those early years shaped him as nothing else did, and though the details have become very familiar to us, their importance cannot be denied.

Stevenson's engineer father was a man of some complexity, not at all the ogrelike Victorian father one assumes from a first impression. For any account of him to make sense, the story of Scotland's recent past needs to be invoked, since he embodied many of its contradictions. Living inside him were strands which the son soon came to know firsthand: the fervor of John Knox; Calvin his mentor; the National Covenant, signed, according to tradition, on February 28, 1638—Covenanters were said to have signed with their own blood to demonstrate the depth of their feelings; the eleven-year rule of Scotland by the Covenanters under Argyll and their avowed aim to create a nation in God's name, ruling the nation by Presbyteries and making church attendance compulsory, raising a Covenanting army to wage a holy war against the English.

By the time Louis was seven the family had moved from the edge of New Town to the very heart of it, at 17 Heriot Row. Thomas Stevenson was representative of a professional class demanding more space and light, and only eighty years before Louis's birth the handsome Georgian squares and fine crescents of New Town were being built, leaving the Old Town around the castle to degenerate into the dangerous slum it became, with its criminals and whores, its medieval wynds and courts, and Britain's first high-rises, ten-story tenements crammed with starving tenants. But Thomas Stevenson and his engineering forebears were shaped by a factor that affected so many Scotsmen after the Treaty of Union of 1707, when Edinburgh lost its status as a national capital. Out of the bitterness of this defeat rose a determination to prevent Edinburgh from becoming a backwater, and the Scottish Enlightenment with its lawyers, philosophers, doctors, and writers changed the town into an "Athens of the North." In part a product of outrage, the Enlightenment carried with it much patriotic nostalgia.

"First and foremost," writes the historian Tom Steel, "the Scottish Enlightenment was the culmination of a national system of education that had its roots in the far-off days of the Reformation. By the middle of the eighteenth century the desire of Calvinists like Knox to have a school in every parish was becoming a reality, certainly in Lowland Scotland, and the fruits of a nation's near-obsession with education showed themselves in the late eighteenth century and well into the nineteenth." The failure of the Forty-five Rebellion (1745) and the departure of Bonnie Prince Charlie the Young Pretender made the English, who assumed all Scots were Jacobites, more determined than ever to undermine Scottish culture. After the slaughter at Culloden, the victorious Hanoverian Cumberland earned himself the nickname "Butcher" for his savage reprisals. Members of Parliament in London considered drastic action, some even advocating the sterilization of all "Jacobite" women. Others thought the Highlands should be cleared and repopulated with people from the south. A vicious act passed by the British government and not repealed for forty years forbade the wearing of Highland dress. Highlanders had already been banned from carrying weapons, even the dirk, primarily a utensil for eating. Emigration began in earnest as a way of escaping a Britain hostile to the Highlanders. Dr. Johnson, on tour in 1773, saw that "Their pride has been crushed by the heavy hand of a vindictive conqueror," and by laws which "make every eye bear witness to sub-jection." Now that the Young Pretender was vanquished, Scotland was effectively severed from her old connections with France and joined to England's Protestantism. Modern Scotland was about to emerge from these afflictions and changes.

The rise of the Scottish Enlightenment was a deliberate attempt to save a culture in danger of extinction, one which went back a thousand years. The nobility in Scotland, finding themselves without a parliament, moved south in large numbers in a search for other sources of power. The new class that emerged to fill the political and social vacuum included men of learning and letters, the "literati" of this Enlightenment, who set out to rival England and be its intellectual superiors.

Any array of names illuminating the Enlightenment would be headed by David Hume, born in Edinburgh in 1711. His informal education and his belief in knowledge gained from experience would have been an example to Thomas Stevenson as well as to his son. In France for three years as a young man, Hume wrote his *Treatise on Human Nature*, spent time in London, published his *Political Discourses*, and became keeper of the Advocates Library in Edinburgh. His *History* brought him fame, and he returned to London on two occasions, each time ending bored by those "barbarians who inhabit the banks of the Thames." Proud of being a Scot, Hume spoke with a dialect broader than Burns's. Braid Scots was widely spoken throughout Lowland Scotland: it had its own vocabulary, pronunciation, and idiom, and Robert Burns fashioned a vigorous poetic language from it.

This is not the place for a history of Scottish culture, but mention should be made of a Scot of even greater importance than Hume. Adam Smith's *An Inquiry into the Nature and Causes of the Wealth of Nations*, published more than two hundred years ago, has never been out of print. A philosopher and economist, he was born in Kirkcaldy in Fife in 1723. In Tom Steel's words, "He left behind a book that, apart from the Bible and *Das Kapital*, perhaps did more than any other to change the Western world." Victorian society with its unrestrained materialism was modified by it, and its influence has reached modern Japan. *The Wealth of Nations* was envisaged as a blueprint for Britain, a way of regulating the post–Industrial Revolution philosophy of laissez-faire for the common good.

A man of the "literati" for whom Stevenson felt a powerful affinity, oppressed as he was in his own youth by a repressive culture which seemed out to "fleg [frighten] mankind frae being good," was Robert Fergusson, born exactly a century before Louis. At twenty he wrote his first poem, "The Daft Days," about the local characters of the filthy Edinburgh streets, and then "Auld Reekie," a masterpiece celebrating the city's most unspeakable citizens, policed after a fashion by the City Guard or "black banditi." By twenty-four his hectic flame had burned out: he died in 1774 in a madhouse. Stevenson's hero-worshiping had its element of morbidity: more than once he thought his own life would be as brief. He admired Fergusson's recklessness and his attack on hypocrisy for their own sakes when he read such lines as

> . . . there's an unco dearth o' grace
> That has nae mansion but the face,
> And never can obtain a part
> In benmost corner of the heart.
> Why should religion make us sad,
> If good frae virtue's to be had?

In his thirties, certain he was going to die, Louis the once-wonderful boy wrote to his friend Henley of his "Fergussonian youth." At the end the ghost was still there at his elbow, the doomed poet born in the same town as himself, wild as he, "both sickly," whispering from the madhouse like a warning.

BEFORE WE CONSIDER Louis's father and the remarkable dynasty of engineers to which he belonged, let us meet Margaret Isabella Balfour, the woman he was fortunate enough to meet and marry. A photograph of her with Louis aged four, looking girlish and chubby, shows a mother little more than a girl, tall and attractive, straight hair parted severely, concentrating on staying still. She married at nineteen in 1848. Louis was her only child. Very different in character from her husband, she adored her son, and he remembered how he loved to be with her, running upstairs to the top flat of their second home, "both of them singing 'We'll all go up to Gatty's room, to Gatty's room,' Gatty being contracted for Grandpapa, my mother's father, who was coming to stay with us." The little boy was called Lou, or "Smout," Scots for any small creature, first by his rather severe father and then by his mother and other members of the family. He was clearly precocious from infancy. His mother in her diary of July 1853 recorded: "Smout's favorite occupation is making a church; he makes a pulpit with a chair and a stool; reads sitting, and then stands up and sings by turns." This must have pleased her simple piety, as did his wish to have the Bible read to sheep and horses, who were ignorant of God. Apart from the influence of the parents, Cummy's teaching was having an obvious effect. "Cummy" was Alison Cunningham, the family nurse, who had joined the household when Louis was eighteen months old. Though she soon made him as fanatically religious as herself, Cummy had to deal with the searching questions of this highly intelligent tiny child. He wanted to know, for instance, why God had made Mary Magdalene "naughty," and, even more to the point, "Why has God got a Hell?"

The family now lived at 1 Inverleith Terrace, a larger house than that at Howard Place but more exposed to Edinburgh's storms and fogs. Stormy nights, with gales ripping at the roof and casements, would tip the fearful boy into nightmares which Cummy had helped to bring about with her gleeful tales of Hell, Evil, and Damnation. A poem, "Childhood," refers grimly to "The long black passage up to bed."

Three years later the family were on the move again, alarmed by doctors advising somewhere less likely to encourage the child's feverish colds and coughs. The Stevensons moved this time to another Georgian terrace, 17 Heriot Row, a south-facing street in the city's

New Town. This was the elegant, genteel environment Louis would know through childhood and adolescence.

The sweet-natured, companionable, and optimistic Margaret Stevenson, called Maggie in the family, was the youngest of thirteen children of the Reverend Lewis Balfour, who spoke broad Scots yet was considered a gentleman, and had married the daughter of the minister of Galston. Margaret was therefore a child of the church on both sides. Her father was a terrifying figure to his children, though surprisingly tender at times, like his son-in-law. Sickly as a youth, he went to the Isle of Wight in an attempt to cure a week chest. He passed this ill health on to his daughter, and probably through her to Louis, whose first serious illness at twenty-nine months, the first of many, was diphtheria. Although the weak lungs which always plagued him could no doubt be traced to the Balfours, the medical history of the Stevensons was also suspect.

Maggie herself, separated from a husband often away traveling on business, suffered poor health from the time of her son's birth through to 1862. This meant that Cummy became to all intents and purposes the boy's "second mother," to use his own words, nursing him devotedly through many a night of feverish illness. When he was thirty he recalled hellish childhood dreams, waking with "my knees and chin together, my soul shaken, my body convulsed with agony." Sometimes his highly nervous temperament would bring on attacks of hysteria. One story goes that he locked himself in his room by accident and wept hysterically, thinking he was trapped forever. A servant was dispatched to bring a locksmith while the boy's father did his best to comfort him by talking gently through the door. Any real stability during Louis's formative years was provided by Cummy, even though paradoxically she was a morbid influence. His tribute to her devotion is moving to this day. "She was more patient than I can suppose of an angel: hours together she would help console me in my paroxysms; and I remember with particular distinctness how she would lift me out of bed and take me, rolled in blankets, to the window, whence I might look forth to the blue night starred with street lamps and see where the gas still burned behind the windows of other sickrooms . . . where also, we told each other, there might be sick little boys and their nurses waiting, like us, for the morning."

It would be easy to condemn Cummy as a bigot, with her hatred of "Popery," of the Continent and its depravity, of playing cards (the devil's picturebooks), of the theatre, of novels. She poured stories of hellfire, ghosts, and persecuted Covenanters into the defenseless child's head, giving him a taste for melodrama and a dread of the night. Only when the country carts clattered in over the cobbles and he heard the drovers bawling and whips cracking around the horses did he know it was daybreak and feel safe again. Cummy's religion was the narrowest Covenanting form of Scottish Presbyterianism, but he remembered her singing and dancing for him, and above all her readings from the Bible. The last time they met, he told her that it was she who gave him a passion for drama. "Me, Master Lou?" she answered. "I never put foot inside a playhouse in my life." "Ay, woman," he said, "but it was the grand dramatic way ye had of reciting the hymns."

Frank McLynn in his biography writes tellingly of the boy's yearning for the presence of his real mother, instead of the absent invalid always in bed till noon. "Goodnight, my jewellest of mothers," he has been recorded as saying. Vowing to call her "mother" so that he remembers "to do it when I'm a big man" gives us a poignant reminder of his sense of loss and his longing for maternal love.

Any account of Louis's father should begin with his grandfather, who died in 1850 just before Robert Louis was born. Robert Stevenson, the grand lighthouse engineer overshadowing all others, entered the virgin profession because of his stepfather, Thomas Smith of Edinburgh. Smith, a shipowner who dealt in lamps and oils, must also have been an engineer of sorts, since the newly created Board of Northern Lighthouses took him on to improve the coal flares in lighthouses by substituting his own oil lamps and reflectors. The stepson, Robert, learned his trade from Smith, and then went far beyond him in accomplishment, as well as cementing the relationship by marrying Jean, his stepfather's daughter by a previous marriage.

Robert's achievements were indeed extraordinary. As first engineer of the Board for forty-seven years he was involved in the building of twenty-three lighthouses in Scotland, introduced his own invention of intermittent lights, and supervised the building of roads, bridges, harbors, canals, and railways. He left his own written account of the construction of the Bell Rock lighthouse, finished before Thomas Stevenson was born. This was his great work, built with crude equipment on a half-submerged reef against all odds. After he died his son Alan went on to raise the Skerryvore lighthouse in 1844, called by Robert Louis in his memorial essay "the noblest of all deep-sea lights." Thomas served under him in this enterprise, and then joined with him in the creation of two further deep-sea lights, Chickens and Dhu Heartach. The brothers went on to build twenty-seven shore lights and twenty-five beacons, and to build many harbors and improve rivers in England as well as Scotland.

In his memorial essay, his son proudly extols Thomas's other achievements, his research into the propagation and reduction of waves, his study of storms—"his sworn adversaries"—and his inventions, unprotected by patents. One was the louver-boarded screen for the protection of meteorological instruments. But his chief claim to fame rests on his pioneering work in the field of optics, bringing to perfection the revolving light his father had initiated. As a result, wrote his son, "In all parts of the world a safer landfall awaits the mariner." Louis went on to relate an anecdote which he was glad to repeat, of a Peruvian who admired the works of Stevenson—but he had never heard of the author of *Dr. Jekyll*: it was the engineer he had in mind.

Thomas Stevenson's firm was known worldwide; they were consulting engineers to the Indian, New Zealand, and Japanese lighthouse boards. In Germany he was called "the Nestor of lighthouse illumination." Honor was longer coming in France, but he was finally recognized and esteemed, as indeed he was in his small circle in Edinburgh: "few men were more beloved . . . where he breathed an air that pleased him, and wherever he went, in railway carriages or hotel smoking rooms, his strange, humorous vein of talk and his transparent honesty raised him up friends and admirers." But in London he was virtually unknown. He seldom went there, and only as part of his work. He refused to dine out, went to the same restaurant, same church, same theatre, and was glad to leave.

Thomas's education was so scrappy that his writer son praised him for succeeding in spite of being so ill-equipped. He was no mathematician, which was curious to say the least for someone practicing applied science. In order to deal with the formulas for the instruments he invented he had to enlist the help of physicists such as Professor Swan, his cousin, and his friend Professor Tait, both of St. Andrews University. As for the lack of patents, this was a matter of principle. Like his father before him he looked on his work as belonging to the nation. All the same he was prosperous enough to employ servants, collect furniture, prints, and pictures, and live in a substantial house. He had never had Greek but retaught himself Latin after leaving school, where he had been "a mere consistent idler." Writing this comment must have pleased the son who wrote in his essay "An Apology for Idlers": "Idleness so called, which does not consist in doing nothing, but in doing a great deal not recognized by the dogmatic formularies of the ruling class, has as good a right to state its position as industry itself." Whitman would have applauded. Natures whose tendency was to brood, like his own and his father's, should, he thought, be left to do so.

Thomas Stevenson read theology voraciously, especially Lactantius, the third-century convert to Christianity. He was a strict adherent to the Scottish Kirk yet thought himself unworthy to be an office-bearer. He never tired of rereading Scott's *Guy Mannering*. Robert Louis called his father's sense of his own unworthiness morbid, like his dwelling on death and the brevity of life. Unlike his wife, who was essentially the peacemaker, equable in temperament, there was a Celtic melancholy flowing under Thomas's thoughts, many of which he kept to himself. He was both stern and soft, the blend wholly Scottish, a man who had been, in his son's words, "an idle eager sentimental youth" whose imagination was romantic, who made up stories during bouts of insomnia that were full of "ships, roadside inns, robbers, old sailors, and commercial travelers before the era of steam." When Louis was enduring his many disturbed nights, his father would sometimes sit at his bedside and slip into his unfolding mind these tales of his own invention. Later, when Louis came to compose and read out the first version of *Treasure Island* in installments for the entertainment of his stepson, Thomas was one of the book's first admirers, to such an extent that he was ready with suggestions of his own as the story developed. This was when father and son were as reconciled as they would ever be, long after the violent family rows that had nearly shipwrecked them for life. The richness of material Stevenson had to draw on came not only from his father but his whole Scottish experience, as he makes clear to Henry James: "A Scottish child hears much of shipwreck, outlying iron skerries, pitiless breakers and great sealights; much of heathery mountains, wild clans and hunted Covenanters. . . ."

The harmony between father and son was hard-won. More than one only child has come to see himself as a rival for his mother's love. When the tension between Louis and Thomas was at its height, he wrote to his friend Mrs. Sitwell: "Today in Glasgow my father went off on some business, and my mother and I wandered about for two hours. We had lunch together, and were very merry over what people at the restaurant would think of us—mother and son they could not have supposed us to be." One is reminded of Paul Morel's delight in his closeness to his mother in *Sons and Lovers*.

Thomas Stevenson was "passionately attached, passionately prejudiced," a man of extremes, short-tempered, genial in company, handicapped by having no firm foothold in life. Without his wife's steadying nature he would have been rudderless. He was a strict Tory who had radical views, and his gallantry toward women led him to favor a marriage law under which any woman could have a divorce on demand, but no man should ever be granted one "on any ground whatever." As if this wasn't extraordinary enough, he founded a Magdalen Mission in Edinburgh and was its main supporter behind the scenes. Other eccentricities included a whimsical belief that dogs had souls, which meant that he felt obliged to greet any stray he met in the street. He could also be seen stopping schoolchildren carrying books to or from school, telling them to learn only what interested them, or if nothing did to avoid book learning altogether. He was an intense, nervous, sometimes anxiety-ridden man, eager to do good and fearing his own inadequacies. When his son broke away from the church, the clashes between them were prolonged and bitter.

If the sickly child in his nursery high in the house felt bewildered by a praying father who gave dinner parties and played cards—which Cummy warned were the work of the devil—what could he have made of this droll man with a "freakish" sense of humor who joined with Cummy in stimulating his interest in drama, especially in the form of miniature theatre? Then highly popular, these miniature stages, with cutout actors and actresses to be pushed on and off stage with tabs of card, could be bought at stationery stores. The eager little boy was soon an addict. Another enthusiast was Jack Yeats, the artist brother of the poet, who not only gobbled up the lurid melodramas, often of pirates and brigands, but was soon writing his own plays for miniature theatre, doing everything himself, drawing the characters and mounting them on cards and coloring them. In Jack Yeats's day as in Stevenson's, most successful plays, if they were suitable, ended up in the miniature theatre. Behind this magical world of cheap melodrama stood a Mr. Skelt, a name to conjure with, whose idea for a juvenile drama was a toy theatre with texts provided, and with the scenery and characters ready to be scissored out and colored. After Skelt, the material was taken over by Parks, Webb, Redington, and Pollock, other producers.

Louis was given his first Skelt for his sixth birthday. The flavor and excitement of it all is captured in his essay "A Penny Plain and Twopence Colored," wherein he lists some of the texts, mostly anonymous, which he avidly collected: *Aladdin, The Red Rover, The Blind Boy, The Old Oak Chest, The Wood Demon, Jack Sheppard, The Miller and His Men, The Smuggler, The Forest of Bondy, Robin Hood, The Waterman, My Poll and My Partner Joe, Three-Fingered Jack, The Terror of Jamaica, The Floating Beacon, The Wreck Ashore, Sixteen-Strong Jack*: on and on they went, "this roll-call of stirring names," a kaleidoscope from a childhood full of changing pictures, echoing in his mind as they receded into the past.

He would go with Cummy and later by himself to a stationer's shop at the corner of Antigua Street and Union Street on Leith Walk, feasting his eyes on the theatre displayed in the window, all in working order, "with a forest set, a combat, and a few robbers carousing in the slides," together with other plays in heaps jumbled up together. Then came the dive inside, to an interior that was dark, smelling of Bibles, and Mr. Smith behind the counter, exasperated by a child too excited to make a choice. Stevenson writes with characteristic honesty that the purchase and the first half-hour at home, "was the summit. Thenceforth the interest declined little by little. The fable, as set forth in the play-book, proved to be not worthy of the scenes and characters: what fable would not?" And before long these childish disappointments were leading him to the dreaming of his own fables.

This now forgotten genre probably originated in London, which had shops specializing in all the trappings, and when Stevenson came to write his essay he realized he had gone south without ever leaving his playroom. Skelt, he remembered, had a strong flavor of England . . . "the hedgerow elms, the thin brick houses, windmills, glimpses of the navigable Thames—England, when I came to visit it, was only Skelt made evident: to cross the border was, for the Scotsman, to come home to Skelt; there was the inn-sign and there the horse-trough, all foreshadowed in the faithful Skelt."

G. K. Chesterton, one of Stevenson's most astute critics, had no doubt that the story of the man begins with what Louis liked to call Skeltery or Skeltdom. "What am I? what are life, art, letters, the world," he declared, "but what my Skelt has made them? He stamped himself upon my immaturity. The world was plain before I knew him, a poor penny world: but soon it was all colored with romance." As a small child, a whole series of ailments kept him inside his own home, and more often than not in his own bedroom. Because he was far from robust he was guarded from the world outside, though he could hear it, see it from his window, and at night fear it. In a strikingly unsentimental poem, "The Land of Counterpane," he does his best to make light of it all:

> When I was sick and lay a-bed
> I had two pillows at my head.
> And all my toys beside me lay
> To keep me happy all the day. . . .
>
> And sometimes sent my ships in fleets
> All up and down the sheets:
> Or brought my trees and houses out,
> And planted cities all about.
>
> I was the giant great and still
> That sits upon the pillow-hill,
> And sees before him, dale and plain,
> The pleasant land of counterpane.

If we think it absurd to say that the images in Stevenson's stories stand out in sharp outline and are in fact all edges, because as a child he began cutting figures out of cardboard, we should read what the wily Chesterton has to say. Stevenson was attracted to the angularity of woodcuts. His maritime figures, commented Chesterton, are all edges, "and they stand by the sea, that is the edge of the world." There is a clarity about a Highland tale by Stevenson. His mountains have little mist, just as his Celts have nothing of Celtic twilight about them. He wanted details to stand out, like the hilt of a sword or a feather sticking out of a hat. Even when he set scenes at night, like the duel in *The Master of Ballantrae*, the emphasis falls on the stiff frost rather than the dark: the candles as rigid as swords, the candle flames as sharp as the stars. His instinct as a craftsman, wrote Chesterton, was that of a man cutting wood, sharp and clean. And he loved splashes of color, as if always conscious of the red gold and blue seas and azure skies of Skeltdom that had so affected him with their simplicity. "How the roads wander, how the castle sits upon the hill, how the sun radiates from behind the cloud, and how the congregated clouds themselves uproll, as stiff as bolsters."

Poetry is never far away in Stevenson, any more than the sea is: and the Skelt influence comes out in him as frugality—not a word one associates with so copious a writer. But he was Scottish to the bone, which means frugal, as well as generous to a fault. And the human wisdom in his work, always lying under the rejoicing of a child which he hung on to all his life, was something out of his own individual temperament that he added on to Skelt rather than found in it. Sickly as he was, this physical frailty left him stranded behind thick walls with a toy theatre and toy soldiers, while outside the abominable Edinburgh weather was either blowing or raining when it wasn't foggy or clogging the streets with snow. The city on its narrow neck of land, exposed to huge winds tearing in from the Atlantic on the west and the North Sea to the east, ironbound in winter and uneasy in summer, with its coal fires and granite houses, had the cold of Puritanism settling in the blood of its citizens in all seasons, and for the time being the isolated boy was happily oblivious. What we can at the very least say about the advent of Mr. Skelt is that it was the first of Stevenson's great escapes.

CHAPTER TWO

The Noise of Pens Writing

T HE SPIRIT OF PLACE was as vividly alive in Stevenson as in any writer one could name, and his native city in all its aspects would live in his imagination wherever he was. Because of his house-bound early years it was as an outsider that he ventured into the Edinburgh streets as a boy. He could almost have been a foreigner. The onslaught of movement and noise must have fascinated as well as frightened him.

In his teens a favorite spot from which to gaze around was Arthur's Seat—the volcanic rock at the opposite end of the Royal Mile to the castle—as exciting "as the hoariest summit of the Alps." Not surprisingly, this youngest member of a family associated with lights for seamen was always sensitive to the lights of Edinburgh, as he was to the sight of water. As McLynn points out, only San Francisco gave more views of the sea from its various vantage points than Edinburgh. And soon the boy was conscious of the unique mingling of town and country, for

Into no other city does the sight of the country enter so far; if you do not meet a butterfly, you shall certainly catch a glimpse of far-away fields upon your walk and the place is full of theatre tricks in the way of scenery. You peep under an arch, you descend stairs that look as if they would land you in a cellar, you turn to the back window of a grimy tenement in a lane—and behold! you are face to face with distant and bright prospects. You turn a corner, and there is the sun going down into the Highland hills. You look down an alley and see ships tacking for the Baltic.

The hills of Fife could be seen on a clear day to the north, where the streets ran down from the corner of Heriot Row and Howe Street to the Firth of Forth. The big parallel streets of New Town, rationally laid out—Queen Street, George Street, and Princess Street—bordered Princess Street Gardens, lying below the great bulk of the Castle which stood as if guarding the slums of Old Town. Waverly Station at the east end of Princess Street with its North Bridge—called by Stevenson "that windiest spot, or high altar, in this northern temple of the winds"—connected the Old Town with the New. Away to the east was Holyrood and the lion shape of Arthur's Seat, while Dean village lay westward by the Water of Leith. Colinton, where his mother's father lived, now a northwest suburb of the city but then a village, was close to the Pentland Hills and would soon be a place Louis loved to visit. The house was always filled with children and next to the church where his grandfather was minister.

Louis was now an author at the age of six, dictating to his mother a juvenile account of Moses, illustrating it with his own drawings, with every Israelite smoking a pipe. From escaping into Skeltdom he now broke out of the closed world of the delicate to the Reverend Lewis Balfour's manse at Colinton, as normal an environment as he could have wished. There were always at least half a dozen cousins to play with as he regained his health in the open air. His essay "The Manse" in *Memories and Portraits* sets the scene. "It was a place in that time like no other: the garden cut into provinces by a great hedge of beech, and overlooked by the church and the terrace of the churchyard, where the tombstones were thick, and after nightfall "spunkies" might be seen to dance, at least by children; flower-pots lying warm in sunshine; laurels and the great yew making elsewhere a pleasing horror of shade; the smell of water rising from all round, with an added tang of papermills; the sound of water everywhere and the sound of mills—the wheel and the dam singing their alternate strains. . . ."

The little boy was half terrified by the old man and sometimes astonished by his sudden impulses of tenderness, when he took Louis in his arms and kissed him after hearing him recite a psalm. In his essay Stevenson recalls seeing him for the last time in his tenth year, his grandfather having walked too far in the teeth of an east wind—a rather fearsome patriarch, hunched near the dining room fire with his white hair, pale face, and bloodshot eyes. His daughter Jane gave him a dose of Gregory's powder, a horrible-tasting medicine which made the old man pull a face. Then he sat as innocent as a child munching a "barley-sugar kiss." When the boy's aunt went to give her nephew a sweet she was stopped at once. No medicine, no sweet. The Reverend Balfour didn't believe in spoiling children.

The old man's thirteen children were scattered over the world, and the boy saw Indian pictures on the walls. Only once did his childhood terrors return, when he was petrified by a violent thunderstorm, and crouched with his cousins under the dining room table. The adult Stevenson remembered as well the river in flood, and his father carrying him wrapped in a blanket through the rain to look at it. Mainly though it was the sunshine and the happiness that stayed in his memory. And the games played with his cousins, especially Willie and Henrietta, on the grass by the water, frightening themselves as children do by imagining a dead man peering at them over the graveyard wall. Louis marched over the lawn pretending to stalk game with an imaginary gun, and they played pirates by the swift-flowing millstream, trying to raise up the devil with incantations from Skelt. His poem "Keepsake Mill" from *A Child's Garden of Verses* is a little hymn of joy commemorating those days.

The household was run by Dr. Balfour's daughter Jane, left nearly blind and deaf as a girl by a fall from a horse and now the "family maid of all work." She had been the chatelaine of the manse since her mother's death in 1844. She spoiled Louis when her father wasn't around, and bought him his first toy soldiers. To the south of Colinton rose the Pentland Hills, which would later mean so much to him. From up there you could see the sea and the mountains, and far down in the lowlands was Edinburgh, "making a great smoke on clear days and spreading her suburbs about her." Trains crawled over the landscape, ships tacked in the Firth, and always there were clouds, sometimes "as large as a parish," driven along by the wind.

"The sight of the outer world refreshed and cheered me," he wrote in "Memoirs of Himself," remembering childhood terrors and black nights, and sickness. Even learning to read at seven he put down to a malady, looking over the pictures of an illustrated paper while recovering from a gastric fever. Then, still only seven, he met a cousin at Heriot Row who would influence his future life profoundly. Robert Alan Mowbray Stevenson, called "Bob" to avoid confusing him with Louis, was the son of Alan Stevenson, the engineer who collaborated with his younger brother Thomas on the Skerryvore lighthouse. Alan succumbed to an unnamed "nervous illness" at the age of forty-five and withdrew from active life for the rest of his days. Bob had a sister, Katherine, but it was Bob who fascinated Louis. Stevenson described him later as "an imaginative child . . . more unfitted for the world, as was shown in the event, than an angel fresh from heaven." The two boys played endlessly together, with tin soldiers and Skelt's theatre, coloring pictures and dressing up as extravagant characters. They invented kingdoms for each other, and these territories even took over their breakfasts. Bob's porridge, heaped with sugar, was a country buried under snow, while Louis used milk on his to create ravines and valleys.

Apart from this intense friendship Louis was a solitary lad, and after the death of Dr. Balfour in 1860 that paradise was no longer open to him. The frequency of his illnesses increased. In the autumn of 1858 he was too weak to sit up in bed for five weeks. He had chickenpox a year later. In 1861 he was ill for six weeks with whooping cough. Before this, in the autumn of 1857, he was enrolled at a preparatory school at Cannonmills. Cummy took him and fetched him back, but endless coughs and colds meant that he was often absent. His first day at school was one he would always remember. How was it that everything wore such a look of sadness that his heart was pierced—"the long empty road, the lines of tall houses, the church upon the hill, the woody hillside garden"—as if everything friendly and familiar had died? He seemed afflicted with a kind of autism. Cummy was no help. If his socks were wet on arrival she would insist on changing them in front of his schoolmates, which hardly made him popular. With the unerring instinct of the young they saw at a glance that he was odd. He longed for the safety of known surroundings which he had thought before as like a cage. Withdrawn from this school he went to somewhere nearer, Mr. Henderson's in India Street, only a stone's throw from his home. Always he would be rescued from the agonies of strangeness by falling ill. Finally, when he was eleven, he entered the Edinburgh Academy, founded by Sir Walter Scott among others in 1824 for the education of gentlemen's sons. This was interrupted two years later when his parents went south to Menton for the sake of his mother's health, and in 1863 he was deposited at a boarding school at Spring Grove, Isleworth, Middlesex. A maternal aunt lived nearby, and her sons were at the same school.

Louis stuck it out until November 12 of that year, then wrote unhappily to his father, "My dear Papa, you told me to tell you whenever I was miserable. I do not feel well and wish to get home. Do take me with you." At the end of the term he was taken to the Riviera and never went back. He was still there with his mother when his father had to return early to Scotland.

Earlier this same year he had been abroad with his family on a trip through Italy, and on to Austria and Germany. Though they visited Genoa, Naples, Rome, Florence, and Venice before journeying down the Rhine, he was apparently impervious to most of the sights, and friends later found it hard to believe he had ever been to Italy. France was his great love. In Italy he was ill on the coach after leaving Rome, and Cummy improvised a bed for him out of cushions. In Florence he was overcome with exhaustion, and Cummy wrote in her diary: "Dear Lew was very much knocked up, but he was able to appear at breakfast next morning. He is not well, poor boy, but I am thankful he is able to be out of bed."

Though always fond of her, Louis was no longer under her thumb. He would make fun of her at the expense of her bigotry. In Nice, Cummy was suspicious of some priests "doing something in a corner curtained off." What infernal popery was this? In fact they were hearing confessions. Louis told her they were playing cards for money, so that her shocked diary entry read, "Is it not very melancholy?"

He had long nourished an ambition to be a soldier when he grew up but gradually realized he would never be strong enough. Attempts to make friends with schoolmates invariably failed because he was useless at sports, and in any case he looked distinctly strange. Also they didn't trust his mouth, about which played something "a little tricksy and mocking." He did once attempt to approach a lame boy, no doubt thinking that as misfits they had something in common, and was sworn at for his pains. One school acquaintance, Baildon, told Stevenson's cousin and first biographer Graham Balfour that "In body he was assuredly badly set up. His limbs were long, lean and spidery, and his chest flat, so as almost to suggest some malnutrition, such sharp corners did his joints make under his clothes. But in his face this was belied. His brow was oval and full over soft brown eyes. . . . The whole face had a tendency to an oval Madonna-like type."

Driven into isolation by a cosseted childhood and an inability to make ordinary connections with others, he dreamed of living in a dream house with his soldiers and had even spotted the very place in the Esterel Mountains outside Cannes, "a pretty house in an orange garden at the angle of the bay. . . ." The congestion of the lungs he was now experiencing, leading to bouts of bleeding throughout his life, led many to believe he was consumptive. At sixteen he was enrolled at one final school before university, Mr. Thompson's, for boys as delicate as himself who had fallen far behind in their learning. It was in Frederick Street, close to home. There was no homework, and afternoon sessions were cut short to allow for preparation of the next day's lessons. The one friend he made there, H. B. Baildon, joined with him to compile a magazine. This was the year in which his first literary effort came to fruition, an outline of the seventeenth-century Covenanters rising. His father, pleased by the choice of subject and his son's determined work, had a hundred copies of the pamphlet printed at his own expense. Before this, during a period with his mother and a private tutor in Torquay, he drafted an early version of *Deacon Brodie*, and wrote a story, "The Plague Seller." Having more time at Thompson's than other schoolboys, he wrote large quantities of doggerel verse. But since the age of six he had been showing signs of an obsession with language. He told his mother once he had dreamt of hearing "the noise of pens writing."

Apart from subjects he chose to study at this last school—French, Latin, and geometry—he went on with his own reading, as he had been doing for years. Shakespeare was familiar to him from an early age, when his mother read *Macbeth* aloud. Browsing in his father's library he came on Scott, and discovered Dumas somewhere else. Thackeray's *Book of Snobs* attracted him when he was astonishingly young, so much so that he wrote an account of the men and women of Peebles in that style before he was thirteen. The Covenanting writers on his father's shelves affected him most deeply, and he was still reading them in Samoa a year before he died.

In spite of physical weakness he did break out on summer holidays at Peebles and North Berwick during the mid-1860s to enjoy physical activities with his cousins Bob and Katherine and presumably other boys there, ingratiating himself by inventing games of pirates too complex for anyone else to master. He was adept at organizing secret expeditions, establishing his headquarters in a cave in the rocks. He also learned to ride, trotting over the sands with Bob and Katherine. His brown pony was "Purgatory," Katherine's was "Heaven," and Bob had a black pony called "Hell." Louis's other pastimes were rambles after dark with bull's-eye lanterns, and something he called "crusoeing," which he defined as "a word that covers all extempore eating in the open air: digging, perhaps, a house under the margin of the links, kindling a fire of the seaware and cooking apples there." There are scenes in *Treasure Island*, *The Black Arrow*, *Kidnapped*, and *Catriona* which have their source in the North Berwick area and its history.

He had lost access to Colinton, but in the summer of 1867, just as he was about to enter university, another Arcadia became available. The Stevenson family rented a country cottage in the village of Swanston in the east Pentlands, mainly to use in the summer months. Only five miles from Edinburgh, it was another world, a perfect base from which to explore the hills. Swanston could be seen from the Castle, as the eponymous hero of *St. Ives* would be told by Flora Gilchrist. Soon he made real contact for the first time with ordinary workers, notably John Todd the shepherd and Robert Young the gardener. Todd, already "the oldest herd on the Pentlands," had fascinating memories of the droving days, when shepherds took flocks into England along old drove roads, sleeping rough on the hillsides and fighting off attacks by sheep stealers. He was not the easiest of men to know, but Louis made a friend of him, thrilled by tales that seemed to him epic, having on them "the dew of man's morning." The old shepherd made the hills live for him, took him on expeditions as the winter light failed, "the shadow of the night darkening on the hills, inscrutable black blots of snow shower moving here and there like night already come, huddles of yellow sheep and dartings of black dogs upon the snow, a bitter air that took you by the throat, unearthly harpings of the wind along the moors. . . ."

When he entered Edinburgh University he already had the secret ambition to be a writer, but let his father believe he would follow the family tradition and be a lighthouse engineer. To this end, as well as Latin and Greek he elected for courses in physics, mathematics, and civil engineering. He took none of it seriously. He was one of those students who prefer to be autodidacts and use their ample leisure time for other purposes. They pick and choose, come and go as they please, and their teachers soon give up on them. Outside the gates the "humming, lamplit city" is always beckoning, and at five o'clock if not before they are free to head for the bright shop windows "under the green glimmer of the winter sunset. The frost tingles in our blood; no proctor lies in wait to intercept us; till the bell sounds again we are the masters of the world: and some portion of our lives is always Saturday."

MOSTLY IT WAS SATURDAY for Stevenson the student. The serious part of his supposed training as a lighthouse engineer came the following summer, when he was in northeast Scotland, sometimes with his father and sometimes alone, learning about marine construction. At first it seemed a big adventure, until boredom set in. In July 1868 he was at Anstruther, Fife, taking note of the harbor works. By September he was at Wick, first with his father and then left to his own devices. He loathed the unsightly, "sub-arctic" town from the outset. The wind never stopped blowing, "a cold, *black* southly wind, with occasional rising showers of rain." The place was devoid of any beauty: no trees, just bare grey shores, grim grey houses, grim grey sea. As for the Highland fishermen, they were "lubberly, stupid, inconceivably lazy and heavy to move," he wrote to his mother. "You bruise against them, tumble over them, elbow them against the wall—all to no purpose: they will not budge. You are forced to leave the pavement at every step." As for the black wind, it never stopped. No one said, "Fine day" or "Good morning." All they ever did was shake their heads and say, "Breezy, breezy!"

What he was really doing at university was following his own nose, reading a tremendous amount (but none of it on the syllabus for an engineering student) and learning how to write. One has only to read his letters to see that they were exercises in technique. In the same September letter to his mother he stumbles on something to the south of awful Wick which does excite him. His apprentice pen goes to work on it with a zest his teachers never see. The coastal scenery is suddenly full of drama, with "Great black chasms, huge black cliffs, rugged and over-hung gullies, natural arches and deep green pools below them, almost too deep to let you see the gleam of sand among the darker weed: there are deep caves too. In one of these lives a tribe of gypsies. The men are always drunk . . . the great villainous-looking fellows are either sleeping off the last debauch or hulking about the cave 'in the horrors.' The cave is deep . . . but they just live among heaped boulders, damp with continual droppings from above, with no more furniture than two or three tin pans, a truss of rotten straw and a few ragged cloaks. In winter the surf bursts into the mouth and often forces them to abandon it."

This was fascinating, much more so than tours of the Scottish lights and harbors, which had seemed romantic in the family histories of legends such as Bell Rock but meant in reality sitting in offices for hours poring over technical diagrams and blueprints. Each time he wrote home it came out as a story: either he couldn't help it or it was part of his vow to learn to write. He had taken a vow and "was always busy on my own private end." His father's criticism of the Pentland Rising missed the point, as it was bound to do. He said that Louis had made it into a story. Now he carried two books about with him everywhere, one to learn from and the other, his notebook, to write in. His loneliness was that of a young man cut off by a secret aim which he could share with no one. He had launched out on an unknown sea which meant solitude, and where no one could help him.

Universities always have their quota of curious students, and he was certainly one of the oddest. Looking back, he described himself as a "lean, idle, ugly, unpopular" fellow who either couldn't or didn't wish to fit in. Such characters, especially those who have been sheltered from childhood, avoiding the rigors of ordinary existence, are often overwhelmed by the commonalty of university life. They either break down or drop out. Ian Bell, one of the best recent writers on Stevenson, paints an expressionist portrait of him at this time: lank hair down on his collar, his face all planes and angles, spindly fingers, "the line of his torso like a question mark." Instead of drowning he chattered nonstop as a way of coping with others and racketed through the squalor of Old Town, dancing through his university years excitedly, now and then withdrawing abruptly into solitude. There was no pressure on him to succeed, and so he failed casually, scraping through with "the merest shadow of an education." It was fortunate that his father set no great store on formal education, and those students who worked diligently because they would have to work later for a living had nothing in common with him. Whatever he ended doing it would be with his family's assistance. Being ill and unhappy through childhood had put him in a special category. As Ian Bell puts it, "Louis suffered, but he did so as a rule in comfortable surroundings."

His character is increasingly hard to pin down. If he had been a painter he could have painted a dozen different aspects of himself, all true. Fizzing with brilliant if showy talk, mischievous and merry, somber, preoccupied, always gregarious, welcomed by his new friends and despised by those outside his little circle who saw only a preposterous charlatan, spoiled and snobbish, he was also cutting himself off on lonely walks through the streets, or beating a retreat to Swanston to commune with nature in the hills. The journey each morning from Heriot Row up the hill to the university meant temptation for so reluctant a student. He went up through the filthy alleys of Old Town and would rather have lingered. Greyfriars Cemetery was a favorite spot; it was where the Covenant was signed. All his life he was drawn to graveyards. Another halt might be Rutherford's bar in Drummond Street: students knew it as "The Pump." Or he could forget lecture rooms and keep walking, out to far-flung villages like Morningside that would soon be swallowed up by the growing city.

AT SWANSTON COTTAGE, which the family were to rent for the next fourteen years, he might have the company of a young friend, David Angus, an engineering assistant employed by Thomas who went on to build the Ailsa Craig lighthouse for the firm. Swanston cottage would be utilized in due course as the home of the heroine of *St. Ives*. By the same process east Lothian vacations turned up in *Catriona*, and jaunts around Queensferry provided material for *Kidnapped*. With Angus, Louis tramped the hills, talking endlessly or rather arguing about politics, sometimes so absorbed that the two found themselves back in the city. It was the time of Louis's brief flirtation with socialism, part of his rebellion against injustice and guilt at his own pampered background. This didn't appear to worry his bourgeois father, and before long his son was a member of Edinburgh University Conservative Club.

He enjoyed dressing up, though he had little aptitude for amateur dramatics, and in debates he failed to shine. His velvet jacket, an essential part of his bohemianism, was no doubt frowned on by his parents, like his long floppy hair, once fair but now turning dark. No doubt they told themselves it was just a phase. In fact he stayed bohemian to the end, even as the laird of his Samoan island. Bohemian affectations at university included attempts at social outrage, such as arriving once on his own doorstep disguised as a rag-and-bone man. Real outrage would occur a little later, when he came out of hiding and confronted his father on the subject of religion.

A legend has come down to us of Stevenson's unshakable cheerfulness, optimism, and exuberance, whereas he was as vulnerable to attacks of depression as anyone. In a letter to his cousin Bob in Cambridge in March 1870 he confessed to being "in the depths again" for no apparent reason. Half determined to get drunk, he went instead to Greyfriars graveyard and stayed there for about two hours "in the depths of wretchedness." His habit of going to churchyards when he felt unhappy is mentioned in "Old Mortality." Heading back to the university he looked down College Wynd "with its clothes poles and harridan faces craning from the windows and its steep narrow roadway clotted with fish barrows and loafing prostitutes." There were two boys near the top holding a jump rope. A sickly little girl jumped up and down while the boys swung the rope, letting loose "the most horrible and filthy oaths" as she did so. At the university he met a nice fellow student who simply wanted to be friendly, but Louis could hardly open his mouth for about ten minutes, which must have been a record. The friend was astonished by this, and even more when Louis, seeing some children playing at marbles in a stable lane, wanted to rush off and buy some for himself.

A lonely childhood can produce disturbance and depressive illness in later years, but sometimes a writer in the making can emerge from the experience of alienation, morbid attachment, and loss and build on the very weaknesses that would cripple others. Contradictions like this are part of the tale of Stevenson. Another is the mastery first of all of essay writing, rather than the storytelling that one would expect to come naturally to someone who at an early age retreated into fantasy. From now on the contradictions multiply. Under the infuriating fey exterior lies a vein of granite, unsuspected by most. He wins admirers, makes enemies, and spreads confusion. He has yet to emerge from his egg.

By the time he came to write to Bob his spirits had lifted, though he was fit for nothing, he mourned, but smoking and reading Baudelaire, adding with typical adolescent posturing, "By the bye, I hope your sisters don't read him: he would have corrupted St. Paul." Louis was not debauched, even by his reading, or ever likely to be, in spite of the mythology that has accumulated since around his days at university. There are stories of drunken whoring in the brothels of Old Town—and there were plenty of them—and even of a fathered bastard, a rumor encouraged no doubt by the *Jekyll and Hyde* novel and by Stevenson's romantic affinity with the ravaged poet Robert Fergusson of a century before. A blacksmith's daughter was supposed to have been made pregnant at Swanston, the romance destroyed by a furious Thomas. Her name was "Claire," who changed into a prostitute, "Kate Drummond," in other versions, a woman Louis had tried to reform. This rollicking picture of the shy student has been shattered by J. C. Furnas's 1952 biography. Furnas could find no foundation of fact in any of the gossip. It would have been hard for Stevenson to engage in a Hyde-like life or sustain any dark chasm of duality in his circumstances, turning up for dinner as he did nearly every evening at Heriot Row, and when his father kept him on such a tight rein as far as finances were concerned. "Twelve pounds a year was my allowance up to twenty-three . . . and although I amplified it by a very consistent embezzlement from my mother, I never had enough to be lavish. My monthly pound was usually spent before the evening of the day on which I received it. . . ."

Yet in spite of Furnas the gossip circulates to this day, as it did when he was a student. It is strange that his parents made nothing of it, or their respectable friends either. Certainly he spent time in brothels, and taverns too, some of them dangerously close to home. Those in Jamaica Street could actually be seen from the rear windows of Heriot Row. There was not such an absolute division as the terms New and Old Town might suggest. "The haunts of the working class extruded, like calloused fingers," writes Bell, "even into the New Town. Rose Street, tucked behind the Princess Street shops, was notorious for prostitution. . . ." Whatever Stevenson did or did not do in these establishments, he would certainly have done plenty of talking, most of which went over the heads of the whores. But he liked their company, and they made a fuss of him while relieving him of his money, calling him Velvet Jacket to amuse themselves, and perhaps affectionately. After all, he treated them as human beings, and would have been gentle and courteous in ways they had not experienced. Brutality was more the norm, and he must have witnessed that too. One imagines him as they must have seen him in the afternoons when they were still in a stupor, waking up after the night's exertions, a foppish figure with gangling limbs, clearly a mama's boy, who tended to laugh hysterically and who couldn't stop talking: some sort of black sheep perhaps, strayed in from the gentry, who might have bleated and been pathetic, but somehow wasn't. A lonely boy.

If he did lose his virginity with them it would have been after drinking more ale than he could manage, to bolster his courage or smother his conscience. There is no way of knowing. He did once become involved romantically with a prostitute, it seems, and then had to extricate himself by not answering the letters that pursued him. To a friend who became his confidante, Mrs. Sitwell, he wrote miserably, "O God, a thing comes back to me that hurts the heart very much. For the first letter she had bought a piece of paper with a sort of coarse flower-arabesque at the top of it."

Chesterton wondered whether the youthful Stevenson was attracted to repellent surroundings in spite of himself, and goes on to speculate that when the boy left his home "he shut the door on a house lined with fairy gold, but he came out on a frightful contrast." The shock of this contrast and the pains of youth he suffered, coming as he did from a tightly observed Puritan tradition where the Sabbath was "more like a day of death than a day of rest," reverberate through *Dr. Jekyll and Mr. Hyde*. Chesterton was convinced that this story, presented as happening in London, "is all the time very unmistakably happening in Edinburgh. More than one of the characters seem to be pure Scots . . . and there is something decidedly Caledonian about Dr. Jekyll." For Chesterton the whole story reeked of a Puritan town and could be some dingy tale "of stiff hypocrisy in a rigid sect or provincial village: it might be a tale of the Middle West savagely dissected in the *Spoon River Anthology*."

The raw youth wrote verse in the style of Whitman, whom he had just discovered and whose glorification of the open road so affected him, to show what a free-spirited rebel he was, at least in his thoughts:

I walk the street smoking my pipe
And I love the daying shop-girl
Who leans with rounded stern to look at the fashions,
And I hate the bustling citizen,
The eager and hurrying man of affairs I hate,
Because he wears his intolerance writ on his face
And every movement and word of him tells me how much he hates
    me.

I love night in the city,
The lighted streets and the swinging gait of harlots.
I love cool pale mornings
In the empty bye-streets
With only here and there a female figure,
A slavey with lifted dress and the key in her hand,
A girl or two at play in a corner of wasteland
Tumbling and showing their legs and crying out to me loosely.

Other early verses, like "Song at Dawn," are strikingly like the poetry Lawrence was producing in Croydon as a teacher, with its yearning wistfulness and hunger for a clean world:

> I see the dawn creep round the world . . .
> Here gradually it floods
> The wooded valleys and the weeds
> And the still smokeless cities.
> The cocks crow up at the farms;
> The sick man's spirit is glad;
> The watch treads brisker about the dew-wet deck:
> The light-keeper locks his desk
> As the lenses turn,
> Faded and yellow.
>
> The unaccountable peace—
> I too drink and am satisfied as with food.
> Fain would I go
> Down by the winding crossroad
> Where at the corner of wet wood
> The blackbird in the early grey and stillness
> Wakes his first song. . . .
>
> At such an hour as this, the heart
> Lies steeped and silent.
> O dreaming, leaning girl,
> Already the grey passes, the white streak
> Brightens above dark woodlands. Day begins.

It has the same emotional beat as that of the young Lawrence, the same awareness of beauty on earth. Richard Aldington, biographer of both Stevenson and Lawrence, exclaims at one point: "How often one feels that RLS in so many ways was a preliminary sketch of D. H. Lawrence!" A letter to Frances Sitwell in 1875 has the authentic Lawrentian mixture of exhaustion, world-weariness, hope, and incipient resilience, the neurasthenic outburst just held in check: "I am so tired, but I am very hopeful. All will be well some time, if it be only when we are dead. One thing I see so clearly. Death is the end neither of joy nor sorrow. Let us pass into the clouds and come up again as grass and flowers: we shall still be this wonderful, shrinking, sentient matter. . . . Consciousness and ganglia and such-like are after all but theories. . . ."

Miraculously the sick boy was banished during Louis's student years. Once out of the coddling nursing-home atmosphere of Heriot Row, he enjoyed the best health he had known so far. In the traditional "town and gown" snowball fight which became a riot, he was robust enough to be prominent, cheered by the crowd in the High Street as he was marched away under police escort. This was the nearest he ever came to feeling a hero.

CHAPTER THREE

The Thunderbolt Has Fallen

A VOYAGE through the Western Isles in August 1870, supposedly to complement his engineering studies, finds Louis writing in some astonishment to tell his parents that he felt amazingly well and was enjoying himself hugely. He was heading for Earraid, an islet off the Isle of Mull which was being used as a base for the construction of the Dhu Heartach lighthouse by the firm. He records this visit in "Memoirs of an Islet." It would be the setting for "The Merry Men" and the scene of David Balfour's struggles in *Kidnapped*.

He traveled by steamer from Glasgow to Oban along the spectacular west coast and through the islands, a trip highly popular with Victorian tourists. The first part of the journey was on the luxurious *Iona*. At Ardrishaig he boarded a small steamer and then transferred to another boat north to Oban. At Iona he disembarked and went on to Earraid. His letter is full of vivid pen-portraits. He was much taken with a girl of seventeen, Amy Sinclair, on the first leg of the journey. "By getting brandy and biscuits and generally coaching up her cousin who was sick I ingratiated myself." When the party halted at Staffa, a tourist stop famous for Fingal's Cave, he made a little more progress before they had to part, Amy and her cousin waving their handkerchiefs "until my arm in answering them was nearly broken." She had "run away with my pen" he apologized to his parents, adding a little pretentiously, "As a psychological study she was quite a discovery to me. I never yet saw a girl so perfectly innocent and fresh, so perfectly modest without the least hint of prudery." His father must have hoped for more on engineering. After Earraid he went on to Portree on the Isle of Skye. Remembering it all in later years, he wrote a touching lament for his lost youth in *Songs of Travel*:

> Sing me a song of a lad that is gone,
>   Say, could that lad be I?
> Merry of soul he sailed on a day
>   Over the sea to Skye. . . .
>
> Give me again all that was there,
>   Give me the sun that shone:
> Give me the eyes, give me the soul,
>   Give me the lad that's gone:
>
> Billow and breeze, islands and seas,
>   Mountains of rain and sun,
> All that was good, all that was fair,
>   All that was me is gone.

On Earraid itself he had stumbled on a dream isle, another paradise he didn't want to leave. In "Memoir of an Islet," written seventeen years later, it all came alive and delicious again, and he felt pangs of loss for a place where

> the ground was all virgin, the world all shut out, the face of things unchanged by any of man's doings. Here was no living presence, save for the limpets on the rocks, for some old, grey, rain-beaten ram that I might rouse out of a ferny den betwixt two boulders, or for the haunting and piping of the gulls. It was older than man; it was found so by incoming Celts and seafaring Norsemen, and Columba's priests. The earthy savor of the bog plants, the rude disorder of the boulders, the inimitable seaside brightness of the air, the brine and the iodine, the lap of the billows among the weedy

reefs, the sudden springing up of a great run of dashing surf along the seafront of the isle, all that I saw and felt my predecessors must have seen and felt with scarce a difference. I steeped myself in open air and in past ages.

As well as being "as gallant as possible" for Miss Sinclair, he met on Skye a man who would one day be invaluable when he became a professional writer. This was Edward Gosse, son of the naturalist, before whom he was uncharacteristically tongue-tied. They did exchange a few words on board the steamer going back to Glasgow, when they entered a loch and were joined by a party of emigrants en route for America. The sound of wailing in the still night from the bereft families left ashore pierced Gosse's heart. He and the young man from Portree were silent after this.

Back he went to the dry-as-dust books he was forced, after a fashion, to study, and those he drank down in secret like a drunkard as that other Louis, the apprentice writer. These vital activities, where he read increasingly widely, experimented with various styles, and devised a program of imitation while waiting to find his own voice have been laid bare without shame in his essay "A College Magazine" for hostile critics to store up and use against him. They would soon accuse him of being an empty vessel, someone with nothing to say, the "sedulous ape" to previous writers, using his own phrase against him. The young writer to be, not yet on his guard against literary malice, could see nothing wrong in owning up to aping work he admired. "I was unsuccessful and I knew it, and tried again and was unsuccessful and always unsuccessful, but at least in these vain bouts I got some practice in rhythm, in harmony, in construction and the coordination of parts." Thus he plowed through Shakespeare, Hazlitt, Lamb, Wordsworth, Sir Thomas Browne, Defoe, Hawthorne, Montaigne, Baudelaire, and Oberman at a steam-engine pace, learning as he went, and was soon feeding his undergraduate appetite on Whitman, a real discovery, and Thoreau, as well as Darwin and Herbert Spencer. The ground he covered is extraordinary. The list kept extending: the New Testament, *Pilgrim's Progress*, Browning and Tennyson, Alexandre Dumas *père* and Meredith. Classics included Virgil, Marcus Aurelius, and Martial—he was especially drawn to the stoicism in Aurelius's *Meditations*, as one would expect. Influences like Ruskin, Keats, Chaucer, Morris, Swinburne, and Carlyle made their presence felt, and the novels of Scott, but nothing supplanted Shakespeare and Meredith, and Hazlitt's essay "On the Spirit of Obligations" was always close to his heart. He must have read at great speed, which was how he later wrote, and none of it seems to have been superficial.

The college magazine he helped to start foundered after four issues, as such enterprises often do. In 1869 he was elected to the Speculative Society, or "Spec," a rather exclusive debating society which still exists, and though not an official university society it had its own salubrious premises, with a Turkish carpet, a library, benches, and a table, the walls hung with pictures, an interior lit with candles and warmed by a fire, where "a member can warm himself and loaf and read: here, in defiance of the Senatus-consults, he can smoke."

It took him a while to find the courage to face this snobbish club's audience, but he gained confidence after delivering his first paper, entitled "The Influence of the Covenanting Persecution on the Scotch Mind." He came to like the atmosphere, both the Spec itself and the talk when they adjourned to Rutherford's afterward. He made important friends there, even if his contributions were unremarkable. Two years after his first paper he gave one arguing that American literature could stand comparison with English. He failed to find a seconder for a motion calling for the abolition of capital punishment. He enjoyed the wit and banter, allowed himself to be swayed by iconoclasts, and read an essay, "Two Questions on the Relationship Between Christ's Teaching and Modern Christianity," a veiled indictment of Scottish religion which anticipated the coming bitter clash with his father.

The Stevensons were already acquainted with Fleeming Jenkin, Edinburgh's first professor of engineering and a teacher Louis respected, if not to the extent of attending many of his classes, and Mrs. Jenkin would call to take tea with Maggie Stevenson. Both she and her husband were prominent in the cultural life of the city: Mrs. Jenkin had established a salon for people interested in the arts. Over tea she made the acquaintance of Maggie's only child, whose soft voice and brilliant if erratic talk enthralled her. She went home to tell her husband of this "young Heine with a Scottish accent," who spoke wittily and with such unconscious authority. Louis's devotion to older women could be said to start with Mrs. Jenkin. Ian Bell suggests intriguingly that this attraction may be explained by early friendships with mature professionals in the "howffs" of Old Town. It makes a change from Freud. Anne Jenkin had invited the bashful tyro to lunch with her husband next day. Louis was soon hero-worshiping Jenkin and calling in on his wife's salon evenings. His respect for the professor perhaps stemmed in part from Jenkin's refusal to give him a certificate of merit at the end of his course. Jenkin said, "There may be doubtful cases; there is no doubt about yours. You simply have not attended my class." The certificate was reluctantly given after much debate, and probably because of the family name.

The suggestion that the Jenkins were surrogate parents, put forward by more than one Stevenson scholar, seems far-fetched. It is more probable that as an only child who sometimes felt himself a rival for his mother's love he was drawn to maternal figures. Close as he was to his mother, her absence because of invalidism and the constant presence of Cummy, "my second mother, my first wife," would have prevented his love from developing into abnormality.

There is no doubt that Jenkin, an older friend rather than a father figure, helped him grow up. He was a polymath who was able to accept the student's waywardness without patronizing. Louis listened to his advice and took note of his strictures. It was an unusual friendship, with admiration on both sides. In his memoir of Jenkin, published in 1888, Stevenson makes clear the strength of the bond between them.

He was also finding kindred spirits of his own age at the university. Acquaintance soon ripened into friendship. All of them were respectable enough to bring round to tea or dinner at Heriot Row. Walter Simpson was now a baronet after the death of his father, the discoverer of chloroform. James Walter Ferrier, son of a distinguished St. Andrews professor, who was to die young of tuberculosis and drink, was the one Louis had reservations about, a disturbing lack of soul and something self-destructive making him uneasy for all Ferrier's "beauty, power, breeding, urbanity and mirth." And there was Charles Baxter, his future financial adviser, the son of a lawyer who became a lawyer himself. Baxter, brawny, thrusting, and confident, was the type of opposite Louis found it hard to resist, just as Henley would soon be.

Simpson had his own flat, which he shared with his brother and sister. It would be handy as a retreat for Louis as relations with his parents worsened. When Louis's cousin Bob, three years his senior, arrived to join this merry band the tempo quickened considerably. Bob, already a dedicated aesthete, was the sworn enemy of convention and the bourgeoisie, a lover of pranks and practical jokes, to which Baxter was also addicted. These jokes were mostly harmless, now and then dubious. A running joke between Louis and Baxter which they kept up for years involved writing letters to each other in vernacular Scots as two religious maniacs. Louis's pseudonym was Johnstone; Baxter was Thomson.

Bob Stevenson was about to influence the course of Louis's life profoundly. He graduated at Cambridge and was back in Edinburgh in 1870. From then on the two, already closely in touch through letters, were like the heavenly twins Castor and Pollux (called by the Greeks the gods of mariners). They had become indispensable to each other. Bob was exciting because the spirit of France was his religion. He smelled of Paris. Studying art in Antwerp later, certain he was destined to be a painter, he wrote to tell his cousin that "I have been so accumstomed to see and do everything with, or with reference to you that being unable to tell you everything day by day to hear what you say and to have you for public audience, world and everything, I am now quite stumped." Louis felt exactly the same, as Bob explained to a friend: "He finds that I have been the whole world for him; that he only talked to other people in order that he might tell me afterwards about the conversation."

This favorite cousin who was such a glamorous figure, heading, so many believed, for great things, would be undermined by the legacy of a stricken father. He did plunge into a painter's life, sharing a studio with Sargent in Paris and having Whistler for a friend. For years he dazzled Louis with his brilliance. In the essay "Talk and Talkers" he is the character "Spring-Heel'd Jack": "He doubles like the serpent, changes and flashes like the shaken kaleidoscope, transmigrates bodily into the views of others, and so, in the twinkling of an eye and with a heady rapture, turns questions inside out and flings them empty before you on the ground like a triumphant conjurer."

Louis's wife resisted the charms of this magician, though meeting him for the first time in France she nearly succumbed, to the extent of seeing him as the one touched with genius rather than his cousin. Before long she was having second thoughts about Bob's moral "backbone," noticing that he "gave like putty." This was shrewd. Louis on the other hand, though he seemed such a frail spirit, had staying power. "That was why Bob never came off," she decided. In a sense she was right. In a few years he would write out of his shifting-sands nature that "We used to think we were like no one else about certain things, but that was a real phase too." Phase or not, Bob would always have the aura of a liberator about him, a man who struck off chains, and it was to his cousin that Louis turned when the parental waves began breaking around his head.

BY APRIL 1871 it was clear that Louis was not going to be an engineer. Thomas had reached this conclusion some time ago and was quick with a compromise. Why not transfer to the law and become an advocate? His son weakly agreed, once again to please his father and because he had no alternative to offer. Before this change of direction he astonished his fellow students by reading a paper to the Royal Scottish Society of Arts "On a New Form of Intermittent Light for Lighthouses." No doubt it was cobbled together with the help of his father. What the rebellious Bob, who kept pouring tales of bohemian life into his cousin's eager ears, thought of this backsliding hasn't been recorded. Louis was caught between two worlds, in thrall to "the most indefatigable, feverish mind I have ever known," about to sit exams before joining a firm of solicitors and unable to convince himself that his ambition to be a writer was anything but a dream. In his head he was revolving like one of his father's lighthouses, shedding light in all directions. His appearance was more eccentric than ever, his hair longer, his velvet jacket never off his back, his felt hat provoking street urchins into catcalls wherever he went.

At the end of July 1872 he escaped from the hated office, a place where "one simply ceases to be the reasoning being and feels *stodged and stupid* about the head," and went on a jaunt to Brussels with Walter Simpson. There they sat under huge trees, drank iced drinks and smoked cigars, and of course talked and talked. Simpson could not have been more of a contrast to himself, "a sincere and somewhat slow nature thinking aloud. . . . He was even ashamed of his own sincere desire to do the right thing. . . . He is the most unready man I ever knew to shine in conversation." Nevertheless Louis liked his friend's droll humor. They made attempts to learn German, went to the opera, and in August Louis was joined by his parents at Baden-Baden.

A rift in the relationship between father and son was suddenly widening. Back in Edinburgh, Bob proposed the formation of a society called Liberty, Justice, and Reverence, or L.J.R. Baxter and Ferrier became members, and the society of four would meet at a pub in Advocate's Close in the High Street. Their society's written constitution opened with the injunction, "Disregard everything our parents have taught us." A copy left, by accident or design, at Heriot Row was picked up by Thomas. The cat was out of the bag. It needn't have been, but when Louis was interrogated as to his religious belief he failed to equivocate, as he had done so often before, and told the shocking truth. On February 2, 1873, he wrote gloomily to Baxter that "if I had foreseen the real hell of everything since, I think I should have lied." He was torn between grief for his parents, who now saw their only son as a vile atheist, and admitting that he was certainly an agnostic. He was twenty-two.

Bob Stevenson, being older, was accused of ruining his uncle's house and his son, and meeting him in the street his uncle told him so. Louis, for his part, as the emotional temperature rose and rose, tried to explain to his parents that he did believe in Christian morality but not in many of the people who called themselves Christians. "O Lord, what a pleasure it is," he mourned in a letter to Baxter, "to have just *damned* the happiness of (probably) the only two people who care a damn about you in the world!" The Stevensons, horrified to think they had raised an infidel, showered recriminations on the son's head. "I have worked for you and gone out of my way for you," cried his father, "and the end of it is that I find you in opposition to the Lord Jesus Christ. . . . I would ten times sooner see you lying in your grave than that you should be shaking the faith of other young men and bringing ruin on other houses as you have brought it upon this." In the company of Bob he had felt boldly piratical, but nothing hurt Louis more than hearing his father say, "I thought to have had someone to help me when I was old."

Thomas Stevenson was far from being the unbending Victorian parent he seems in this crisis. In the event he was as stoical as his son would prove to be: he had indulged his son before and would do so again. Not that the grievous wound ever properly healed. In an attempt to defuse arguments and avoid quarrels in the painfully tense household, Louis was given a study of his own on the top floor of Heriot Row. Then in July he was relieved to be packed off for a long holiday with his Balfour cousin Maud, whose husband was the Rector of Cockfield, Suffolk, presumably in the hope that he would come to his senses. The atmosphere at home was stiff with disapproval and he needed no urging.

He went to say goodbye. Standing before his morose father he felt a fraud and a coward. What was he doing but running away? He avoided his mother's bewildered eyes. All his certainty and youthful resolve left him: words out of books rushed through his mind like blasphemies, like devils. Bob's laughter filled his ears with mockery.

Where was his conceit now? He longed to be reconciled with the father he loved, but how could he explain, in the face of such piety, that he was right—or was he? Everything confused him, pulled him this way and that—a believer who repudiated the Kirk, a sensualist and an ascetic, bound to his home and family but with treachery in his heart. In despair he wrote again to Baxter, "Here is a good cross with a vengeance, and all rough with rusty nails that tear your fingers, only it is not I that have to carry it alone: I hold the light end, but the heavy burden falls on those two."

Louis was hardly ever at home in England, and the English seemed to put a chill on him. But something happened while he was in Suffolk that changed all that, at least for a time. Guests at the rectory already were a Mrs. Frances Sitwell and her small son. She had married a clergyman at seventeen and was now living apart from him. Through a Victorian veil drawn over her past—she had lost one child—Louis guessed that her husband was "of unfortunate temperament and uncongenial habits." He may have been an alcoholic. Clever as well as beautiful, she was thirty-four to Louis's twenty-two, and there was a man in the offing, the literary and art critic Sidney Colvin, who would have married her if that was possible. It wasn't, and he was prepared to wait. Mrs. Sitwell supported herself with freelance literary work and by working as secretary to the College for Men and Women in Queen's Square, London.

From the first he was bowled over by the Madonna-like Mrs. Sitwell trailing her sad past, and by her vivacious, intelligent responses. There is no doubt that she did respond to this extraordinary apparition, hardly there physically, an elfin lad, gauche, spoilt, who looked at her so intensely, as if he could plumb all her secrets. She was used to admirers but here was someone different. She must have been flattered by such passionate attentiveness. Soon aware of his inconsistencies, she saw that through them ran a real capacity for feeling. They talked and read poetry together, she kept a ladylike distance between them physically, and perhaps realized before long that she had become a muse. It had probably happened before, but not so romantically. This curious being was flamboyant without superficiality, almost as if some force was acting through him. She called Colvin over to meet this remarkable prodigy. Long after Stevenson's death Colvin wrote a testimony in which he tried to pin down this chameleonlike creature's charm. In his opinion Mrs. Sitwell had not been mistaken. In one person Louis seemed to combine all ages, "the unfaded freshness of a child, the ardent outlook and adventurous daydreams of a boy, the steadfast courage of manhood, the quick sympathetic tenderness of a woman, and already . . . an almost uncanny share of the ripe life-wisdom of old age." As a tribute it is not as sugary as some, and clearly the impact Louis had was considerable.

Louis for his part was describing Frances Sitwell's effect on him in a letter of July 1873 to his mother. He had also, though he did not yet know it, found a mentor in Colvin, a man who would introduce him to publishers and editors and promote his interests tirelessly, if not always uncritically. Two years before his death Stevenson dictated a fragment of autobiography to his stepdaughter, acknowledging that it was Colvin who "paved my way in letters: it was he who set before me, and still, as I write, keeps before me a difficult standard of achievement."

To his mother on July 29 he writes joyfully: "My dear Mother, I am too happy to be much of a correspondent. Mrs. Sitwell is most delightful; so is the small boy, so is the Professor; so is the weather, and the place."

But not, one presumes, the people in general, when he began to walk about and explore his surroundings. In his essay "The Foreigner at Home" he makes clear his reservations:

> The first shock of English society is like a cold plunge. It is possible that the Scot comes looking for too much, and to be sure his first experiment will be in the wrong direction. Yet surely his complaint is grounded: surely the speech of Englishmen is too often lacking in generous ardor, the better part of the man too often withheld from the social commerce, and the contact of mind with mind evaded as with terror. . . .
>
> The fact remains: in spite of the difference of blood and lan-

guage, the Lowlander feels himself the sentimental countryman of the Highlander. When they meet abroad they fall upon each other's necks in spirit: even at home there is a kind of clannish intimacy in their talk. But from his compatriot in the south the Lowlander stands consciously apart. He has had a different training: he obeys different laws . . . his eyes are not at home in an English landscape or with English houses; his ear continues to remark the English speech; and even though his tongue acquire the Southern knack, he will still have a strong Scotch accent of the mind.

IN EDINBURGH AGAIN, Louis resumed fragile relations with his wounded father, desperately sorry for him but unwilling to recant. They went for walks together, and there were stubborn silences at times between them, with Louis struggling to avoid giving further offense. Meanwhile the letters he poured at Mrs. Sitwell were growing more ardent by the week. Later in his life he thought it best to burn those he received from her, so we are unable to see how she handled what were now his love letters. She is supposed to have sweetly rebuffed him once in London when he tried to cross the firm line she had drawn, in an attempt to express himself physically, but seemingly she did nothing to cut herself off from the young man's flood of adoration. By the end of August he was using an intimate name for her, Claire, and would soon be unburdening all his woes concerning the awkward truce with his parents. "O God, I feel very hollow and strange just now. I had to go out to get supper and the streets were wonderfully cool and dark, with all sorts of curious illuminations at odd corners from the lamps; and I could not help fancying as I went along all sorts of foolish things—*chansons*—about showing all these places to you, Claire, some other night; which is not to be. Dear, I would not have missed last month for eternity. . . . It is very hard to stop talking to you tonight, for I can't do anything else. Sleep well, and be strong. I *will* try to be worthy of you and of *him*." The "him" refers to Colvin, who had already been instrumental in getting his essay "On Roads" taken by the *Portfolio* after *The Saturday Review* had rejected it. It was his first essay to be published and given the accolade of payment. In thrall to Mrs. Sitwell and the inchoate desires she was inspiring, he lost temporarily the compulsion to escape from Edinburgh and even the urge to write. He was living inside himself, not even noticing the "precipitous city" he had wanted to flee. His life was chaotically emotional as he lived from day to day for a letter from Suffolk or London, and if none came he would be desperate. The domination by his Madonna was of his own doing, almost as if he needed the sexual charge it provided. He was rescued from this morass by sheer chance. He and his father met Edward Strathearn Gordon, the government's chief Scottish law officer, whom Thomas knew, when they were on a train. The lord advocate suggested that Louis should study for the English bar. As this would be near to Mrs. Sitwell, the lovelorn young man accepted at once. London was also the place to further his literary ambitions, to take advantage of the connections Sidney Colvin could provide.

Ian Bell notes perceptively that a pattern to Stevenson's career was becoming clear, namely that "when things were going well, disaster was not far behind." No sooner had Louis installed himself in London than disaster struck. It is easy to see why he should crack under the strain he had been living with. A throat infection led to a complete physical collapse. Dr. Andrew Clark, faced with his feverish and emaciated patient, immediately ruled out further study, ordered a diet to fatten Louis up, suspected consumption and prescribed rest and a warm climate such as the south of France. The Stevensons, hurrying to London in a panic, were advised to let their son have a holiday on the Riviera by himself. Colvin may have advised the doctor that on the evidence of his letters Louis was close to a breakdown and should be given a respite from his parents, from guilt, from Edinburgh.

He set off shakily, delighted to escape the dust of English laws and wrote a swift note to Frances Sitwell: "I do look forward to the sun and I go with a great store of contentment—bah! what a mean word—of living happiness that I can scarce keep bottled down in my weather-beaten body." Here we have the oscillation between near extinction and rapture that would occur again and again and characterize his life journey. He had half his span of years yet to live. His first proper letter to her after being ordered south would be from Avignon. His destination was Menton.

CHAPTER FOUR

Remember That I Come
of a Gloomy Family

*I*RONY OF IRONIES, he had been made to come south, where he had always secretly wanted to be. Wandering about in Avignon and on the other side of the Rhone like a ghost, absorbing the "southernness and Provençality," he felt literally a nervous wreck, babyishly afraid of rudeness, jumping out of his skin at any sudden noise. He didn't know what day of the week it was. He was horribly restless, unable to write anything to anyone except to her, his confidante. His friends in Edinburgh and his cousin could have been on another planet. Were they still the same band, merry and bright as ever? It had been so vital, all that, the seizures of infectious laughter, the sense of being a band of angels, joyously alive and kicking in each other's company, united against a world of absurdity and leveling hostile criticism at all its hypocrisies by the very act of being themselves. They had invented a nonsense word, Jink, conveying nothing to anyone else but to them it meant the time they spent together as initiates of their own secret society. What did it mean now? Much later he would see his cousin as a kind of savior and try to find words for his gratitude: "The mere return of Bob changed at once and for ever the course of my life: I can give you an idea of my relief only by saying that I was at last able to breathe. The miserable isolation in which I had languished was no more in season, and I began to be happy. To have no one to whom you can speak your thoughts is but a slight trial . . . but to be young, to be daily making fresh discoveries and fabricating new theories of life . . . and never to have a confidant, is an astounding misery."

Driven on by his restlessness, no more than a bag of bones with all his nerves horribly inflamed, he reached Marseilles and then at last Menton, which he knew already from being there as a child with his mother. Menton, a very dull place according to the publisher William Chambers, was full of recuperating English invalids, lodged comfortably in the half-dozen hotels that were there expressly to cater to them. Louis handed over his baggage to a hotel porter and started off unwisely on one of his hikes. He had landed in one of the principal British sanatoria abroad, according to the historian John Pemble. Hot, dry climates were favored by Victorian medical science. Louis was a Francophile by instinct, and though his mind was confused and he was unsure of his direction, none of it mattered. His spirits soared. One is reminded of the revelation experienced by van Gogh arriving in Arles for the first time, throwing open his window to let in the aroma from a sea of blossom. "Suddenly," Louis wrote to Frances Sitwell, "I was met by a great volley of odors out of the lemon and orange gardens, and the past linked on to the present, and in a moment, in the twinkling of an eye, the whole scene fell before me into order, and I was at home."

Order was what he desperately lacked, and always sought to achieve, in the emotional chaos of his life. He came to terms with the chaos, and when he decided to marry he chose well. His wife was an organizer. Until his marriage he was driven by divisions and contradictory impulses as much as by constant illness. As a writer he was strumming without real purpose, an aesthete and a phenomenon rather than a real artist, until his no-nonsense wife sat him down to do directed work.

His moment of epiphany on the road was no more than a moment: his soaring spirits soon collapsed. His body was simply worn out. He felt like someone with premature senility. On November 21, 1873, he again confided what he would have been ashamed to tell anyone else: "If you knew how old I felt. I am sure this is what age brings with it, this carelessness, this disenchantment, this continual bodily weariness. I am a man of seventy. O Medes, kill me, or make me young again!" He wrote to Charles Baxter, but only to ask how things were in Edinburgh and say he was expecting *Leaves of Grass*. Two days later he managed to get to Nice, more dead than alive, for an examination by a Dr. Bennet, who "agrees with Dr. Clark that there is no disease." Disoriented, he had difficulty finding his way back to the station. He was more than once about to give way and shout at strangers out of sheer rage, but thought if he did he would burst into tears or have a fit. His confidence was nonexistent, so much so that he lost the ability to speak French. At the station he crawled up the steps and simply sat there, steeping himself in sunshine, "until the evening began to fall and the air to grow chilly." He accepted now, after his worst day since leaving London, that he was a physical wreck. Slowly, as he sat about with other middle-class invalids, his body began to mend and his mental health with it. It is easy to see how Fanny Sitwell's protective instincts were aroused as she received these disturbing letters, sometimes wildly happy but often showing him at such a low ebb that he seemed not far removed from despair. To cope with his anxiety he tried opium (laudanum and morphine), prescribed by his doctor as a cough suppressant, but never went the way of so many of his artist contemporaries to become an addict. Gradually, as time went on, Mrs. Sitwell ceased to be his "beloved" or his "Consuelo," a name lifted from George Sand. Baulked by her refusal to be disloyal to Colvin, he solved the problem of his turbulent feelings by writing to her as a son to his mother. It was a characteristic solution.

One factor in his slow recovery was the renewed love and concern showed by his father. Louis had been writing at length to Thomas, worriedly explaining that his break from cover was in no sense a personal attack, and trying to clarify his ideas on morality and religion. His father replied at once with a telegram: "Quite satisfied with your letter—keep your mind easy." For Louis, his head full of turmoil, this must have been music to his ears. What he didn't know, but discovered later, was that his parents feared he was losing his mind and sought to humor him.

As he began to calm down and look around him, he started work on the first essay to gain him real attention. He made slow progress, reporting to Mrs. Sitwell as he got moving. As David Daiches points out, "Ordered South" is the only piece of writing in which Stevenson owns up to being an invalid. But he was finding out that no matter what one wrote, the urgent thing was to impose order on one's view of the world. Stevenson's responses throughout his life were those of a man who has come close to death, repudiates it, fights through, and sees the world with new eyes, like someone who has been given another chance. Lawrence too conveys this sometimes primal freshness, and so does Chekhov. But only in "Ordered South" is the process of convalescence being openly paraded. There are touches of the young exquisite, and if he had been a painter he would have been called mannerist, but there is also a new realism, something bracing, a firm grip on generalizations which only now and then become pretentious. His essay appeared in *Macmillan's Magazine* in May 1874 and then was reprinted in 1881 in the volume *Virginibus Puerisque*. He was still groping after his own voice, and the style veers about as he blends impressions of France and the Midi with memories of home, where he was on surer ground. He felt homesick in his lonelier moments for

> the hale rough weather; for the tracery of the frost upon his windowpanes at morning, the reluctant descent of the first flakes, and the white roofs relieved against the somber sky. And yet the stuff of which these yearnings are made is of the flimsiest. . . .

If the temperature in Menton fell a little, if a chilly wind came down from the snowy Alps behind him, he lost his longing for the north. Grim scenes of the Edinburgh streets came into his mind; tramps huddled hopelessly in doorways, the

flinching gait of barefoot children on the icy pavement; the sheen
of the rainy streets towards afternoon; the meager anatomy of the
poor defined by the clinging of wet garments; the high canorous
note of the Northeaster on days when the very houses seem to
stiffen with cold: these, and such as these, crowd back upon
him. . . .

He remembered the icy blasts, the damp sea fog, the *haar* of the
east coast of Scotland, the oppressive presence of John Knox, the
deathly claustrophobia of the Sabbath, and realized again how lucky
he was.

As well as "Ordered South," he tinkered with essays on Whitman, Victor Hugo, John Knox, and Mary, Queen of Scots. Colvin had
interested *Macmillan's* in him, and they suggested something on
Savonarola. Instead he turned to Whitman, teasing out the American
poet's feminine side and trying the experiment of getting people to
guess the sex of the writer of Whitman's "Civil War Memoranda," in
which the poet nursed the wounded of both armies. "More than one
woman, on whom I tried the experiment, immediately claimed the
writer for a fellow-woman." The essay appeared eventually in *Familiar Studies*.

He was alone until December, when Colvin came out to see him
during the Christmas season. He saw at a glance that Louis was far
from himself, "without tangible disease, but very weak and ailing."
In the New Year Louis wrote to his mother that he had moved with
Colvin from the Hotel du Pavillon to the Hotel Mirabeau in the East
Bay, which was more congenial in every way and the food wonderful.
Also he had shaken off the "horrid English" at the Pavillon. They
spoke French at the Mirabeau, and soon Louis could report that his
conversational French was improving. Better still, the hotel had a
cosmopolitan atmosphere, which made him feel he had truly escaped
Edinburgh. Bob would have been at home here. Though Louis often
felt a need for solitude, the gregarious side of him always responded
to lively company. His spirits rose. Colvin interestingly called him a
"type-hunter."

All the same he was unhappy at the thought of his father, and the contrariness of his own behavior toward him. It was as if the upheaval within him had come from nowhere, like a convulsion. How could he have thought his father deserved such treatment, a man who had labored as much for him as for anyone, giving up his liberty to do so? He wished he could pay his way in the world instead of having his father subsidize his convalescence. Colvin overpraised him yet didn't exactly encourage him to believe that literature could provide for him full-time. How about a job of some kind? Louis knew a great deal, but not how to earn a living. He thought guiltily of fellow students at the university "who followed the plow in summertime to pay their college fees in winter." Ten years later, in "Lay Morals," he questioned the justice of it all:

> When he thought of all the other young men of singular promise, upright, good, the prop of families, who must remain at home to die, with all their possibilities lost to life and mankind, and how he, by one more unmerited favor, was chosen out from all these others to survive, he felt as if there was no life, no labor, no devotion of soul and body that could repay and justify these partialities. . . . Like many invalids he supposed that he would die. Now should he die, he saw no means of repaying this huge loan which, by the hands of his father, mankind had advanced him for his sickness. In that case it would be lost money.

From the stance he had decided on, writing as an author miraculously free of physical handicaps, he felt bound to describe this dilemma, which stayed with him until he became a best-seller, as something happening to "a friend of mine."

His cousin Bob had fallen strangely silent, so he launched into a long letter which made clear at the outset that he was still a nervous wreck. He was on a visit to Monaco with Colvin, sitting in the sun on a seat behind the Casino. The band was tuning up, but should he risk going in? The last time he had ventured inside to a concert "the brass made me quite mad and all my nerves got tense and stiff like whipcord." He moved adroitly to more cheerful matters. "Has the sun of

Jink then set? God forbid, as St. Paul would say. . . ." Here at Menton he must have seemed an age away from their elaborate jokes.

Sounding ill at ease, he did his best to do what he guessed Bob expected and sought to amuse him by retelling a story of Colvin's. "Courbet's grand climax of realism was a picture called *La Baigneuse* of a great, fat, obese *bourgeoise* clambering out of a bath with her big bum turned to you. It was the ugliest thing on record. The Empress had been looking at a picture of Rosa Bonheur's of a lot of percheron horses—those great white draft horses with immense quarters." Seeing Courbet's *Baigneuse*, she said, "Is that a percheron?"

He mentions dining with Colvin and Sir Charles Dilke, a radical politician, and his wife. Dilke was the man who had been held up to ridicule a few years before with his proposal for abolishing the monarchy: he was about thirty, "and just Hell on laughing at jokes— his joke, your joke, my joke, anybody's joke."

His time at the Mirabeau after Colvin departed was enlivened by an influx of energy, by the glorious situation, the moon rising over Italy, the plane trees, the aroma of violets, and most of all by the residents: boisterous Americans, the daughters of an English clergyman, a hairy French artist, and two "brilliantly accomplished and culti- vated" Georgian sisters. Madame Zassersky and Madame Garschine had two children in tow. They were both married but had come to France minus their husbands for some mysterious reason. Louis, who loved to be with children, started spending time with them. Nelitchka, the younger child, was two and a half. Louis was soon de- scribing her to Mrs. Sitwell as "a little polyglot button" and "a hell of a jolly kid." The child of eight apparently belonged to Madame Gar- schine. Louis was bewildered, later learning that the elder sister, Madame Zassersky, was a princess who had borne ten children and written popular comedies. Her frankness upset him. He had no expe- rience in dealing with direct talk from a lady. He told Mrs. Sitwell that he thought they simply found him amusing and were trying to make a fool of him. "I am to them as some undiscovered animal. They do not seem to cultivate RLS's in Muscovy."

He took tea with them at a villa they had rented, only coming to the hotel for meals. There he found the situation even harder to handle. Madame Garschine embarrassed him with her flirtatious manner. He was inexperienced yet on strangely familiar ground, involved again with an older woman, a wife separated from her husband, and once again it was a mother. He was deep into the work of George Sand and must have wondered if he had landed in one of her novels. His discomfiture would have melted away if he could have taken into account her light, accomplished handling of him.

Children were less complicated. He was much taken with Marie, the daughter of an American couple. In his eyes she was "grace itself, and comes leaping and dancing simply like a wave." When he came to write his essay "Notes on the Movements of Young Children," which the *Portfolio* published in August 1874, he was able to draw on his friendships with these three little girls.

To keep himself buoyant and in motion he planned books. One was to be called *Four Great Scotsmen*, containing essays on John Knox, David Hume, Robert Burns, and Walter Scott. Only those on Knox and Burns got written. Notes for the Burns essay referred to "the sentimental side that there is in most Scotsmen, his poor troubled existence, how far his poems were his personally, and how far national, the question of the framework of society in Scotland and its fatal effect upon its finest natures." Scott, a sane, courageous, admirable man, epitomized for him the birth of Romance, in a dawn that was "all sunset; snobbery, conservatism, the wrong thread in History, and notably in that of his own land." He was brooding on Scottish character, Scottish society, Scottish history, reading that would find its place in *Kidnapped*, *The Master of Ballantrae*, and *Weir of Hermiston*. He also wanted to write fiction but found it hard to get a footing. He envisaged a series of Covenanting stories: a notebook of this period lists the titles of projected stories under the heading "Covenanting Story Book."

Diversions such as Colvin's visit and the exotic Russian sisters helped him through the exile of winter at Menton. Not long before he left for Paris in April, anxious to see Bob again on his way back to Scotland, he met the scholar and poet Andrew Lang, who was also wintering in Menton with lung trouble. Lang was unimpressed by the twenty-three-year-old at first, not knowing what to make of this Scot who seemed "more like a lass than a lad . . . brown hair worn at greater length than is common." He thought him every inch an aesthete, with his big blue cloak fastened with a snake buckle and his Tyrolese hat. He was struck by his large, lucid eyes. Soon they were warm friends. The cloak was found for Louis by Colvin, who had looked for something suited to his taste, picturesque and colorful.

Bob's letters from Antwerp had disturbed Louis, who picked up an undertone of loneliness which made him wonder if "the world has gone more unfortunately for him." But their reunion reassured him; his cousin was in good spirits, hoping to find "a nice woman." A note to Mrs. Sitwell on his last night in Menton gave her his Paris address, Hotel St. Romain, rue St. Roch. "God help us all, this is a rough world," he ended, and drew a line to signify the end of a chapter.

WHETHER MADAME GARSCHINE had been playing games with him or really hankered after an affair, it was no more than a comical, confusing interlude now. As soon as she changed tack and adopted a maternal role toward him he knew where he was. Passion muddled things, as it had with Frances Sitwell. And he could enjoy being with the children. Was he foreseeing a childless future for himself when he wrote to his mother, "Kids are what is the matter with me"? He told Fanny Sitwell less obscurely, "I sometimes hate the children I see in the street—you know what I mean by hate—wish they were somewhere else and not there to mock me; and sometimes again, I don't know how to go by them for love of them, especially the wee ones."

Paris beckoned, and so did Bob, his spiritual twin. As well as Bob's letters from Antwerp sounding downcast, there was bad news from home. Bob's father had quarreled with Thomas, who still alleged that his son had led Louis astray. And Bob's sister Katherine was in marital difficulties. She had gone against the wishes of her family and married Sydney de Mattos, a Cambridge atheist, and now the marriage was falling to pieces. Later she divorced him and went off with her children—like Fanny Sitwell, like the Russian sisters, and like Louis's future wife.

After the warmth of Menton the Paris weather spoke to him of the north. But he made for the city instinctively, like so many artists of his time and since. Walter Benjamin calls it "the capital of the nineteenth century." Even before he set off his mother cabled her disapproval: after all, the suspect cousin was there. Would their son never learn? He replied evasively, "Well, I didn't approve of it particularly myself. I only did it to be sooner able to come home." He was leading the double life of so many sons who feel unable to make the truth about themselves palatable.

In fact he was turning plans over in his mind to go with Bob on a painting trip to Fontainebleau. He also thought halfheartedly of studying Roman law at Göttingen—anything to avoid sentencing himself to more of the same at Heriot Row. The truth was he had no stomach for either. He realized that he was still far from well. His eager cousin took him round his old haunts, out to impress him with his intimacy with real bohemia, real starving artists, real studios, and cafés where one could eat cheaply and on credit.

Trotting round like a tourist, Louis had no need to fake a response. He saw why so many generations had derived spiritual food from this city. On the verge of falling in love with Paris at first sight, seeing the brilliant posters pasted on round pillars, hearing the shouts of glaziers and grocers as he walked the streets, wandering through the village that was rural Montmartre with its trees, vineyards, windmills, and panoramic views, he was overwhelmed by the color on all sides—swarms of soldiers everywhere in red trousers—and by the sheer pace of it all; masons at work on their huge lumps of stone and buildings rising on all sides. The jolting contrast between the peacock elegance of rich women with their top-hatted escorts and the poor, the beggars and the workmen, coopers trading barrels, men with carts hawking clothes, boilers of hot water being trundled through the streets for anyone wanting a bath, never failed to amaze him. The great river too, its slow barges and its serenity, was an artery along which the whole blood of the city seemed to flow.

He was taken to the Louvre and came out dazed by its sheer weight of art, plunging back into the living theatre of the streets. What made it unlike anywhere else, making Edinburgh shrink in comparison, was not only the level of street noise, the horse dung, the ammonia reek, the dirt, but the unceasing bustle and optimism of the crowds, the yelling and the traffic, wagons of all sizes and buses pulled by horses. Every house and alley had its allure, no matter how decrepit; even the peeling paint on the shutters somehow contributed to an originality that had evolved over centuries.

Yet by the end of his stay Louis knew he would never be a fully committed bohemian, freezing in some garret, any more than he was ever an out-and-out rebel. He was not robust enough, and family ties pulled more strongly than this life of freedom which fascinated but failed to engage him. Bob was short of money for essentials like food, and so was he. He had already accused himself in his conscience of being a social parasite, sponging on his father and inwardly resenting it. As so often when he was confronted with a dilemma, he solved it by falling ill. Not that there was anything bogus about it; he ran a fever, was disabled by raging headaches, sweated profusely at night, and developed a nervous facial tic. He alarmed his Paris doctor who thought he might have smallpox or typhoid symptoms. He sent a mournful report to his parents: "I am bronchial a bit and cough and have mucous membrane over the best part of me and my eyes are the laughablest deformed loopholes you ever saw: and withal my lungs are all right." His semi-hysterical mother beseeched him to come home, so back he went. At least as a sick man he would be "a prince," he thought.

He knew his parents better than they knew themselves, but this gave him no satisfaction. He felt slippery and disloyal. Thomas swallowed down any vexation he may have felt, and Maggie was just grateful to find her son still sane. Louis, fortunate to have such a patient father, was immediately made guilty by his forbearance.

Thomas raised his son's allowance to seven pounds a month. Fears over his precarious health prevented his parents from sanctioning his move to Göttingen. He agreed dutifully enough, reading again for examinations to the Scottish bar. He drew closer to his mother than he had ever been. Edinburgh was now the enemy. His spirits sank, then lifted when he got out to Swanston. It was only the beginning of May and the cottage was six hundred feet above sea level. It had sleeted on the morning he wrote to Fanny Sitwell to say that everything was wintry but he was "jolly, having finished Victor Hugo . . . just looking round to see what I should next take up."

He spent time with Fleeming Jenkin, still his main mentor. Thomas and Maggie fully approved of that friendship, even if they withheld judgment on the more worldly Sidney Colvin and Fanny Sitwell in London. In the summer he dabbled in the law, was again occupied with the Jenkins and their amateur theatricals, at which he was never more than fair, and did plenty of traveling. By the autumn his cordial relations with his father had deteriorated, and he sent the results of his mournful self-analysis to Fanny: "I have discovered why I get on always so ill, am always so nasty, so much worse than myself, with my parents; it is because they take me at my worst, seek out my faults, and never give me any credit." This was shifting the blame with a vengeance, and in an effort to convince himself he kept worrying at it like a terrier. "I once wrote to you to tell how you should do with me; how it was only by getting on my weak side, looking for the best, and always taking it for granted that I should do the best before it is done, that you will ever get the best out of me." With his parents, it all happened in reverse, it seemed. Because they expected him to be not good, "I am never good, because they never seem to see me when I am good." It was insoluble.

He went sailing with his friends Simpson and Baxter on the lighthouse yacht *Heron*, cruising the Hebrides and hearing of Simpson's common-law marriage. He wrote what amounted to a declaration of the new state of affairs between him and Fanny, telling her that he was not yet a man but still "a peevish and a spoiled child."

That was about to change. The R.L.S. she had come to know was no more: "he is dead." The passion he had felt was over too. What he wanted was for her to see him as strong and helpful, a good friend, rather than the dead weight he must have been in the past. He begged her to believe it was so, and then it would be so. He was doing his utmost to be honest, if more than a little fearful of slipping back into his previous unrequited role. Indeed he did falter that winter—always a bad time for him—and suddenly poured out a confession which Fanny would have preferred not to read: "O, I do hate this damned life that I lead. Work, work, work; that's all right, it's amusing; but I want women and I want pleasure. John Knox had a better time of it than I, with his godly females all leaving their husbands to follow after him. I would I were John Knox; I hate living like a hermit." As if wanting to hurt her, he said he wished he did not love her so much, but had learned not to go down that path for both their sakes. He was good, he was changed, adding plaintively, "I am, am I not?"

His parents took him on holiday with them to Wales and the West Country. Then he slipped his reins and used Andrew Lang as a reason to visit Oxford. Colvin had invited him to stay with him in Hampstead, and he would be close to Fanny. Through Colvin he became a member of the Savile Club, a new, unstuffy London establishment, which he hoped would help bring him into contact with literary London. He had a flair for essays, but the three pounds eight shillings he had got for "On Roads" and the five pounds for "Ordered South" were barely more than the monthly allowance from his father. He was aware, though not yet acutely, of the mountain to climb that fiction represented, and certainly realized that the only real money to be earned was by writing novels.

COLVIN HAD INTRODUCED HIM to Andrew Lang, he had met Gosse on his own account in the Hebrides, and now Leslie Stephen, editor of the *Cornhill*, put him in touch with W. E. Henley. Louis had not met anyone remotely like him. It would be true to say that his doubts about the literary life were put to flight in an instant by the personality of this literary pugilist. They would be comrades, collaborators, and, in the end, enemies.

He must have had to remind himself that he was meeting a man of letters. Leslie Stephen took the "young Heine" to visit Henley in the Old Surgical Hospital at Edinburgh. Louis came face to face with a "crippled colossus" who made up for a middling talent by an exuberant lust for life. He had tuberculosis of the bones, had already lost one foot, and was in danger of losing the other. Joseph Lister saved his right foot, after eighteen months of painful scraping of the bone. The man's fortitude in bearing this agonizing treatment was what most impressed Louis initially. Stoicism would always count with him. Henley's early years had been all hospitals. He came of a large, poor family in Gloucestershire and was another aspiring writer like his visitor, though already involved with magazines. His father was a provincial bookseller. They took to each other directly, and for very different reasons. The heavily built figure on the bed playing tunes on a tin whistle was larger than life, as pugnacious as Charles Baxter, with the same liking for drink. Bearded, jovial, extrovert, he was only a year older than the young Scot but assumed a paternal role, sensing at once what he would call Louis's "feminine force." He must also have been quickly aware that his visitor's mind was malleable and in ferment, and this too appealed to him. As he established himself as a London editor, critic, and poet of Empire, he collected protégés, soon to be known as "Henley's young men," perhaps as a bulwark, perhaps to provide himself with the comforting loyalty of disciples. He is unread now but became well known as a New Imperialist in late Victorian days, famous for these lines from "Invictus":

I am the master of my fate:
  I am the captain of my soul.

Louis, meeting him for the first time, admired the stricken man's courage and came away exalted. He told Fanny Sitwell of the little room with two beds and a couple of sick children in the other bed; a girl came in to visit the children, and played dominoes on the counterpane with them: the gas flared and crackled, the fire burned in a dull economical way: Stephen and I sat on a couple of chairs, and the poor fellow sat up in his bed with his hair and beard all tangled, and talked as cheerfully as if he had been in a King's palace. . . .

What volumes that word "economical" speaks—a foretaste of the writer to come. Richard Aldington in his book on Stevenson sought to convey the impact of Henley by likening his quality of self-confidence and belief in himself and his power to communicate it with "the gift which Lawrence gave so lavishly to the few who knew him at all intimately." But Henley was no Lawrence: he reacted angrily to criticism and was liable to be jealous of other friends of Stevenson. Andrew Lang went so far as to say that Stevenson possessed the power of making other men fall in love with him. Henley undoubtedly saw Stevenson as having "feminine" appeal. His poem "Apparition," a portrait of Stevenson and one of his best efforts, hints as much, especially in a suppressed version containing the phrase "feminine force," using "Cleopatra" instead of the later "Antony." All the biographers reproduce it, and it is worth repeating:

Thin-legged, thin chested, slight unspeakably,
Neat-footed, and weak-fingered: in his face—
Lean, dark-boned, curved of beak and touched with race,
Bold-lipped, rich-tinted, mutable as the sea,
The brown eyes radiant with vivacity—
There shines a brilliant and romantic grace,
A spirit intense and rare, with trace on trace
of passion, impudence and energy.
Valiant in velvet, light in ragged luck,
Most vain, most generous, sternly critical,
Buffoon and lover, poet and sensualist:
A deal of Ariel, just a streak of Puck,
Much Antony, of Hamlet most of all,
And something of the shorter catechist!

As the final line confirms, Louis was still a Christian, and would remain one all his days. On Samoa he would instruct his native servants in hymn singing and even preach them sermons, like Livingstone in Africa. Henley, a brash egotist, sent a complimentary copy of his poem to Heriot Row, inscribing it to Mrs. Stevenson. She liked some of it but objected to the words "vain" and "sensualist" applied to her son. Henley ignored her.

The two rapidly became inseparable. Louis was a constant visitor to the infirmary. As soon as the crippled poet could sit up, Louis dragged an armchair along the pavement from Heriot Row, unable to pay for transport. When it was spring he managed to get his friend down the long stone stairs for a carriage ride, reporting triumphantly to Fanny Sitwell that "it is now just the top of spring with us. The whole country is mad with green. To see the cherry blossom bitten out upon the black firs, and the black firs bitten out of the blue sky, was a sight to set before a king. You can imagine what it was to a man who has been eighteen months in a hospital ward. The look on his face was wine to me." Here is the black-and-white woodcut prose of a man as convalescent as his new friend. Again and again he would experience the rapturous feeling of rebirth that a sick man knows who has been near death and has life revealed to him as if for the first time. And revelation it was: he saw the look of ecstasy on Henley's face and it was his too. The stir of birds, the fizzing green of springtime was stirring blissfully inside himself.

Both men continued with essay-writing and reviewing, but Henley, who had come up in a hard school, had an aptitude for making a living which Louis always lacked. Fortunately Louis had an indulgent father, and thanked his stars for it. To please him he went docilely on with his law studies. On July 16, 1875, he was admitted to the Scottish bar. He dressed up imposingly in wig and gown for a photograph of himself as a barrister, and that was the beginning and end of it. Fleeming Jenkin, well aware of the truth behind the pretense, wrote to him sardonically, "Accept my hearty thanks on being done with it." Although real vagabondage had not yet begun for him, he realized it was imminent. Needless to say, the man who had worked most powerfully on him as an intercessor, freeing him from threatening spirits, most of all from what impeded him within himself, was not Henley but Bob. His cousin, showing him by his example that one could be independent of others, could exorcise those things which made one an outsider, never really at home, pointed the way. Bob was his weapon, as he was Bob's heroic figure. Hence the exalted language Bob used whenever he spoke of Louis.

A letter to his mother as early as October of the previous year from Euston Station, after wandering around Wales, Buckinghamshire, and Oxford, showed the extent of his self-knowledge. No doubt she thought he was writing foolishly and wildly yet again, but he was never more serious. He asked her not to be vexed at his absences, then made a solemn declaration. She must understand, and

> (I want to say this in a letter) that I shall be a nomad, more or less, until my days be done. You don't know how I used to long for it in the old days: how I used to go and look at the trains leaving, and wish to go with them. . . . I *must* be a bit of a vagabond; it's your own fault after all, isn't it? You shouldn't have had a tramp for a son!

A brass plate that read R. L. Stevenson, Advocate was fastened to the front door of 17 Heriot Row. To set him going, Stevenson senior presented him with a thousand pounds. As Ian Bell remarks caustically, "The trials of RLS, and there were many, did not include starvation." Though when he reached America he came close to it.

There is no legal career worth mentioning, and the enormous sum of money disappeared with amazing rapidity. Ten years later Louis wrote ruefully, "I always fall on my feet, but I am constrained to add that the best part of my legs seems to be my father." Where did it go, all this largesse? Some went on loans or gifts to Henley, to Colvin, to Bob—who was always on the point of being broke—and to Bob's penniless sister. He turned down two briefs, pleading illness, and traveled off to spend more money in France, now a favorite destination. His cousin introduced him to the delights of artists' colonies at Barbizon, the Hotel Siron, where Bob's artist friends congregated, and the Forest of Fontainebleau. Wine, food, and books swallowed up the rest. In a burst of Bob-inspired euphoria he decided that he was no longer a lawyer.

It sounds like feckless idleness. The truth was that he was working hard at essays and articles and slowly getting himself known, if not making much money. How he got down to work while being constantly on the move can be best understood by realizing that he was always stimulated by change, as Lawrence would be after him. Periods in France were proving fruitful. An essay on Victor Hugo, prompted by Colvin, was something of a breakthrough, both materially and because it marked the beginning of his mastery of style. It earned him the splendid sum of sixteen guineas. He went on to break fresh ground with his essay on "John Knox and His Relations to Women," describing as laughable Knox's denunciation of women as agents of the devil and at the same time drawing them to his banner like a magnet. It appeared in *Macmillan's Magazine* and was later reprinted in *Familiar Studies*. He fell foul of authority for taking issue on the current glorification of Burns when an article commissioned by the *Encyclopaedia Britannica* was rejected. The editors found it "too frankly critical, and too little in accordance with Scotch tradition." In a fit of Calvinism, Louis condemned Burns's treatment of women and asserted that his debt to his predecessor Robert Fergusson was barely acknowledged. Tackling three poets, Villon, Burns, and Fergusson, he saw Burns as a man who "had trifled with life and must pay the penalty," Fergusson as "the poor, white-faced, drunken, vicious boy," and Villon as a thief ending on the gallows as he deserved, "a sinister dog . . . with a look in his eye and the loose flexible mouth that goes with wit and an overweening sensual temperament." He passed judgment on all three with the morality of a Covenanter, yet felt unable to withhold sympathy. He wrote a story about Villon entitled "A Lodging for the Night" and as if thinking of himself muses on the irony of Villon the thief having his purse stolen: "In many ways an artistic nature unfits a man for practical existence."

*

BOB WAS NOW spending the summers painting at Fontainebleau. Joining him there for some part of every year till 1879, Louis got to know the forest of Fontainebleau and the valley of the Loire. He felt at home with Bob's artist friends, and accepted as himself, as he never really did in Edinburgh. What was eccentric and commented on there at home was not worth a second look here. Soon he was blissfully in love with France for the sense of freedom it gave him. There was something adult and tolerant about the French, and they regarded art, like wine, as part of ordinary life. He was happy, he could breathe. Steeped in French literature from the fifteenth century onward—Villon, Dumas, Baudelaire, Hugo, Balzac, Flaubert, though he drew back from the pernicious naturalism of Zola—he found the transition easy and natural. He detected aspects of himself in the poets, in Musset, Verlaine, and Heine. One wonders what he would have made of Rimbaud, that other literary vagabond with an urge to slough off civilization.

He had stumbled on another Arcadia and was soon drunk on it. The lonely isolation of his youth seemed a bad dream. Certain traits of French character bothered him, but he loved the eating and drinking in the open air, and Barbizon appealed to him because it was primitive. It all seduced him into idleness: why struggle? There was nothing to do except wander. Paul Potts in his 1949 tribute to Whitman wrote that "Literature indeed has many great men, but he was her only great child." Stevenson might have been another if it had not been for his future wife.

The Barbizon School was in decline, the great painters associated with it no longer active. Rousseau was dead, Millet about to die. Their ghosts lived still in the vast forests of Fontainebleau. Stevenson's stepson Lloyd Osbourne remarked in a memoir that his stepfather was mentally "half a Frenchman: in taste, habits and prepossessions he was almost totally French. Not only did he speak

French admirably and read it like his mother-tongue . . . but he was really more at home in France than anywhere else."

In his essay "Fontainebleau," written in the 1880s, he remembered the delights and wonders, and especially that haven, Siron's, where

> you could get your coffee or cold milk and set forth into the forest. The doves had perhaps wakened you, fluttering into your chamber; and on the threshold of the inn you were met by the aroma of the forest. Close by were the great aisles, the mossy boulders, the interminable field of forest shadow. There you were free to dream and wander. And at noon, and again at six o'clock, a good meal awaited you on Siron's table. The whole of your accommodation . . . cost you five francs a day; your bill was never offered you until you asked for it; and if you were out of luck's way you might depart for where you pleased and leave it pending.

What could be better? Life was so wonderful, he thought he had tumbled into heaven. As he acknowledged, he had been set free in Edinburgh by the arrival of his freebooting cousin: now his bohemian friends and Barbizon itself completed his liberation. Bob, a shining figure among this community of artists, knew many of his companions from Paris. He had a studio on the Boulevard Saint Michel where he kept open house. The Siron set opened to include Louis when he first turned up, but as a relation rather than as someone making an impression in his own right. This was not a problem. If he played second fiddle to Bob he had no objection. As the elder cousin, Bob would lead the way for some time to come.

One person who did take note of Louis was Will Low, the American painter, as he became acquainted with this young man who looked less attractive than his conventionally handsome cousin but was a witty and entertaining conversationalist. Recalling him after Stevenson's death, he wrote, "It was not a handsome face until he spoke, and then I can hardly imagine that any could deny the appeal of the vivacious eyes, the humor or pathos of the mobile mouth, with its lurking suggestion of the great god Pan at times. . . ." As well as remembering the seductive charm he was struck, like Henley, Lang, and many others, by something feminine in his responses. He could burst into tears if emotionally overwrought, but this was hardly unusual among these high-strung artistic temperaments.

This brings us straight to the quality in Stevenson which has inspired much psychoanalytical speculation in recent biographers. Will Low thought that "Fascination and charm are not qualities which Anglo-Saxon youths are prone to acknowledge, in manly avoidance of their supposedly feminizing effect, but it was undoubtedly this attractive power which RLS held so strongly through life." Clearly he saw Louis as a youth rather than a man: he would look youthful to the end of his days. And he would go on appealing to men like Will Low, from homosexuals like John Addington Symonds to those difficult to categorize like Henry James. As one might expect, he excited jealousy in his admirers. Henley was jealous of Fanny Osbourne, who felt threatened by Henley's love, and Colvin himself, writes Jenni Calder, "was not above jealousy."

By 1875 Bob had overcome the inhibitions of his background and had moved a model into his studio to live with him. He liked to tantalize Louis with references to his Paris girl, who was not exactly beautiful but "a burning fiery furnace really." In the summer of 1876 Louis traveled over to join Bob again at Barbizon, only to discover that he was at nearby Grez to investigate the intrusion of two American females into the Hotel Chevillon, very much a male preserve like the Hotel Siron. Louis knew Grez-sur-Loing: he had been there with Bob, Low, and Walter Simpson, with whom he planned to go canoeing on the river. Word came back from Grez that Bob had succumbed to the charms of the invaders, settling in with them amiably as a willing prisoner. Louis, intrigued, went after him. He got there in time for dinner. An adventure awaited him that would take him away from France and Europe forever, though not yet. In his first book, *An Inland Voyage*, he wrote that "the most beautiful adventures are not those we go to seek" and went on to speculate on a journey as "a headlong, forthright tide, that bears away man with his fancies like a straw, and runs fast in time and space." The adventure he would one day embark on with an American woman ten years older than himself, in some ways a remarkably uncomplaining woman, was certainly "headlong, forthright," and so was she.

CHAPTER FIVE

To Marry Is to Domesticate
the Recording Angel

C HARACTERISTICALLY, Louis made his entrance into the dining room of the Hotel Chevillon as dramatically as possible.
The assembled company of friends were always amused by his
touches of theatre, and he was not one to disappoint them. The window was open, so he jumped through it, applauded with shouts and
laughter. The American, Mrs. Fanny Osbourne, naturally thought he
was mad. Someone explained that he was the younger cousin of Bob,
about whom she had already gone into rhapsodies in letters home.
"He is exactly like one of Ouida's heroes," she gushed, with his "wonderful grace and perfect figure . . . the best painter here, a charming
musician, speaks all languages, does all sorts of feats of strength, and
has no ambition." Spellbound she may have been, or pretended to be,
but she was sharp-eyed enough to see that he was going nowhere.

Fanny Vandegrift Osbourne had come to Grez with her teenage
daughter Belle, who was cutting a swathe among the susceptible
artists with her dark gypsy beauty. Mother and daughter were often
taken for sisters: Fanny, thirty-six when she first met Louis, looked to
be in her late twenties, with her wild dark hair brushed back behind

her ears. A photograph of 1875 shows an independent woman wearing a velvet-edged jacket over a tight black dress. A white scarf knotted at her throat declares her to be a romantic heroine in her own eyes. Grez, when she discovered it, was not yet famous for its artists but would soon be associated with Delius and Sisley, among others. As for the group clustered merrily around Bob, it was the loose commune to which Louis referred in *Travels with a Donkey* when he wrote of having had "some experience of lay phalansteries of an artistic not to say bacchanalian character." He had borrowed the odd word *phalanstère* from his reading in Charles Fourier, the French utopian socialist, and the cell of living he later established with his family and entourage in Samoa must have gone some way toward fulfilling his dream of a place set apart from civilization. It would be remarkably like the fantasy that Lawrence would call Rananim, a big house on the other side of the world into which he would put his mother and a few friends, and live a communal life with other men. Grez, with its warmth and color, would feed the dream.

Fanny might have been enamored of the Scottish Apollo whom she found attractive even when he was drunk, but Bob had fallen for Belle. This was the situation when Louis vaulted unknowingly into the dining room of the Chevillon to delight the assorted company sitting around the long refectory table. Oil lamps illuminated the scene, jugs of wine passed to and fro, the night air circulated, moths fluttered and banged against the glass funnels of the lamps. Fanny's little boy Lloyd saw a shadowy figure outside and then in came the dusty Louis in his slouch hat, a knapsack on his back. Fanny had been absorbing tales of the "two mad Stevensons": now she could compare them. Her sources of information were unreliable to say the least; her friend in San Francisco heard that Bob was dying from the effects of his wild living, had taken holy orders to please his mother and then quit. He had spent a large fortune, so she believed, and "is considered a little mad." Louis she described as having a face like Raphael: the poor fellow was dying of consumption, overeducated, dissipated, the heir to an immense fortune which he would never live to inherit. As if this wasn't inaccurate enough, she believed that his parents were both near to insanity, "and I am quite sure the son is." The two men's saving grace, it seems, was their gentlemanliness. This was not snobbery, though she had her snobbish side. It was her American view of two men who were clearly honorable.

Fanny Osbourne had arrived in Paris from California earlier that year after separating, not for the first time, from her husband. Sam Osbourne, sitting beside her at the hotel table as she chatted with Louis, had come over in a hurry to be at his youngest child's sickbed. Poor Hervey was dying from scrofulous tuberculosis. Father and mother sat watching the little boy's bones sticking through his skin, which oozed blood. It was a vile death. Fanny, who had been studying art in Antwerp and waiting desperately for money from America which failed to come, was told about Grez, and the family settled in at the Chevillon while the mother recuperated. Their young boy Samuel Lloyd, afterward known as Lloyd, had not been well, and Fanny had become neurotically anxious about him since Hervey's death. He soon blossomed in the clean country air.

Sam Osbourne did not hang about for long. The loss of Hervey did not bring them closer, and Sam was out of his element in these arty surroundings. He loved his children and they adored him, but if he was to earn any kind of living he had to go back. Also there were other attractions to being in California. The Osbournes' volatile marriage had staggered through nearly twenty years of philandering, recriminations, and passionate reunions.

Fanny Vandegrift, born in 1840, had grown up in Indianapolis, then a rowdy, rapidly developing town. She was the eldest of seven, her forebears Dutch and Swedish. Her father Jacob was a sometime farmer who could turn his hand to anything, and Fanny was allowed to run wild on a series of ranches. Self-reliance was necessary for survival in this environment, and though Fanny later put it about that she was of pioneering stock, Jacob Vandegrift soon moved into this new town in the Midwest. He was in turn a timber merchant, real estate agent, and smallholder. Her mother was short, of Swedish descent, and it was from her that Fanny got her small stature. Her skin was olive-colored, her hair dark like her complexion. Always a tiny child, she grew up a tomboy, devil-may-care, climbing trees like a boy and made to keep out of the sun by a grandmother who told her that dark was ugly.

In common with Louis she experienced a childhood saturated with prayers and bloodthirsty bedtime stories: she had been baptized in the Presbyterian faith at the age of two in a total immersion ceremony in the White River. At seventeen, short-legged, swarthy, with small feet and beautiful eyes, one could read her character by looking at her stocky body and determined jaw. Her blend of sensuality and spirit made her popular. "There was scarcely a tree in the place that did not bear somewhere the name or initials of Fanny Vandegrift," recalled her sister Nellie.

One admirer was Sam Osbourne. Twenty-one, he was a town Romeo. He could have had anyone but wanted her. His prospects couldn't have been more promising. Secretary to the governor of Indiana, a blond Southerner who exuded Southern manners, tall, personable, his character had yet to reveal itself. Sam's family had reservations about Fanny, finding her "cold and distant," but Sam had no doubts. Possibly already pregnant when she married at seventeen, she gave birth to a daughter, Isobel, soon to be known as Belle.

After a few years Sam was already a troubled man, restlessly casting about for some excuse to drift off. His chance came with the outbreak of the Civil War. Indiana fought for the Union, and Sam went off to war with a captain's commission. The girl who had learned to ride, use a rifle, and hand-roll cigarettes in her teens was left alone with her baby. Sam saw no action, and after six months he had had enough.

EIGHTEEN MONTHS LATER he had devised another adventure for himself. His tubercular brother-in-law George, married to Fanny's sister Josephine, was traveling to California, and Sam accompanied him. George died on the road, leaving Sam to push on alone to the coast. From there, and with the saloon women with whom he usually dallied, he headed for Nevada, hoping to strike it rich in the silver mines. He had arranged for Fanny to follow him to California and she got there via Panama, only to find herself on the move again and fending for herself. The pioneering childhood she claimed as hers may never have existed, but now she was about to acquire frontier skills as a young mother with a child. Sam as usual had gone on ahead. Fanny tracked him down in a Nevada silver camp, where she tried to set up home in a camp shack as the only woman among tough miners. She learned to cook like a gypsy, ignored Indians peering in at the window, rolled and smoked her cigarettes, and was glad she could shoot. Meanwhile Sam came and went. By the time she came to be uprooted again she could kill and butcher a pig. No wonder Louis admired a woman who seemed ready for anything.

Virginia City was the next stop. There Sam seemed to settle down, taking a job as clerk to the local court. This was a rough town, with plenty of diversions for a man whose eye was always prone to roam. Quickly bored with clerking, this time bitten with the bug for gold, he made for Montana with a comrade. Word came back that he had been killed by Indians. Whether or not she believed it, Fanny, now in a cheap hotel in San Francisco with her daughter, eked out a living by needlework. Rows and reconciliations had become the norm in her marriage, her husband unfaithful so often that she was probably relieved to class herself a widow.

In Austin, the mining camp in Nevada, she had established a relationship with John Lloyd, a Welshman who devoted himself to her and apparently asked nothing in return. He was in San Francisco when the ever-wandering Sam reappeared out of the blue in 1868. Amazingly his wife took him back. He took work as a court stenographer at ten dollars a day. This was riches to Fanny. They bought a cottage over the bay in Oakland, and for a time a semblance of domestic bliss descended. It produced a son, Samuel Lloyd. Sam Osbourne, always a warm, plausible fellow, was happy to make friends with Fanny's Welsh admirer, inviting the now respectable bank clerk over to Sunday dinner. One wonders if he was that kind of man who takes pleasure in sharing his wife, or merely glad to have her distracted.

Long-suffering but no doormat, Fanny had quite a temper according to Sam's mother. For years she had sought to turn a blind eye to her husband's secrets and lies. Finally and inevitably it all ended in rage and tears: she had no more stomach for his infidelities. Between them they agreed on a trial separation, and Fanny retreated with her children to live with her parents in Indiana.

Incredibly by 1869 she was back with Sam yet again. The attraction is hard to fathom when one considers the misery he inflicted. At least he had proved himself capable of being a good if sporadic provider. He was good-humored, generous with his money when he was flush, and loved his children. Perhaps it was the home of her own that beckoned, after the attempt to share one with her parents. A second son, the ill-fated Hervey, was born from the reconciliation.

It may well be that this capable, self-dramatizing woman who claimed she had second sight developed a taste for a life that had never ceased being eventful, "like a dazed rush on a railroad express." After all, Sam Osbourne was anything but boring. His daughter adored him. In her remembrance of him he comes across as likeable, as such feckless characters often are for those exempt from responsibilities:

> I cannot remember ever hearing a cross word from my father. If he would ask me to sew on a button, or darn some socks, and it wasn't done, instead of scolding like most fathers he'd stick a notice on my mirror: "Miss Handsome's attention is directed to her Papa's socks" or "Miss Osbourne's Papa is now buttonless."

Fanny was spirited, impulsive, brave when she had to be, but had never managed to take charge of her own life. Nor had it been her good fortune to have someone dependable looking after her. "I have always wanted to be taken care of," she wrote sadly, long after it became clear that by throwing in her lot with Louis she would in effect be his nurse, as well as, at times, sister and mother. But she started off as his fellow adventurer, and Stevenson's biographer Jenni Calder says truly that her decision to get on a train with her three children to the East Coast for embarkation to Europe was her first real step toward independence.

How did she reach the pitch of confidence necessary to launch herself off into the unknown? It was a triumph of will over unfavorable circumstances, and she had received some encouragement from a young Irish-American lawyer who became her mentor. First she had joined Belle at the San Francisco School of Design, enrolling in art as a mature student. Timothy Reardon, head of the Mercantile Library, befriended her. He was well read and had a "European" attitude. Reardon was a bachelor who would provide legal advice when she came to divorce Sam. He urged her to read French and German, to go on with her painting, to write, and to envisage another life for herself. So did a clutch of loyal friends in San Francisco, after she joined Belle to study art under Virgil Williams.

Belle had an admirer in a young California painter, Joe Strong, and it is possible that her mother's flirtation with Reardon became serious for a while. But she had no intention of tying herself down with anyone. Sam's infidelities were once again blatant, and she was intent on creating a separate life for herself. Though she would never be in any sense a committed artist, she needed a reason to travel to Europe. Enrolling for art studies in Antwerp gave purpose to what was essentially a flight from Sam. In 1874 these were risky tactics for a woman on her own, so to scotch rumor she took along her children and also a friend, Kate, from San Francisco.

In Antwerp there were snags: the city was too conservative to accept female students. At this point the golden-haired Hervey fell ill. A doctor sent the distraught mother to Paris, where she and Belle would have no trouble gaining admittance to life classes. Sam had agreed to send funds, but the monthly payments were erratic, sometimes nonexistent. They led a wretchedly pinched life, which Lloyd vividly remembered as an adult. "We were miserably poor," he wrote. "It seems to me that I was always hungry; I can remember yet how I used to glue myself to the bakers' windows and stare longingly at the bread within."

Louis, chatting volubly in the Chevillon dining room with this strong-jawed American, found her attractive but would have had no inkling of the kind of woman she was. Indeed she would have been entirely outside his experience. Bruce Chatwin, an Englishman married to an American, speaks of the extra fascination any transatlantic affair holds for both sides, "combining the charm of the exotic with an ease of communication." Not that anything happened at this first meeting, or for some time to come. Fanny, for her part, a bereaved woman of thirty-five trailing a "history," with flecks of grey in her defiantly short hair, must have seen the thin, fey young man growing a wispy moustache as an innocent abroad, a mere boy, as in a real sense he was. She did not take to him at first. To an American he would have seemed affected, somewhat perverse. At any rate he was altogether too exaggerated and strung out for her to grasp. His cousin was more interesting, his humor easier to handle, and in any case Bob was obviously the dominant figure at Grez. The men flirted with Belle, Frank O'Meara falling in love with her, and made a fuss of Fanny. The nightmare of the recent past began to recede in this idyllic playground as she sat painting in the meadows under a white umbrella and lunched in the shade of trees. "Mama is ever so much better and is getting prettier every day," her daughter wrote home. The fainting fits at the *atelier* in Paris after Hervey's death were no more.

Louis, out of his depth, had nevertheless registered the circumstances of this forthright woman who was, in his own words, "in no sense ordinary." She was both tough and tender, and he responded to both qualities. In the communal atmosphere of Grez he was content to observe while staying mostly ignored. Belle in a letter home enthusiastically conveyed the scene. "We generally congregate down in the garden by the big tree after dinner. Mama swings in the hammock, looking as pretty as possible, and we all form a group around her on the grass, Louis and Bob Stevenson babbling about boats, while Simpson, seated nearby, fans himself with a large white fan."

Presumably the monthly installments of cash from San Francisco had been restored, for Fanny departed at the end of the summer with her children to a modest apartment at 5 rue Douay in Montmartre. The two "mad Stevensons" were among her first visitors. They were sweet, and they thrilled her with their exhilarating company. She may have been behaving like a coquette, but after all the years of betrayal and humiliation at the hands of Sam Osbourne it was hardly surprising. She had broken out with a vengeance. Before leaving for home Louis took rooms nearby and became a regular caller. Lloyd would call out happily, "Luly is coming." Yet nothing developed that could be called serious for nearly two years.

Writing to Timothy Reardon from Grez, Fanny had stoked up his jealousy, perhaps unable to resist sharing a triumph which after all he had helped bring about:

> I am known among the villagers as "the beautiful American" and they crowd round to look at me. I don't care so much. Isn't it funny that they should do that? It was a long time before I could believe that I was not mistaken. Only think! Some artists came from a distant town to see me. I never dared to ask what they thought. I don't mind, on the contrary I think it is all very nice.

In Edinburgh again, Louis was busier than ever with ideas for essays and plans to move. Suddenly life had become richer, more complex, threatening disorder. He wrote "A Defense of Idlers," "Virginibus Puerisque," and "Charles of Orleans" and was trying his hand at fiction, attempting a novel and writing an "outrageous" long story which was meant to be an exercise in depravity. He was hardly the man for it. Hardest of all for him was the writing of dialogue. He told Bob in a letter that he was getting nowhere. "I have been working like Hell at stories and have, up to the present, failed. I have never hitherto given enough attention to the buggers speaking—my dialogue is as weak as soda water. . . ." If the time was a fertile one, it was also confusing. What did he want? Where was he heading? He thought he might have the makings of a travel writer. Or should he be married? The second essay of *Virginibus Puerisque* was a meditation on marriage, as if he strove for some clarity in his thoughts. The "something" unclear was no doubt the woman he had met at Grez, who as yet only half attended to him but who kept haunting his memory.

The prospect of marriage, however, was a sobering one. "Times are changed with him who marries," he wrote wryly. You couldn't wander any more; the road lay ahead and it was long, straight, and dusty. Being an idler, so attractive when you were single, was no longer an option. "You have wilfully introduced a witness into your life" and therefore must stand up straight "and put a name to your actions." His father would have approved of most of his reasoning, though not the self-mockery of the conclusion: "To marry is to domesticate the Recording Angel. Once you are married there is nothing left for you, not even suicide, but to be good."

There was also the threat posed by marriage to his long-cherished youth, by which he meant a quality one hung on to, that he called the "unfading boyishness of hope." By marrying he would be risking a great deal of his inner self, a renunciation so costly that it might well kill off "the green enchanted forest of his boyhood." In his view it was criminal to deny that element in a man that connected us to our original natural state, "For as the race of man, after centuries of civilization, still keeps some traits of their barbarian fathers, so man the individual is not altogether quit of youth when he is already old and honored. . . ." These problems with his idea of marriage would be swept aside in due course by someone with reservations of a less abstract kind, someone more strong-minded if less imaginative than himself.

He still wrote to the other Fanny, Mrs. Sitwell, beginning his letters to this muse "My Dearest Mother," but the correspondence was faltering. He spent time with the Jenkins in the West Highlands, and then made for Antwerp to begin a canoeing trip with the near-silent Simpson. This expedition had been planned when they were both at Grez. The scheme was to journey by water from Antwerp to Grez, and then on a series of rivers, the Loing, Loire, Saône, and Rhône, ending at the Mediterranean. As far as Louis was concerned, the justification for the jaunt was the material it would provide for a book, his first.

THEY SET OFF in their canoes, named the *Arethusa* and the *Cigarette*, Louis armed with his notebook and his professional purpose. It was a near disaster from the start. They were dogged by constant rain and flooding nearly all the way. Visibility was poor, and they couldn't see much farther than the towing paths or the banks. They put up at inns and were once mistaken for peddlers, the door slammed in their faces. Nevertheless Louis got his book out of it and was shamed by critics who praised him. He was never able to fool himself about the worth of his work. He ought to have done better, and he would, one day. Later he read *An Inland Voyage* again and told his mother he found it "thin, mildly cheery, and strained."

In this first book a casual aside reveals his compulsion to escape which he had been conscious of for years. In Mauberge he identified himself with an unlikely little man who drove the hotel omnibus. Unprepossessing he might be, but with a spark

> of something human in his soul. He had heard of our little journey, and came to me at once in envious sympathy. How he longed to travel! he told me. How he longed to be somewhere else, and see the round world before he went into the grave! . . . But it is an evil age for the gypsily inclined among men.
>
> About three in the afternoon the whole establishment of the Grand Cerf accompanied us to the water's edge. The man of the omnibus was there with haggard eyes. Poor cagebird! Do I not remember the time when I myself haunted the station, to watch train after train carry its complement of free men into the night, and read the names of distant places on the time-bills with indescribable longings?

Louis could handle and grasp character in his essays—many of them were biographical portraits—and this interest in the clash of personality with circumstance would eventually lead him to the writing of stories. For the moment he had cast himself as a character in a true story whose outcome he could not foresee. In October he was back in Paris with his cousin, seeing the Osbournes on an almost daily basis. By January 1877 he had given his parents Fanny's apartment as his forwarding address. Fanny, enjoying herself for the first time in years, had decided against returning to America for the present.

Bob's passion was still Belle, though she was now more interested in Frank O'Meara, the young Irish painter she had met in Grez. Fanny still had reservations about his cousin Louis, the man Belle called "a nice-looking ugly man." Fanny saw him more romantically now as a "tall, gaunt Scotsman" who reminded her of Raphael. He had immense charm, but she was disconcerted by his erudition, his flights of fancy, and an air of dissipation and ill-health. She still thought he might be dying of consumption. Bob had assured her that he was a gentleman and "you can trust him and depend upon him." Like many other older women, she responded to his waiflike quality, but what was she to make of a young man whose emotions flowed as freely as a woman's, who suddenly erupted in laughter that had an edge of hysteria to it, and was quite likely to burst into tears and throw himself on the floor? It was most embarrassing. "One doesn't know what to do, whether to offer him a pocket handkerchief or look out of the window."

Some of Louis's actions at this time were undoubtedly attention-seeking. Andrew Lang described meeting him in an Edinburgh drawing room. When he thought he was being overlooked he took off his coat and sat there in his shirtsleeves until his hostess said, "You might as well put your coat on again, no one is taking any notice of you." Henley said maliciously after his death that Louis found mirrors too irresistible to pass without looking into them.

Certainly he responded to admiration like a flower to the sun, especially from a woman. In *An Inland Voyage* he wrote, "If a man finds a woman admires him, were it only for his acquaintance with geography, he will begin at once to build upon the admiration."

What did he make of Fanny at this time, before he was in intimate relation with her, and long before he acknowledged a mannish aspect to her which led him to call her in letters "My dear fellow" and "My dearest little man"? In his celebration of her in a late poem he writes:

Tiger and tiger lily,
She plays a double part,
All woman in the body,
And all the man at heart.
She shall be brave and tender,
She shall be soft and high,
She to lie in my bosom
And *he* to fight and die.

In his essay on marriage he foresaw that he was in for a fight, which he welcomed with more than a hint of ambivalence, writing that "And yet when all has been said, the man who should hold back from marriage is in the same case with him who runs away from battle."

FOR ALL HIS eccentric behavior and emotional outbursts he was becoming more mature, reviewing his own situation with real awareness. Essentially honest when it came to facing himself, he was never able to delude himself for long. In Edinburgh again in November he wrote his essay "On Falling in Love" which was published in February 1877 in the *Cornhill*.

By the time he wrote his essay on wedlock he had clearly made up his mind that he ought to be married, even though "One is almost tempted to hint that it does not matter whom you marry." Women, he thought, tended to benefit from marriage, and men did not. Fanny must have wondered whether she had encountered yet another overgrown boy, like her philandering husband. But Louis was also perceptive, only too aware of the problems of communication between the sexes, which he compared to the "incompatibility of the Latin and Teuton races."

When he came to write "On Falling in Love" at the time of his growing intimacy with Fanny, he acknowledged the clap of revelation and the "pang" of curiosity without losing his power of analysis.

It is scarcely a passionate piece. One wonders if he was indeed "in love," until the separation brought about by her departure changed everything for him. He did describe falling in love as "the only event in life which really astonishes a man and startles him out of his pre- pared opinions" and went on to speak of it as "the one illogical adven- ture, the one thing of which we are tempted to think as supernatural, in our trite and reasonable world." He saw embarrassment as well as pleasure in it, with the pair venturing into a dark room like children, unable to declare anything. The "trouble" they were in they could read in each other's eyes. Delicately he tried to pin down something that was essentially wordless, where "as soon as the man knows what is in his own heart, he is sure of what is in the woman's." He knew too how fleeting it was, "all the things of a moment," in fact any- thing but eternal. It was a game likely to dissolve, but to see that was not to withdraw from it.

As well as delving into his own feelings, Louis was able to ob- serve at close quarters the huge-eyed Belle and her amorous entangle- ments. Bob Stevenson was in hot pursuit, and he could be "wolfish." Lloyd Osbourne remembered him as "a dark, roughly dressed man as lithe and graceful as a Mexican vaquero," smiling pleasantly with a mocking expression "which reminded you of the wolf in *Little Red Riding Hood*." This might have terrified her young brother, but not Belle. She had now got herself involved in the name of love with two men and was enjoying the attentions of both.

Fanny's own emotional condition at this early stage is unclear. As a woman approaching middle age she was certainly no child enter- ing a dark room. She must have been wary of the risk of disgrace for a married woman not yet divorced who regarded herself as respectable, with a daughter on hand who was bound to see everything and was far from naive. But she was lonely, far from home, and it was good to feel desirable again. She had also got it into her head that the Steven- sons were a very wealthy family. And this scrawny Scot, obviously not long for this world, whose hysterical laughing fits could only be stopped if someone bent back his fingers, had made it clear he was drawn to her.

Fanny hung on in France to see what would happen. Louis had speculated in his Whitman essay that "the majority of women . . . live all-of-a-piece and unconsciously, as a tree grows, without caring to put a name upon their acts or motives." Bruce Chatwin suggests that Fanny had developed a distaste for aggressive males and perhaps for sex altogether, and the death of her youngest son had given her a guilty urge "to save someone or something." Louis, he writes waspishly, "awoke her salvationist impulses."

For whatever motives, Fanny hung on. She was still procrastinating months later. John Lloyd waited devotedly to see her again. Timothy Reardon, becoming exasperated, had been led to believe she was soon coming home. The errant Sam was missing his children and asking for a last chance, vowing to turn over a new leaf. These were Victorian times: Fanny was not about to admit sharing a bed with an ill lover who valued her more than she had ever been valued before, though it was the truth. Louis, longing to be open with his parents about this secret life, had to be content with gestures of triumph. He had met an attractive woman and her daughter at a party. "I am in a new quarter," he wrote obscurely, "and flame about in a leisurely way," hinting in another letter that he was lunching in a dairy café and was told of a woman who had come over to study art, "and now she can't do it, feels herself like a fish out of water in the life, and yet is ashamed to give in and go back."

WHAT HAS BEEN CALLED the high adventure of Stevenson's life was now about to unfold. After his death the gathering legend of the romantic hero produced its own inevitable reaction, as critics and biographers in the 1920s found the "heaving syrup of appreciation" hard to stomach. George Moore, for instance, thought Stevenson a clever fake, dazzling his readers with mere style, and in midcentury F. R. Leavis saw fit to exclude him from his "Great Tradition." The fault-finding is still with us. Any study of Stevenson today has to take account of Bruce Chatwin, his latest critic, whose onslaught seems remarkably prescient regarding his own fate.

Chatwin's admirers have seen him as touched with genius. Like Louis, he was a prodigy. His blue eyes had a fanatic gleam. He hero-worshiped Stevenson to begin with, so obsessed with him that he went deliberately to live in Edinburgh and got himself enrolled in Stevenson's university. By the time he came to dismiss his hero, both as a man and a writer, it was important for him to do so violently. His 1974 article in the *Times Literary Supplement* is that of someone facing both ways at once. The truth is that he found resemblances to himself too disturbing to be borne. He attacked the mirror that James Pope-Hennessy's biography of Stevenson must have held up to him.

Some of these parallels that he detested so much are startling, as are Chatwin's harsh words and often spiteful insights. No doubt he understood Stevenson and was deeply affected by him. It was as if he had to destroy this fascination or be dominated for the rest of his days. He implies throughout that Stevenson was a charlatan, was "profoundly self-centered and had a morbid concern for his public image." There is no denying that Stevenson went in for occasional posturing, enjoyed fancy dress, dreamed of being a soldier, and tried on different identities. Like Chatwin, he was an only child and his mother's darling. Friends of Chatwin remember his own unnerving laugh "like a wild hyena, whoops and away it went."

The list of similarities gets longer. Louis, with "the pack on his back, always happier to be somewhere else," is exactly, says Susanna Clapp, how many people saw Chatwin. He too had Louis's gift of making himself irresistible to both sexes, just as he had, it seems, Louis's ability to render those he met "slaves to a rare, authentic and irresistible charm." Both, when you talked to them, could make you feel the most important person, and whenever they were around "you felt awfully happy." Both were self-styled nomads with one eye on Walt Whitman's Open Road. Both married self-reliant, tomboyish American women. Both died in their forties in a welter of syco-phancy, rumor, and myth. Louis's "hysterical gaiety in the face of fatal illness," as Chatwin put it, was echoed uncannily when Chatwin died after weeks of wild excitement and fantasy.

The youthful Stevenson who had arrived at Cockfield Rectory to meet Mrs. Sitwell in his velveteen jacket and straw hat, knapsack on his back, was closely related, writes J. C. Furnas in his biography, "to a style of youngster already rife in British universities and later imitated in the States with pious Anglophilia—very young, very witty, very impulsive, very cultivated, very promising, very picturesque, very high-strung, very generous, and oh so sensitive. Rupert Brooke was the peak of the development." This picture, comments Susannah Clapp, fits Chatwin very well—his marvelous good looks must have equaled Brooke's. And Chatwin's talk, filled with "an extraordinary jumble of the abstruse, the exotic, the savage and the sophisticated," delivered at tremendous speed, puts one immediately in mind of Sydney Colvin's recollection of his brilliant young friend, his "pure poetic eloquence . . . grave argument and criticism, riotous freaks of fancy, flashes of nonsense more illuminating than wisdom" that "streamed from him inexhaustibly."

CHAPTER SIX

The Great Affair Is to Move

F OR LOUIS, 1877 was a repeat of the previous year. He joined
Bob, Fanny, Belle, and Lloyd at Grez, where he had known such
unexpected happiness. He and his cousin must have looked a pair of
wonder-figures from a land not to be guessed at, Bob in his wide-
brimmed hat, striped stockings, and piratical neckerchief, Louis in
his straw hat and cloak and the now permanent velvet jacket. But the
wonder was not in what they wore, it was in how they were, and that
they were such an obvious pair: the heavenly twins. Louis was there
until mid-July. Then he tore himself away, flitted back to England,
and joined his parents on a tour of Cornwall, all the time eating his
heart out to be in Paris with Fanny. With his new impetus to prove
himself like "a goad in my flesh," he felt bound to "work, work,
work." He pushed out ideas for essays and articles to Leslie Stephen
and tried his hand at stories that fell by the wayside. His one success
with fiction, though he called it "bosh," was "Will o' the Mill," which
the *Cornhill* published the following year.

Cornwall he didn't much care for, but then nothing that was not
France would be to his taste. To him it was as bleak as bleakest Scot-
land and "nothing like so pointed and characteristic." He was glad
Frances Sitwell liked his Villon, and he liked it himself because it was

vivid. He was aiming for vividness now rather than style; having hit on the ingredient he saw as "the real line of country," and he was determined now to be readable if nothing else. One wonders whether the American was already making her influence felt. He was a poor correspondent, he told friends, occupied with his own "blarsted immortal works" to the exclusion of all else, but keeping occupied was now his religion, "so that a man should have his life in his own pocket, and never be thrown out of work by anything." He was dreaming as always of being finally independent of his father, though that was years away.

By September he was back at Fanny's side in Paris, with another forwarding address for his mail—which of course was hers. He had not yet moved in with her. Then in the early winter he was afflicted with a chronic eye infection. Fanny took charge of him, nursing him for the first of many times to come. They were now effectively living together. It was yet another of his illnesses which moved things along for him. If there had been any other woman hidden away in his life before Louis and Fanny finally became lovers, as some biographers have speculated, there was no one now, and the evidence is flimsy. He was as incapable of deception as his father. The stand against Burns in his essay was in part a rejection of his philandering, which could be read as a warning to himself. "It is the punishment of Don Juanism," he had written, "to create continually false positions—relations in life which are wrong in themselves and which it is equally wrong to break or to perpetuate. . . ."

Fanny, solely responsible for him, panicked when he showed no improvement. The first of her famous telegrams signaling a state of emergency went to Bob, asking him to take his sick cousin home. Louis was now nearly blind with conjunctivitis. Unfortunately Bob was ill himself in Edinburgh. Fanny, hobbling about with a bad foot, wired Colvin, a friend she had yet to meet, wrapped Louis up, and somehow transported him to London. It was November.

She knew no one in the city, and Colvin arranged for Mrs. Sitwell to take her in. They both liked her and made a fuss of her in their restrained English fashion. Louis had gone back home and she was not sure how to act, grateful though she was for their hospitality. Also she was curious to put faces to these unknown people she had heard much about. Taking tea with these murmuring foreigners in Bayswater she soon felt she was being patronized. In a letter to America she describes feeling so out of place in Mrs. Sitwell's house that she ended up in a corner like an exotic animal. There she sat listening to the innocuous Colvin and the "stately, beautiful Mrs. Sitwell" as they talked to her in their correct English about the progress of literature and the arts. She declared that she was rather afraid of them, a statement hard to believe from this resourceful, assertive, and earthy character who could march into a gunsmith in Antwerp to have her firearm cleaned. Certainly she was being arch when she added that they occasionally came down to her level and "petted me as they would stroke a kitten."

She was no kitten, but what exactly was she? Commentators have been divided into pro- and anti-Fanny—she was that kind of woman. Frank McLynn calls her bluntly "a very rum creature indeed." Lodging with Mrs. Sitwell gave her the opportunity to know her paramour's friends at close quarters and get to grips with the London scene. There were soon pro- and anti-Fanny factions as Louis's friends divided, but this was not exactly her doing, and at first all went well. Partly the divisions opened up because of the possessiveness he inspired. There was also a great deal of snobbery. She met her bitter enemy of the future in Mrs. Sitwell's salon, and that too went smoothly. Initially Henley must have been easier to deal with than more duplicitous callers. At least she knew where she was with this noisy, raffish fellow, heavily bearded, who waved his crutches at her while he argued and spoke frankly.

Colvin was one who found merit in her personality, praised her eagerness and devotion, her "supple and elastic" build, and admired her small, "beautifully modeled" hands and feet. He took note of her pearly white teeth and quaint speech and suggested alarmingly, though without irony, that her looks and character were Napoleonic. He stayed on her side from the beginning, unlike Henry James with his reference to her as a "poor, barbarous and merely *instinctive* lady."

Later James would become an ardent supporter. His sister Alice, however, stuck by her first impressions, convinced that she had met a savage . . . "such egotism and so naked! giving me the strangest feeling of being in the presence of an unclothed being."

Fanny for her part was skeptical of this whole London crowd but was shrewd enough to keep her dislike to herself. She would not do so for long. She came from a tough world they knew nothing about, had visceral reactions to people and circumstances she encountered, and believed she possessed extrasensory powers. The occult would always be one of her interests. If her thought processes were a mystery to some, that was because she kept in touch with her instincts. Louis in a fit of temper once called her a peasant. She never forgave him. Her belief in spirituality and the supernatural were mixed with vulgarity, her love with egoism. Her deadliest critic would be her future daughter-in-law Katherine Osbourne, who was to maintain in her testimony that Fanny's will

> could have conquered provinces, but all her ambition was turned to subjugating all the individuals about her. She was clairvoyant, uncannily so, she watched and studied everyone to turn anything her way or to thwart any of their plans and ambitions that were aside her use. . . .

Debunkers of Fanny have used this woman as their main source, though Katherine's motives for depicting her mother-in-law so harshly are questionable, as will be seen. Fanny's biographer finds her muddled, and like a caricature of her subject's darker side.

In Katherine's opinion Fanny could have been another Annie Besant. She loved dramas and mysteries that only she could sense, felt she had the power within her to help and comfort people, and seemed always to encounter people weaker than herself, lost souls who seemed drawn to her. Sadly, wrote Katherine Osbourne, she lacked industry and ambition. There was something striking about her eyes, but they were

> cattish, cruel, always moving in quick little jerks sideways. . . .
> She never outgrew childhood and it seemed to me that she be-

longed to the childhood of the race—the first beginnings of the race—in some dark-skinned peoples. But she was not feminine, she was more a man. Her one great service to Stevenson was the pleasure she took in listening to his tales—and he always wanted a listener. I do not think she was mad, but of the year 10,000 B.C. and a pure romancer.

In Edinburgh, nursing his afflicted eyes as well as his half-mended relationship with his worried parents, Louis tried to clarify for himself his moral position with regard to Fanny. It seems clear that he was now sexually committed. Where did he go from here? What was honorable for a young man with scruples who saw the French attitude to women as "indecent"? Fanny, an experienced and older woman, was clearly able to take care of herself, but the situation was after all illicit, and he could be seen to be taking advantage. For a man who saw women as sexual victims, this was intolerable. The relationship could be made decent only by her divorcing Sam and marrying him, if indeed that was what she wanted. He was still not sure. Soon he would have to come clean with his parents about a position they were bound to find appalling, one that he hadn't in fact sought. Or was he deluding himself? He had struggled to make his peace with his father without sacrificing his principles, such as they were: sometimes he thought they were in tatters. Now he was poised to deliver his deadliest blow yet.

He confided some of his hopes and fears in a letter to Henley in December 1877. In order to work he had to light the gas and have it burning all day long, the weather was so dark. So, he could have said, was the weather inside himself. But, taken the circumstances, he was not as black at heart as he might have been. Nevertheless it was a strange time to be writing his "Gospel According to Walt Whitman," making a fair job, in his opinion, of dealing with the American poet's "ranting optimism." He was also churning out copy for a new magazine called *London*, edited by Henley, in which Fanny, now an aspiring writer herself, had become involved. Never lacking in self-confidence, she was helping to choose or reject writers, even handing out criticism whether asked for or not. The magazine lasted barely two years but had the merit for Louis of encouraging his apprentice fiction. Henley not only printed his stories but kept padding out the periodical with his own bad verse.

Although *The Suicide Club* was Louis's book, the idea for it was Bob's, based on a series of linked stories in the style of the *Thousand and One Nights* that was running in the magazine. Louis had a poor opinion of the book, but the satire worked. In it a group of rich parasites meet to drink champagne and play cards in order to decide who will put an end to the tedium of it all. The important thing for anyone about to end his life was to do it like a gentleman.

After skirting around literary matters in his letter to Henley, the "positively" lonely Louis made his now famous declaration. He might be a miserable widower but he kept working, not reproaching God or disowning the universe because he had problems.

> And do I not love? and am I not loved? and have I not friends who are the pride of my heart? O no, I'll have none of your blues; I'll be lonely, for I can't help it; and I'll hate to go to bed, where there is no dear head upon the pillow, for I can't help that either, God help me; but I'll make no mountain of my little molehill, and pull no damnable faces at the derisive stars. . . .

He was apart from Fanny over Christmas, doing his best to be festive with his parents and their friends. Fanny had reverted to being a nurse again, this time taking care of the ailing Bob in Paris. When Louis had been struck half blind in the early winter, Bob was in the throes of a breakdown in Edinburgh which has not been described but may have been similar to the depressive illness disabling his father. Now he was being looked after by a woman eager to know all he could tell her about his cousin.

Louis, casting about for distraction, had "a kick at the stern works of that melancholy puppy and humbug Daniel Deronda . . . the Prince of Prigs, the literary abomination of desolation in the way of manhood, a type which is enough to make a man foreswear the love of women." He was writing to Patchet Martin in Australia, the first person to send him a fan letter.

In Paris himself early in the New Year, he enlisted the help of Colvin and Mrs. Sitwell in reconciling his parents to the fact of Fanny's existence and their son's hopes for a future life with her. Thomas Stevenson had a soft spot for Mrs. Sitwell, and when she vouched for the unknown Fanny's character it must have reassured him. All the same the news, delicately put though it was, must have been shocking. Louis asked his father over, so as to explain the matter face to face in all its complexity, and in February 1878 Thomas was in Paris, seeing his twenty-seven-year-old son at a separate address. The advanced views he held on women's rights may even have gone in Louis's favor, at least to a certain extent. He does not seem to have met Fanny, and probably hoped that when the American returned home to sort out her affairs the relationship would fizzle.

Once his father was back at Heriot Row, a guilt-ridden Louis sat down in a busy café to write something he knew his father would welcome, a statement of his Christian beliefs. Behind the attempt could have been a Fanny advising her lover not to throw away the only financial security he was likely to have for the foreseeable future. Apparently the meeting had gone surprisingly well, with Thomas, resigned now to his son as some sort of rebel, making less fuss than was expected. When they parted, Louis promised to spend Easter with his parents, knowing how important it was for his father to have his family around him on Good Friday and Easter Sunday.

His café letter is a curious if well-meaning attempt to turn Christianity, "a very wise, noble and strange doctrine," into something as practical as Buddhism. Christ, he now thinks, "was of all doctors (if you will let me use the word) one of the least ascetic." To live out the Gospels in his understanding "consists in making oneself very little in order to avoid many knocks; in preferring others, in order that even when we lose we shall find some pleasure in the event; in putting our desires outside of ourselves, in another ship, so to speak, so that when the worst happens there will be something left." If all this was puzzling to Stevenson senior, the conclusion at least would have been a comfort. "Everything has been, in one way or another, bringing me a little nearer to what I think you would like me to be." And he ended with a hope that clearly came from the heart. "I hope I have taken a step towards . . . more intimate relations with you. But don't expect too much of me. I am a narrow and a sad person. Try to take me as I am."

Suddenly he was felled by another of his pulmonary illnesses. The more cynical critics have suggested that this seemed a signal for Fanny to be mentally disturbed. It was a pattern that went on repeating itself, for whatever reason or unreason. Louis, at his wit's end, wrote to Mrs. Sitwell from the Hotel Canterbury on the Boulevard Haussmann, "I wish I could say she is well; her nerves are quite gone; one day I find her in heaven, the next in hell." He thought her condition would improve if he could get her to Grez, but that was some way off and he was desperately "in need of coin." Sam's allowance often failed to arrive. As he recovered from his own attack he complained of weakness, trudging round in an overcoat which he feared to leave behind, even when it was mild. He returned home to spend Easter with his parents as arranged, but soon hastened back. He was trying to support Fanny and her family as well as himself on the money his father allowed him. He tried to obtain loans from Henley, who was always hard pressed, and Baxter, then in June was forced to take his one and only job, if one can call it that, as secretary to Fleeming Jenkin, at that time a juror at the Paris Exposition. It is hard to imagine Louis in a paid position. He drew a modest salary and was allowed plenty of time off to visit Fanny and her children at Grez. Then disaster struck. Sam Osbourne, whom they had been expecting on another trip to Europe, sent his wife an ultimatum. There would be no further maintenance from him unless she returned.

In August Fanny crossed to London for the boat train and her transatlantic voyage. Bob was there at Dover to escort her and her family to his digs in Chelsea. Louis, working in London now as an assistant editor on Henley's magazine *London*, though it too could hardly be called a job, came to see them off at the station. He was drawn and silent, fighting down his anger and despondency at the thought of Sam Osbourne's power over him. He was nearly twenty-eight. What had he achieved? Crucified by having to wait for the train to move he strode off on his thin legs, his brown ulster pulled round his shoulders. Lloyd was hurt because his "Luly" walked away without once looking back.

UNABLE TO STAND his own company in Edinburgh now that his love was six thousand miles away, Louis decided on a twelve-day walking tour in the Midi, where at any rate the sun should be shining and the weather warm. He was overlooking the altitude: the region he settled on was the high Cévennes with its granite uplands, which he thought might be similar in some respects to the Highlands. It was essential that he do something. In his state of mind he was in danger of sinking like a stone. "I find it damned hard work to keep up a good countenance in this world nowadays, harder than anyone knows, and I hope you may never have cause," he wrote to Baxter, "to feel one half as sad as I feel." It was true that "all's squared with my people," but only because his parents believed that their son's moral crisis was over. He was not living illicitly with "that woman" any longer.

His interest in the Cévennes had been stirred by reading George Sand's *Le Marquis de Villemer*. As well as having a desperate need to be on his own, he thought there might be a book in the project. *An Inland Voyage* had not done well. He took himself off to Le Monastier in the Cevenol hills in September to make his preparations, and to finish revising the pieces for his second book, *Edinburgh: Picturesque Notes*. Charles Baxter, ever loyal, had loaned him some stake money.

A fortnight later he was ready to set off. His intention was to hike over some of the wildest and highest terrain in France, crossing the borders of four *départements*—the Haute Loire, the Lozère, the Ardèche, and Gard. At the highest point, on the savage upland peaks of the central Cévennes, he would traverse ridges that were between 4,000 and 5,500 feet. "You walk against the sky," writes the literary sleuth Richard Holmes, "with chain after chain of hills rolling southwards at your feet."

What gave him the idea of a donkey is hard to say, except that in 1878 it must have been a practical way to transport one's equipment. Nowadays the Stevensonian pilgrim can go by car. And Louis was in need of assistance, for he was intent on carrying his huge homemade sleeping bag, green waterproof on the outside, lined inside with sheep's fur, meant to serve as a saddlebag during the day; two changes of clothes; a Scottish railway plaid; a spirit lamp and cooking pan; candles and a lantern; a jackknife costing twenty francs, with assorted blades; a leather water bottle; an eighty-page schoolboy's exercise book to contain his notes; blocks of dark chocolate; tins of Bologna sausage, and, just before he started, a leg of mutton and a bottle of red wine. Other necessities included papers for rolling cigarettes, tobacco, a revolver, and, strangest of all, an egg whisk so that he could make the egg-and-brandy nog he liked with his morning coffee. He also took along a few books, one of which was the French edition of Peyrat's *Histoire des Pasteurs du Désert*.

It was October before he set out. The small donkey cost him sixty-five francs and a glass of brandy. He called her Modestine. Richard Holmes, in his book *Footsteps*, says he was first captivated, as a child of the 1960s, by *An Inland Voyage*, a book that would enthrall few young men today. But Holmes, an indefatigable and subtle investigator of journeys, goes searching at eighteen for the traces of *un Ecossais*, a Scotsman, who walked on foot through the Cévennes uplands. He has fun with the misunderstandings as he tries to explain to the man in the local grocer's van giving him a lift to Le Monastier why he has come. Finally he pulls *Travels with a Donkey* out of his rucksack. "Ah, *that*," shouts the driver. "I understand, I understand! You are on the traces of Monsieur Robert Louis Steamson. Bravo, bravo!"

In a passage not used in the final edition of *Travels*, Louis dwelt on the ways in which the people and their landscape curiously resembled Scotland:

They have abrupt, uncouth, Fifeshire manners, and accost you as if you were trespassing, with an "*où est-ce que vous allez?*" only translat-

able into the Lowland "Whau'r ye Gaun?" They keep the Scottish
Sabbath. . . . Again, this people is eager to proselytize: and the
post-master's daughter used to argue with me by the half hour
about my heresy. . . . I have heard its reverse process going on between a Scots woman and a French girl; and the arguments in the
two cases were identical. . . .

His donkey, Modestine, was female, as he discovered later, a
beast about the size of a Newfoundland dog and the color of a mouse.
She was soon giving him grief, shedding her load without warning,
refusing to climb hills and veering off the path toward the nearest
shade. A peasant he encountered advised him to cut a thorn switch
from a hedge and use it on the animal's flanks. He did so and was
soon revolted by the brutality he had been forced into, writing in his
journal that "The sound of my own blows sickened me." Finding out
that Modestine was female only made things worse, for "this increased my horror of my own cruelty."

At Le Bouchet, the heartsore Louis who had taken on this
toughest walk of his life—and he was a prodigious walker—so as to
stop thinking of Fanny, found himself having to share the same inn
room as a married couple from Alais. This was normal practice at the
time, but the woman was disturbingly young and Louis embarrassed.
"*Honi soit qui mal y pense*: but I was sufficiently sophisticated to feel
abashed. I kept my eyes to myself as much as I could, and I know
nothing of the woman except that she had beautiful arms, full white
and shapely: whether she slept naked or in her slip, I declare I know
not; only her arms were bare." He was resigned to celibacy, but it
hardly helped that he had tasted the married state.

The weather worsened in less than a week. He lost his bearings,
fell into bogs, wandered through the tangled undergrowth of woods,
and came to the village of Fouzilhac, a godforsaken place where no
one would help him when he asked to be put on the path to Chey-
lard. The light was falling and he looked terrible, soaked and covered
in mud, the smell of brandy on his breath. Nothing is more dismal
than the south of France when you are cold and wet, the rain slopping

around shoes chosen for southern warmth. The rain came down heavier than ever. The lanterns held up to his face half-blinded him, and "I plowed distressfully among stones and rubbish heaps." He knocked at more doors but no one answered. It stopped raining but the cold wind kept blowing. Louis would always be at his most determined and gritty at moments like this. He pitched camp in a beech woods that sheltered him in the blackness like a cave. He tethered the drenched Modestine to a branch, broke half his black bread for her supper, lay down his sleeping bag, and crawled into it, lying there exhausted like a "*bambino*." Feeling hungry, he had a revolting meal of Bologna sausage and chocolate, washing the mixture down with neat brandy.

He woke up next morning to find Modestine tied to her branch, standing tranquilly across the path. He had survived a bad situation without sinking into despair or losing his temper. Overhead the sky was full of shreds of cloud, the weather still wild and as cold as ever. For some unaccountable reason he felt in excellent spirits. He wrote later:

> Ulysses, left on Ithaca, and with a mind unsettled by the goddess, was not more pleasantly astray. I have been after an adventure all my life, a pure dispassionate adventure, such as befell early and heroic voyagers; and thus to be found by morning in a random wayside nook in Gevaudan—not knowing north from south, as strange to my surroundings as the first man upon the earth, an inland castaway—was to find a fraction of my daydreams realized.

"A PURE DISPASSIONATE ADVENTURE" expresses perfectly his hunger for heroism. Though even his detractors have conceded that Stevenson was a talented storyteller who became a consummate stylist, he was perhaps most original in his character, his spirit. D. H. Lawrence opens *Sea and Sardinia*, an account of his journey on foot through the savage middle of an island full of chaotic squalor, with the words, "Comes over one an absolute necessity to move." Forty-six years earlier his British predecessor was writing of his own incurable restlessness and his longing to throw off civilization and its ills like this: "For my part, I travel not to go anywhere, but to go. I travel for travel's sake. The great affair is to move, to feel the need and hitches of our life more nearly: to come down off this feather-bed of civilization and find the globe granite underfoot. . . ."

Chekhov, another weak-chested literary nomad and a near contemporary, asking about facilities for relieving himself in the howling wilderness of Siberia he had planned to cross, was told he needed only to carry a stick, to beat off the wolves. Louis seemed to have no dread of either wolves or brigands—he had heard rumors of both—but he greatly feared dogs, the bane of his life. "A dog is vastly braver, and is besides supported by the sense of duty." To a self-styled tramp like himself, the sound of a dog's insistent bark "represents the sedentary and respectable world in its most hostile form. . . . I both detest and fear them."

Hiking through these French highlands he stopped for meals now and then at *auberges*, or "hedge-inns" as he liked to call them. The people of the inn were not the same as the rude peasants on the road. Once you shared their hearth you ceased to be a stranger and they were invariably friendly and considerate. The accommodation was rough and ready, the table provided with a glass, "a whang of bread," and an iron fork. The traveler was expected to eat with his own knife and might be surprised by the visit of a fat sow grunting under the table and rubbing against his legs. "Anyone who has a fancy to wash must do so at the common table." The old landlord at one such *auberge* had nicer manners than his wife, who said cuttingly, "My man knows nothing, he is like the beasts." It was said without contempt, and the old man nodded amiably in agreement. When he heard of Louis's difficulty with his donkey he at once fashioned him a goad, a wand with an eighth of an inch of pin at the end. "Thenceforward Modestine was my slave. A prick, and she passed the most inviting stable door. A prick, and she broke forth into a gallant little trot that devoured the miles."

He crossed over the Allier by an old stone bridge and approached with trepidation the Trappist monastery of Our Lady of the

Snows. Drawing near to the place and driving his "secular" donkey before him, he felt a pang of something like terror. "This it is to have had a Protestant education." But the hospitality of the monks was welcome, and there is humor in his account of their attempts to convert him, his defense of Protestantism and "the faith of his mother," which must have delighted his father after their recent conflict.

He went on to L'Estampe and then made for Mont Lozère. Near the summit he slept out under the stars. The passage recording it is a rhapsody.

> Night is a dead monotonous period under a roof; but in the open world it passes lightly, with its stars and dews and perfumes, and the hours are marked by the changing face of Nature. What seems a kind of temporal death to people choked between walls and curtains is only a light and living slumber to the man who sleeps a-field. All night long he can hear Nature breathing deeply and freely. . . .

He ascended the Pic de Finiels and then went down from the summit to Le Pont-de-Montvert in the Tarn Valley. He was now in the country of the Camisards, Protestant country, and it thrilled him to be there. The Camisards had been the "Covenanters of the South": they organized themselves and had a military and religious hierarchy like their Scottish counterparts, if on a smaller scale, "in a land where the tyranny of the Church produced the Camisard rebellion." Louis came to believe, when he researched them later in the Advocates' Library in Edinburgh for his book, that the spirit of these southern Covenanters was lighter in conscience than those who took to the hills in Scotland. "They knew they were on God's side, with a knowledge that has no parallel among the Scots; for the Scots, although they might be certain of the cause, could never rest confident in the person."

There is more than one Stevenson marching resolutely onward through the pages of this little book. The Covenanter reborn, the Bunyan pilgrim, the Protestant heretic among the Trappists, the Victorian hippy setting out to find himself, the fool lost and blundering—all put in their appearance. Chatwin, predictably scathing, dismisses *Travels* as "the prototype of the incompetent undergraduate voyage," a Don Quixote getting nowhere. Richard Holmes in a fine essay calls the journey an initiation, a trial set by Louis himself to discover whether he could survive on his own. And sometimes it was touch and go. He refers at one moment of crisis to "this disgusting journal," when "black care" sits on his knapsack and he feels like a dead man, teetering on the brink of falling ill. A voyage is a piece of autobiography and that's all, he decides.

Then a night in the open air saves him. Waking up one night at two in the morning he is initiated into a secret. This is a "resurrection" time that only shepherds and countrymen know, when "Cattle wake on the meadows; sheep break their fast on dewy hillsides and change to a new lair among the ferns; and houseless men, who have lain down with the fowls, open their dim eyes and behold the beauty of the night." He listens to the "indescribable, quiet talk" of the runnel over the stones. His cigarette creates a speck of light on his silver gypsy ring, the highest light in the whole landscape.

He had undertaken the journey to distract himself and to prove that he could stand alone, rather than sit miserably at home missing Fanny. One day the voice he heard of a woman singing underneath the trees betrayed him back. The ballad "seemed to be about love and a *bel amour*, her handsome sweetheart, and I wished I could have taken up the strain and answered her." He told Bob that his cousin would find in his travel book "mere protestations to Fanny," and it was true that, fully alive though he felt at times, "as if life had begun again afresh," there was something sadly lacking in the paradise he had regained. Most of the protestations disappeared from the published edition, and there are few signs anyway in the original version, published in 1978 as *Cévennes Journal: Notes on a Journey Through the French Highlands*. But he drafted what was in effect a proposal of marriage when he wrote that

I could have wished for a companion, to be near me in the starlight, silent and not moving if you like, but ever near and within touch. For there is, after all, a sort of fellowship more quiet even than solitude, and which, rightly understood, is solitude made perfect. And to live out of doors with the woman a man loves is of all lives the most complete and free. . . .

He came at last to the St.-Jean-du-Gard plain, shed a tear over Modestine when he came to leave her, then sold her for thirty francs less than he paid. Returning via Alès, Lyons, Autun, and Paris, he was back in "the Bastille of civilization" by the beginning of November. He eked out a few days with Colvin in Cambridge, unable to write anything but "ditchwater," and tried to flesh out his travel notes. In Edinburgh for Christmas he went on working at his book and hoped for news of Fanny. Henley came up to spend a week with him at Swanston in mid-January and was given the manuscript to read. *Travels with a Donkey* was published in June 1879. He told Bob, "I've got thirty quid for it, and should have had fifty," but money was the last thing on his mind. Fanny had been his muse when he heard a woman sighing and wrote "love is the great amulet which makes the world a garden," and he pined for her. He thought there was some good stuff in the book here and there. All his mother knew was that the prodigal was back safe and sound. In her diary she recorded: "At *last* on the 21st [of December] after being more than six months away Louis came home."

The reviews were, as they say, mixed. The *Spectator* found it "a very readable volume." Already literary opinions were beginning to divide, like his friends on the subject of Fanny. *Frazer's Magazine* damned him as a dilettante who wrote prettily, "one of those darlings of fortune who, having no natural hardships of their own, find a piquant gratification in inventing a few artificial ones. . . . This is the last whim of exquisite youth."

He published a story, "Providence and the Guitar," started work on one of his best short stories, "The Pavilion on the Links," a complicated thriller that he finished in the States, and wrote more of the Prince Florizel stories that make up *New Arabian Nights*. Then he walked straight into a literary dead end, thanks to Henley, who had married in April 1878, lived in Shepherd's Bush, and was now permanently hard up. The idea of a play based on the infamous Deacon Brodie was Louis's: he had drafted the play ten years earlier and then abandoned it. Deacon Brodie was a respectable Edinburgh businessman who lived a life of crime at night. The theme of the double had long fascinated Louis, and he needed money as badly in his way as Henley. This was the spur. Henley talked his friend into a collaboration, certain they could make a fortune. If Louis had little talent as a playwright, Henley had less. They worked on the drama of Brodie's life for three months before Christmas, Louis scribbling drafts in the Savile Club and then walking to Shepherd's Bush to confer with his partner. At Swanston in the New Year they were polishing the melodrama. It was submitted to Henry Irving, who left it lying around for a year before rejecting it. Henley, his belief in it unshaken, had the effort printed while Louis was in America, and managed to get it produced in Bradford, Aberdeen, and finally London, but nowhere successfully. Brooding over these failures led him to think that this attempt and others later were the fault of his collaborator for not devoting himself more single-mindedly to plays.

Louis's essay on Burns appeared in the *Cornhill*. Undeterred by the rejection of the piece he had written for the *Encyclopaedia Britannica*, he had been inspired by Leslie Stephen's encouragement to write a fuller study. He set to work with the aim of demolishing the icon which still remains intact. He praised the poems but leveled an attack on the poet's life and character which has earned him the label of hypocrite. Who was he to object to Burns's immorality when he was involved in an adulterous affair? Ian Bell has seen that it was really the poet's selfishness that Louis was unable to stomach. Burns was a man who "trifled with life." The legend of the poet dying of drink was itself a lie, for as Louis points out, others have drunk more. "He died of being Robert Burns, and there is no levity in such a statement of the case; for shall we not, one and all, deserve a similar epithet?" He recoiled from his subject like Chatwin writing of Stevenson, as if he had recognized something unsupportable in his own character. His study of Burns was at the same time an exercise in self-examination.

Writing to Edmund Gosse while he was working on the essay, he told him, "I made a kind of chronological table of his various loves and lusts, and have been comparatively speechless ever since." Had his own youth in Old Town risen up to haunt and accuse him? He was on surer ground with the poems, full of admiration for "The Twa Dogs" and the "Address to the Unco Guid," adding with his anti-English bias that even a common Englishman could glimpse their merits "as it were from Pisgah."

Louis, shuttling restlessly back and forth between Edinburgh and London, was exhibiting the stresses and strains he had been inventing for Brodie. The rising literary star, in and out of the Savile Club and getting to know George Meredith at Box Hill, was acting bizarrely when night fell, wandering through the London streets in clothes that made him look like a tramp. His parents had begun to worry again about his state of mind and so had his friends. Did he secretly hope to be arrested? It had happened to him once before, in France, on his canoeing trip with Simpson. Briefly alone, he was challenged by a gendarme and found to be without papers. Losing his temper, he was held in the *préfecture* until the aristocratic Simpson sauntered in to vouch for the "beggar."

The "black care" that settled on his knapsack in the Cévennes had returned to perch on his shoulder. Edmund Gosse, accustomed to Louis being as fired with "ranting optimism" as Whitman, calling him "the Great Exhilarator . . . my emblem of Life," wondered in a letter what was wrong. Louis could only say, "I can do no work at all. It all lies aside. I want—I want—a holiday; I want to be happy: I want the sun or the moon or something. I want the object of my affections badly. . . . I envy you your wife, your home, your child—I was going to say your cat."

Fanny's letters, wild, rambling, and disjointed, were making him anything but happy. It was no wonder he could settle to nothing. He had suicidal impulses, not for the first time, but his father's morality, not to mention Cummy's, always won out. Well-meaning advice from Colvin and others, urging him to give up his infatuation, confused him even further. Fanny seemed unable to give him a straight answer to any question. In short she was procrastinating again. So far as Louis could make out, she had done nothing about a divorce. From Sam's point of view a divorce would have been humiliating, and in Victorian times it was no easy matter. Her lover, tormented with doubts, was beginning to wonder if Fanny, with her instinct for secrecy, had in fact put her husband in the picture with regard to Louis, or had she taken the line of least resistance and slid back into another patched-up marriage? Louis doubted the strength of her will, faced with Sam's charm and the consolations of a settled family home. As a court stenographer to the Bureau of Mines, Sam now moved with his family to Monterey. Louis was deluged with a mishmash of family news he could not have cared less about: Belle had run off with the young painter Joe Strong; Fanny's sister was marrying a Mexican saloon-keeper.

Fanny's letters grew wilder, which convinced Louis that she was again mentally unstable, as she had been for a time in Paris. Pressed by Louis to make up her mind, tempted by the security he might one day be able to provide with his inheritance, she veered around, paralyzed by indecision. Evidently her letters were making no sense. Louis, driven by frustration to confide in someone, turned to Baxter, who was soon out of his depth and passing on his worries to Colvin. The half-understood problem was circulating farcically from one friend to another. Colvin told Gosse that Louis, who had "been to pieces" recently, had at last "got quite a sane letter from an intelligible address in Spanish California." Perplexed as everyone else, he ended, "What next, who shall tell?"

In the midst of this chaos the luckless suitor wrote in May from the Savile Club to his mother: "I have been in such a muddle about my plans that I did not know what to write." Before landing in this morass he had been consolidating the beginnings of a literary reputation. This too was at a standstill.

Suddenly we find him sending twenty pounds to Fanny's only brother Jacob, ostensibly to help him establish himself after arriving in California, but more likely to pass on to his sister. He took himself off for a short holiday at Lernay-la Ville, bought twenty pounds' worth of copies of *Travels with a Donkey* to present to friends, then in July wrote to his mother from London, "After a desperate struggle with the elements of every sort and principally money, I arrived last night in London the possessor of four shillings."

Everything came to a head at the end of July 1879 in the form of an urgent telegram from Fanny. No one knows what it contained, but it may well have been prompted by Sam's flight to San Francisco with another of his mistresses. Most of the speculation assumes a cry for help in Fanny's inimitable style: her taste for melodrama was becoming well known. But what form of words could have sounded so desperate that Louis immediately sprang into action, his predicament at an end? "Our nature lies in movement," wrote Pascal in his *Pensées*. Louis had been living on his stoicism for the best part of a year. He must have thanked his stars that he was now on the move at last, moving with the swiftness of someone who is compelled to act no matter what the consequences might be. Nothing less would have set him upon the most improbable course of his life.

PART II

CHAPTER SEVEN

A Shipful of Failures

F OR MONTHS Louis had been turning over the possibility of a journey to California. What was extraordinary was the fact that he had now shed all his uncertainty. It was like waking from a nightmare, and probably no one was more astonished than himself. He parted amicably from his parents at Waverley Station—they were off to take the waters at Gilsand—and hurried to London to talk his decision over with his friends. He felt strong, determined, convinced of the rightness of his action. In "Lay Morals" he had written in March this year, "Life is no longer a tale of betrayals and regrets, for the man now lives as a whole; his consciousness now moves on uninterrupted like a river; through all the extremes and ups and downs of passion he remains approvingly conscious of himself."

Needless to say his friends saw nothing of this inevitability he was feeling. At first they thought he was dramatizing, something he had always done when discussing his problems, fears, and family troubles, whether in person or in his letters. They assumed he had come for advice. Nothing was further from his mind. He always wanted to talk, but in reality he was dispensing with them and their supremely bourgeois head-wagging. Colvin and Henley were quick to point out that he was risking everything—his poor health, his literary career, the peace he had reconstructed with his parents—to voyage over three thousand miles of ocean and another three thousand of unknown wilderness—and for what? For a reunion with a woman who had shown signs of being unhinged, and who had not even committed herself to him definitely. His scheme was just madness, "a mere freak" as Gosse put it bluntly. When his father eventually heard of it he said it was a "sinful, mad business" and put the blame on Herbert Spencer for undermining his son's faith.

Louis wrote a letter to his father and asked Colvin to forward it. One thing is clear: this was no romantic impulse, as legend would have us believe. He was twenty-nine, and after his dalliance with Fanny at Grez and in Paris he had no illusions about the woman he was traveling to meet. Nor, judging by his essays, was his view of love and marriage a romantic one. In his view marriage was a battle which a man should not shirk. Falling in love he acknowledged as "the one illogical adventure." This was no headlong pursuit of the beloved. In "Lay Morals" he wrote of man being tormented

> by a very imperious physical desire; it spoils his rest, it is not to be denied; doctors will tell you, not I, how it is a physical need like the want of food or slumber. In the satisfaction of this desire, as it first appears, the soul sparingly takes part; nay, it unsparingly regrets and disapproves the satisfaction. But let a man love a woman as far as he is capable of love; and for the random affection of the body there is substituted a steady determination, a consent of all his powers and faculties, which supersedes, adopts and commands all others. . . .

Louis tried to resolve these contradictions in a piece of fiction, "The Story of a Lie," which he had put to one side in the summer, working on it as he crossed the Atlantic in the hope of raising money toward his expedition. Baxter, the only one to be trusted with his forwarding address, had managed to borrow something against the promise of future literary work. One such work was a book on the subject of emigration which he was turning over in his mind before he had even become an emigrant.

Thomas Stevenson, nervous, intense, devout, melancholy in disposition, a civil engineer "by whose devices the great sea lights...now shine more brightly...."

Maggie Stevenson, Louis's mother: sweet-natured, companionable and optimistic, the youngest of thirteen children of the Reverend Lewis Balfour. Suffering poor health, this "jewellest of mothers" was often the absent invalid.

Stability during Louis's formative years was provided by Alison Cunningham, or "Cummy," the family nurse, who terrified her charge with stories of hellfire, ghosts, and persecuted Covenanters, yet would comfort him in his "paroxysms" in the small hours.

Father and son: Thomas Stevenson and the sixteen-year-old Louis, already impossibly thin, at Peebles, 1866.

Louis, age twenty-eight, etching after a pencil sketch by Fanny Osbourne.

Louis, left alone in Monterey—his future wife awaiting a divorce in Oakland—found lodgings in this house belonging to Dr. Heinz, a local physician.

This portrait of Fanny at the time of her marriage shows a woman about to become as much nurse as wife to her sick husband. Forty years of age to Louis's thirty, she described herself on the marriage certificate as a widow.

The newly married Stevensons shared this farmhouse in the Vale of Atholl with Louis's parents in 1881, his breakout year as a writer. He wrote much of his "first book," *Treasure Island*, here in atrocious September weather.

He had dreamed of big skies, open seas, adventure, heat—and the fast schooner *Casco*, chartered by his wife in San Francisco, symbolized it all. A new life begins in the vast Pacific.

Now famous but no longer a tourist, feeling a brother to native chiefs, Louis sits with his friend, the extraordinary Kalakaua, last king of Hawaii.

The barefoot, enraptured author as man of action on the bowsprit of the *Equator* in 1889 as he neared Samoa, his final home and resting place.

Louis and Fanny island-hopping on the *SS Janet Nicholl*.

Vailima, meaning Five Waters, complete at last: the walls blue, the roof
red corrugated iron, door and window frames dark green.

Louis, half
escapee and half
patriot, in
Australia a year
before his death.

The South Seas
Don Quixote with
his stepson and
two favorite
Samoans, 1894.

Louis dictating fiction to his "amanuensis," Belle Strong, 1892.

In 1897 a plinth was added to Louis's tomb, flanked by two bronze plaques. One in Samoan carried images of a thistle and a hibiscus, together with Ruth's speech to Naomi. On the other was Louis's own Requiem, written years before in San Francisco.

He had failed to heed the advice of Colvin, Gosse, Henley, and the rest because he saw them suddenly as timid naysayers. He was weirdly cheerful, perhaps intoxicated by his own daring. These friends of his would never take a chance, and chance was what America represented for him. He had read his Whitman and been rocked by the vision of a young, ramshackle, half-finished nation in the making. "For many years," he would write in *The Amateur Emigrant*, "America was to me a sort of promised land." Perhaps he imagined a huge empty wilderness where he would live out the great adventure he had dreamed of in the Cévennes, a place where there was room for everyone. Maybe too he was in flight from a fate as a bourgeois litterateur which he felt closing in on him, and dreaded. An educated tramp, asked to define the term vagrant, said, "Vagrancy is a symptom of a society that's gone wrong, a society that does not cater for the needs of the individual. A vagrant is someone who thinks he's escaping to something, when in actual fact he's escaping from something."

It was no wonder that the calls to reason by his alarmed friends fell on deaf ears. While he listened to their sage words he had the steamship ticket for New York in his pocket, purchased for eight guineas at the Anchor Steamship Line's office in Hanover Street, Edinburgh. From now on he would lead the itinerant life in earnest, one that he had only played at until this moment. The prediction to his mother in October 1874 that he would be a nomad to the end of his days was about to come true. "To move exhilarates, to stay cripples," wrote Bruce Chatwin in a notebook studded with quotations but for once quoting himself. "In the symbol of the Journey lies our principal dilemma. Where does happiness lie?"

Chatwin is illuminating on the origins of our need to wander, if not on Stevenson's character. He labored for ten years to produce a book on the nature of nomadism, only to have his project founder in chaos. He was left sitting before a huge pile of contradictory fragments which stubbornly refused to cohere. The notebooks he accumulated were crammed with abstruse quotations, from the famous to the most humble, from Baudelaire and Robert Burton to a vagrant encountered on the road who, when questioned about his involuntary compulsion to wander, said, "It's like the tides was pulling you along the highway. I'm like the Arctic tern, guv'nor. That's a bird. A beautiful white bird that flies from the North Pole to the South and back again."

It is possible of course that the abbreviated message of Fanny's cable sounded so hysterical and despairing that a feeling of near panic gripped him, forcing him into action. Or was it that he could not stand any more scrambled half-truths, and had to find out for himself how things stood? Whatever she had said or not said, he was now a changed man, a man with a mission, an arrow of desire. He had uprooted himself from friends and family, and the break was quick and clean. Now at last he was on his way, his existence dramatically simplified. The words he scribbled to Colvin enclosing the letter to his father reveal someone scarcely able to believe what was happening. His state of mind seemed like that of a somnambulist. He had never felt more vividly alive, and yet as if he was about to die he made his will. One can see him struggling to make sense of the whole enterprise. No man is of any use, he wrote

unless he has dared everything. I feel just now as if I had, and so might become a man. . . . I have never been so detached from life. I feel as if I cared for nobody, and as for myself I cannot fully believe in my own existence. I seem to have died last night. . . . The weather is threatening; I have a strange, rather horrible sense of the sea before me, and can see no further into the future. I can say honestly I have at this moment neither a regret, a hope, a fear or an inclination. . . . I never was in such a state. . . . I have just made my will. God bless you and keep you, is the prayer of the husk which once contained RLS.

THE MAN WHO went down the Clyde on August 7, 1879, to Greenock and then shipped out on the *Devonia* was a poor man, but not bone-poor like the steerage passengers he would soon get to know intimately. It would take some time to sink in that he wanted more than "the stuffy old show" in London could ever offer, and was off in search of something else, bigger, brighter, and cleaner, as well as a woman who would wander the globe with him. He makes clear on the first page of *The Amateur Emigrant* that he had been advised to pay an extra two guineas so as to have a table to work on. And in no time, embarking in the company of the jobless of Scotland and Northern England, mixing with Swedes, Italians, Irish, Jewish refugees from pogroms, he became classless, nameless, a nobody. At once he felt like a fugitive. On the boat taking them to the *Devonia* "anyone . . . might have supposed we were all absconding from the law." Two of the women were weeping. Nobody spoke. The limp dandified author of little travel jaunts lasting no more than a fortnight, narratives that smack of "what I did on my vacation," would soon cease to be a European "gentleman." He was anxious to see the worst of emigrant life, and indeed he would.

He seems to have had some sort of primitive partition around his table, but his spot was only a precarious oasis set down in the accommodation called steerage at the stern, in evil-smelling holds below the waterline. His fellow steerage-class passengers regarded him as peculiar because he spent most of each day writing. He may have been an outsider, but in a real sense everyone was. Soon he identified with his fellows completely. "We were a company of the rejected; the drunken, the incompetent, the weak, the prodigal, all who had been unable to prevail against circumstances in the one land, were now fleeing pitifully to another; and though one or two might still succeed, all had already failed. We were a shipful of failures, the broken men of England." He had little trouble including himself in that description. Though unaware of the fact, he was taking part in what has been described as the most important mass odyssey of modern history. He had joined a tide of millions who, like him, saw America as golden, a promised land.

No matter how dire the conditions in which he found himself, Louis was never dreary for long. He was no down-and-out Orwell, joylessly slumming for slumming's sake. And though he would soon be disgusted by the snobbery of the first-class passengers, he had no illusions about British workmen, some of whom were soon telling him of their "skulking, shirking and malingering," seeing nothing dishonest in doing half an hour's work for an hour's pay and sneaking off to the pub when the boss turned his back. Worse, they were living on pipe dreams. A change of landscape would not prevent them getting drunk and blaming everyone but themselves for their misfortunes.

As he got to know his companions better it seemed to him that the Scots were the most doleful of all, since the land of their birth had never taught them how to be happy. The historian Henry Buckle, author of *The History of English Civilization*, described Scottish life during the century from the Reformation to the end of the Covenant risings as a life in which "Whatever was natural was wrong. The clergy deprived the people of their holidays, their amusements, their shows, their games, and their sports; they repressed every appearance of joy, they forbade all merriment, they stopped all festivities, they choked up every avenue by which pleasure could enter, and they spread over the country a universal gloom. . . ." If Louis was escaping from the slowly closing trap of being a respectable man of letters or a hack in Grub Street like Henley, he was also in flight from the land of his birth.

There are touches of grim humor in the rite of passage he documented. He managed to detach himself somewhat so that he could see himself as conducting an experiment. How long could a man sink, how far, and yet remain himself? It took a brass plate on a lavatory door to remind him that he had once been a gentleman. He may have had no rosy view beforehand of the proletariat, but even before embarking he had been aware of calamitous times, of a Glasgow as good as dead commercially, of whole streets of houses standing deserted by the Tyne, "the cellar-doors broken and removed for firewood," of closed factories, useless strikes, and starving girls.

On board ship he talked with other men, commenting on the

food and the vileness of the steerage accommodation. Children ran up and down stairways and on decks, finding each other "like dogs" and introducing themselves without delay. "What do you call your mither?" "Mawmaw" was one reply he heard, "indicating, I fancy, a shade of difference in the social scale." Here was an observer of the human condition meticulously at work. The children were soon all in a band and thick as thieves, while their parents and relatives were still cautiously putting out feelers "on the outskirts of acquaintance." He was enchanted by one unlikely little boy of three whose family belonged to Steerage 4 and 5. He ran about the ship like a melody, "an ugly, merry, unbreached child" with his lint-white hair all tangled, his face smeared with suet and treacle, falling over and jumping up again so gracefully that Louis thought him beautiful when in motion. Banging with a tin spoon on a tin cup he was nothing less than "a little triumph of the human species." And notice how this observer avoids toppling into sentimentality. Even when the child's mother and the rest of his family lay sick and lifeless around him, he sat upright in the midst of them and piped away "in the pleasant heartlessness of infancy."

Though Louis invariably came into his own as a sailor, after his experience of sailing round the coasts and islands of Scotland as a trainee engineer and on holidays with friends, he had no illusions about the sea. Delmore Schwartz has called it "the fatal, merciless, passionate ocean," and Stevenson would have concurred. To escape the poisonous smells below he was soon finding a shelter on deck near a fire-hole and making himself as snug as possible for the night. On one balmy night he loved the gentle cradling movement the ship made, and remembered later hearing when half asleep "the beautiful sea-cry 'All's well!' I know nothing, whether for poetry or music, that can surpass the effect of these two syllables in the darkness of a night at sea."

Most of the passengers were bitterly discontented, except for one or two who had been so near starvation that they'd climbed aboard as if chased by the devil. Yet even in the inferno below decks there were songfests, before seasickness laid many of them low. As the voyage continued he was repelled more and more by the atrocious stench in steerage, tasting in the throat like a horrible cheese. He saw a fellow passenger who had been sick and lay with his head in his vomit. This kind of uncompromising description would render his book unpublishable in Victorian times.

He went around taking note of human behavior in its worst and best aspects. It had dawned on him that he was not only voyaging away from his country but "out of myself." And by doing so he was learning more about the value of men than he could ever have done by staying sheltered at home.

He was particularly impressed by a white-faced fellow Scot playing his fiddle to an audience of white-faced women, and concluded that humanly speaking it was more important to scrape away, even if it was badly, than to "write huge works upon recondite subjects." When the man paused, Louis went up and told him he was a happy man, carrying happiness about with him in his fiddle-case, "and he seemed alive to the fact." Louis was realizing too that you cannot run away from a weakness. The only fortune worth having was an aim in life, and that was found in the heart. In fact "emigration has to be done before we climb aboard the vessel." He met a miserable specimen, another fellow Scot called Mackay, who was adrift like a dead stick, crippled by a puritanism which had divorced him from nature and thinned out his instincts, leaving him with material greed and little else.

There was a change of weather, the sun shone, and he was glad to witness the lift in everyone's spirits. "We got in a cluster like bees, sitting between each other's feet under the lee of deck-houses." People began to laugh, to tell stories. Children were clambering about the shrouds like monkeys, white faces took on color from the wind and sunlight. Louis found himself in demand, rolling cigarettes and earning admiration for it. All that marred the scene was the intrusion of three cabin passengers, a gentleman and two ladies, who picked their way through the riffraff with little titters of amusement "and a

Lady-Bountiful air about nothing, which galled me to the quick." Louis was no radical, always believing that one person was as good as another, but these swells doing a little slumming infuriated him. Somehow they managed to convey insults by their very presence. "They seemed to throw their clothes in our faces." He had no time either for the revolutionary talkers who saw revolution as the cure for all evils. Some hated the church, and all hated the masters. In America, they naively insisted, they would find justice and money; all the evils they had known, some visited on them by themselves, would disappear once they had crossed the Atlantic, that Great Divide.

A man called Jones pointed out a young woman to him. She wore a ragged old jacket and a bit of a sealskin cap on her head. The puzzling thing was her look of refinement and the self-sacrificing way she cared for a heavy, dull man like a ditcher in rough clothes who rarely said anything. He was "dog-sick," and he had this delicate, sad woman tending him constantly. The man was a stowaway. The story went round, true or not, that she was also without money or a ticket, and the man she petted so selflessly was the father of a family who had left his wife and children to travel with her.

Louis earned the nickname of "Shakespeare" by his insistence on somehow managing to write at his table. He completed "The Story of a Lie," with its central figure, Dick Naesby, an obvious self-portrait. It was another attempt to analyze the fraught relationship between his father and himself. Reflecting on the creation of characters, he wrote, "To begin to understand is to begin to sympathize; for comprehension comes only when we have stated another's faults and virtues in terms of our own. Hence the proverbial toleration of artists for their own evil creation."

How a workingman saw the difference between England and America was summed up for him by a fellow passenger as their eleven-day voyage drew to a close. "In America," the man said, "you get pies and pudding." And on all sides he heard warnings: don't speak to strangers in the streets of New York or you might be cheated and beaten. Take care when entering a hotel to be on your toes at all hours if you wanted to emerge again with your money and baggage. "You would have thought we were about to land on a cannibal island."

ON THE SECOND SUNDAY of the voyage he looked out for the first time on the low shores of New York harbor. It was before noon. By six he was setting foot in America, more precisely on West Street. He had befriended Jones, the man who had pointed out the stowaway and his girl, and Jones seemed a man with an air of competence. The rain was pouring down and continued for the next thirty-six hours. They trundled off in an open baggage wagon, sitting on some straw. Nothing could have been more unpromising. The steady downpour flooded the roads, the restaurants smelled of wet people, wet clothing. They lodged for the night in Reunion House, a dollar-a-day rooming house run by an Irishman named Mitchell.

Jones must have been there before; he was well known. Louis accepted the offer of a cigar and was soon out of doors, determined to experience the New York streets. Still the rain hammered down. He and Jones and two Scots lads, recent immigrants, made a party of four. The two Scots had been six weeks in the city and were still out of work. Louis, who had been thin enough when he embarked, had lost fourteen pounds and looked dangerously emaciated. The lads soon left. Louis hunted in the rain for a French restaurant with French waiters and French cooking, presumably to console himself. Eventually he found one. The French coffee was good, the wine so-so.

He went trailing round, soaked to the skin, finding a post office, a bank, and a chemist for advice about a nonstop itching which he was told was caused by a liver complaint. He was hardly cheered by a letter he collected postmarked California, telling him that Fanny had "inflammation of the brain." The terrible voyage he had endured didn't prevent him from writing to Henley that the trip was "otherwise great fun; passengers singing and spewing lustily, and the stormy winds did blow."

In the rooming house on his first night he shared a cramped room with Jones. An inner window looked into another room where three men snored and mumbled all night long. Jones took the one bed and Louis lay down on the floor. Half the night he sat up naked to the waist, scratching at his tormenting itch.

His "nightmare wanderings" in New York began next day. He went in search of money changers, publishers, and a bookseller where he loaded himself down with "six fat volumes" of George Bancroft's *History of the United States*. All the time he was getting wetter, if that was possible. By the time he got back to Mitchell's his shoes, coat, trousers, and even his socks were drenched. Time was running out. If he was to make the train he would have to unpack his dry clothes and leave all his wet things behind. It was a bad start and would get steadily worse. The behavior of the New Yorkers he encountered baffled him: either they shoved him aside or went out of their way to help him.

Reaching the ferry he was confronted by the chaos of four boatloads of emigrants heading for the one train. Open carts heaped with bedding stood in the downpour. "There was a Babel of bewildered men, women and children." Getting on the New Jersey ferry and fighting to stay upright among these huddled masses was "an evil dream." He was pushed and elbowed into a long shed reaching downhill from West Street to the river. At last he was on board, creeping over the river in the dark like a wounded duck, the ferry wallowing to port with its freight of wet and silent emigrants.

Then came the dreadful stampede of the New Jersey landing. It was like a battle. "Children fell, and were picked up to be rewarded by a blow. One child who had lost her parents screamed steadily and with increasing shrillness, as though verging towards a fit . . . but no one else seemed so much as to remark her distress; and I am ashamed to say that I ran among the rest." The rain fell as heavily as ever. Louis was too exhausted to reach the railway station without resting: he sat down twice with his bundles in the wet. Then he had to camp with all the others on a windy, gaslit platform before being allowed into the cars. Cold, wet, and clamor had reduced everyone to a mute stupor, himself included. Trying to fight off his dejection, he rummaged through his luggage for, of all things, a clothes brush, brushing his trousers as hard as he could to expel the water and warm his blood at the same time.

It was night and the train was rattling through it; that was all he knew. Somehow, squatting down, he managed to doze off after seeing the lights of Philadelphia. He slept and woke, and nodded off again, waking on the Tuesday morning with the train halted in the middle of nowhere. He got out to stretch his legs, rubbing his eyes. It was not quite England, not quite France. A green open country stretched away on all sides. Something was different, but what was it? He came to the conclusion that the sunrise in America had more purple, brown, and smoky orange in it, more like sunset than the gold and scarlet of sunrises at home.

Each time they halted at a station there was a mad scramble to buy food. The coffee had always run out before he could get to it, and the only food he could buy was fruit. He had written to Colvin just before landing in New York: "At least if I fail in my great purpose I shall see some wild life in the West and visit both Florida and Labrador ere my return. But I don't yet know if I have the courage to stick with life without it. Man, I was sick, sick, sick of this last year." The letter, full of uncertainty about his future, seemed to be saying that without Fanny at his side he would lose all belief in himself. Now, heading west like countless travelers before him, itching madly with scabies or eczema, hungry, out on his feet from lack of sleep, and with no idea what to expect at his journey's end, he was at the end of his tether. "I had no idea," he scrawled to Colvin, "how easy it was to commit suicide. There seems nothing left of me; I died a while ago; I do not know who it is that is traveling."

He stood for hours like a hollowed-out ghost gazing out as they passed villages, carts, highways, taking in the smell of woods, rivers, and ploughed earth, his spirit rising and falling like the hills on the horizon. The weather slowly improved until there were no clouds, only baking sunshine. He asked the brakeman the name of a river and was told it was the Susquehanna. He thought the beauty of the name so apt for the shining river and its valley that his euphoria, which he had thought gone for good, came back in the form of a chorus of names of the states and territories of America. There were surely "few poems with a nobler music for the ear."

In a waiting room at Pittsburgh he had his first meal for thirty hours. He went on into Ohio, which was different from anything he had expected, the country as flat as Holland but not in any way dull. They crawled over huge plains which stretched unbroken to the Rocky Mountains. The tall corn was pleasant to the eye, the townships evoked summer evenings on the stoop. Then one morning a freezing chill struck his blood and bones, which a native pronounced "a fever and ague morning." Courteous as ever, Louis was trying to be of service to a Dutch widow by buying fruits and candies for her children, carrying her parcels, and even sleeping on the floor so that she could have his seat. In spite of all his efforts she didn't disguise her distrust of him, or perhaps she was alarmed by his ghastly physical appearance. Typically he respected her honest dislike of him. Getting out at Chicago she said, "I am sure we all *ought* to be very much obliged to you."

At Chicago, passengers like him who were going west had to catch a bus to the station of a different railroad. The "Windy City" seemed a great and gloomy place. In a third-class waiting room he sat down to a dish of ham and eggs. When it was time to find his train and climb aboard he realized how utterly dog-tired he was, walking along the platform like a man in a dream. He scarcely had the strength to carry his valise, his knapsack, his rug, and those cumbersome tomes of Bancroft's *History*. Bent like an old man, hot, feverish, and thirsty, he became conscious of a great darkness around him, "an internal darkness." He was dangerously weak and unwell. Finding an empty bench on the train he sank into it like a bundle of rags. A cheerful, rosy little German sat down beside him, babbling away "nineteen to the dozen" about pickpockets and God knows what else, but Louis was too far gone to understand him. The German got off somewhere in the suburbs and the train went on into the darkness.

He woke up next morning surprised to be still alive, feeling cheerful for no reason whatsoever. At Burlington, Iowa, he got out and ate a good breakfast of porridge with sweet milk, and coffee with hotcakes. They were on the Mississippi. A drunk clambered in at a place called Creston. He got a free ride as far as Cromwell, then the conductor threw him out. Louis was impressed by the precision of the action, "in three motions, exact as a piece of drill." The train was already gathering speed but the drunk landed on his feet and went staggering back along the track. All around him Louis was hearing English spoken, "but I knew I was in a foreign land."

At nearly nine that night he arrived at the Pacific Transfer Station near Council Bluffs, Iowa, on the eastern banks of the Missouri River, which provided a kind of hostel for emigrants. The next afternoon he stood in front of Emigrant House, waiting with more than a hundred others to be "sorted and boxed" for the onward journey toward the Pacific Coast. The three cars allotted to emigrants were segregated—families in one, single men in another, and Chinese coolies in the third. Twenty baggage wagons were coupled on at the rear. That evening the enormous train rattled out of the transfer station and over the Missouri to Omaha.

As before, meals were taken by the wayside. These pauses were always drawn out, since their train had to give way to expresses and anything else which had right of way. All the same it was hazardous trying to eat with one eye on the train, which might suddenly move off with no "All Aboard" warning. Washing was no joke either. The primitive ritual involved filling a tin bowl at a water filter and kneeling with it on the rocking observation platform. You hung on to the rail with one hand and splashed cold water on yourself with the other.

Louis had fallen foul of hotel clerks in France, whose insolence made his blood boil. He now added train conductors to his list of dislikes. They treated all the emigrants with contempt. He asked one official three times when the train would stop for dinner, and was ignored each time. The one source of information and contact with the outside world was the newsboy, plying his trade with papers and other commodities. Even so Louis was bewildered by what he called the "uncivil kindness" of the American character.

He was in a sorry state, "like a man at death's door." His body, he reported to Henley, was "all to whistles; I don't eat; my blood has broken out into a kind of blister, blain, blight and itch business . . . but man, I can sleep. The car in front of mine is chock full of Chinese." The incessant itching could have been caused by a mite under the skin. He sat at the end of the car, trying to hold the door open with his foot to gulp down some fresh air as the door catch was broken. When the newsboy came by with his box of merchandise Louis did his best to move his leg, but twice he was caught unawares. The lad kicked his foot out of the way without a word, though Louis apologized. Suddenly the lad, who had noticed how ill he was, touched his shoulder and made him a present of a large juicy pear "out of a tender heart." For the rest of the journey he was kindness itself, loaning him papers and even coming to sit beside him in an effort to cheer him up.

Crossing Nebraska as he scrawled a letter to Henley, he felt as if he were at sea, the world he looked out on from his dangerous perch on top of a fruit wagon was so utterly featureless. The crawling train seemed the only live thing, the rail tracks stretching from horizon to horizon like the cue on a billiard table. All he could hear above the roar of the train was the chirp of grasshoppers, "a noise like the winding up of countless clocks and watches." You could get a sickness of the vision, he was told, if you lived like a settler on these empty plains.

He reached Wyoming more dead than alive, which his fellow emigrants seemed to find laughable. "My illness is a subject of great mirth," he told Henley, "and I smile rather sickly at their jests." No longer able to sleep he tottered about at night, picking his way across prostrate bodies, opening a window for fresh air, and looking out on an infinity of blackness. "They that long for morning have never longed for it more earnestly than I."

He changed trains again at Ogden, Utah, from the Union Pacific to the Central Pacific line. Emigration now struck him as a pathetic illusion for these men and families hoping for an El Dorado. He told himself that they were driven by something else, as old as the race; "wages, indeed, are only one consideration out of many; for we are a race of gypsies, and love change and travel for themselves." But he was beginning to loathe his fellow whites as he observed them. They thought themselves superior to the coolies, when they were nothing of the sort. The Chinese kept themselves cleaner than the rest of the passengers, they were fastidious in their hygiene, and "Their forefathers watched the stars before mine had begun to keep pigs." He also felt strong sympathy for the cheated, exploited, and slaughtered red man. He saw plains Indians hanging around at way-side halts, degraded specimens subjected to guffaws and catcalls from semi-literate emigrants of "a truly Cockney baseness. I was ashamed for the thing called civilization." He encountered one female settler who came selling milk at a wayside station and saw "it would have been fatuous arrogance to pity such a woman" for all the bleakness of her existence. She sold milk with rare grace and yet the place where she lived was ghastly, "showing nothing homelike but the burning fire."

Westward the train ran on, and the talk he heard was as obsessional as the talk he had listened to on the ship, returning time and again to the themes of hard times, short rations, and hope. Cornish, Scots, Irish, Dutch, Poles, Hungarians, Swedes, and even Americans were all hungrily in search of a better land and better wages. "Hunger, you would have thought, came out of the east like the sun, and the evening was made of edible gold." Now they were passing other emigrant trains going back east, their passengers crying out from the windows in a wailing chorus, urging them to "Come back." Again and again Louis heard the same haunting cry, "dismal to my heart." What had they discovered, these retreating emigrants, that had been so utterly disheartening?

Now they were in Nevada, traveling all day from Toano through alkali and sand desert "horrible to man," and bare sagebrush country that was equally uninviting. They reached Elko at suppertime and he saw his first hoboes. They had been riding the rods under the train and they took off fast, running madly across open ground. Louis wished he could have become acquainted with these "land stowaways." Next day the train was laboring to the summit of the Donner Pass in the high Sierras. They were near the gateway to California at last.

A companion woke him in the night. He followed the man out to the rear platform. The train had halted at a siding. The night was clear, moonlit. Then he was transfixed by a clamor of falling water close at hand among the mountains. The night air struck chill but tasted good, and it was strangely familiar, like being in the Highlands. Louis went back to sleep "with a grateful mountain feeling at my heart."

Next morning he sat up and was confused. Was it day or night? They were descending through a long snowshed. Suddenly they shot clear into the open and he caught a glimpse of a huge pine-forested ravine to his left, a foaming river, and a sky "already colored with the fires of dawn." The endless deserts had been left behind. "Every spire of pine along the hill-top, every trouty pool along that mountain river, was more dear to me than a blood relation. Few people have praised God more happily than I did."

Down they dropped in a triumphant swooping descent, down through Blue Canyon, Alta, Dutch Flat, dropping thousands of feet through all the old mining camps and through a sea of mountain forests toward the coast. Everyone was suddenly childishly delighted, and Louis no different from the rest. The sun stopped punishing them with oppressive heat. At every little town they could hear the cocks crowing for the new day and the new country.

By the afternoon they had reached Sacramento, which seemed all gardens in a paradise of corn. Next day before dawn they came to a final halt at the Oakland side of San Francisco Bay. Crossing over on the ferry, the bay was perfection, with not a ripple or stain to spoil it. The sun rose in glory, bathing the city hills with golden light. Louis would one day celebrate his love for this city in *The Wrecker*.

CHAPTER EIGHT

All Kinds of Miseries Here

SOON HE WAS on a train again and urging it to go faster, this time a narrow track to Salinas. There he climbed on the stage to Monterey. His garb, a blue serge suit and bowler hat, must have been the most unlikely attire he ever wore. Close to collapse, he made his way to the Mexican household where Fanny was boarding with her children. The boy was eagerly waiting for him. "Luly's coming," Fanny had said to Lloyd a few days before. Lloyd remembered him long afterward walking into the room "and the outcry of delight that greeted him, the incoherence of laughter, the tears, the heart-swelling joy of reunion." But the Scottish suitor who was the boy's hero had shrunk to a scarecrow, and Fanny was curiously apprehensive. She must have seen him as anything but a knight-errant. In fact he was an embarrassment. With her marital position still unresolved, his reception was a cool one.

Frank McLynn warns that Lloyd Osbourne has become "part of the RLS mythmaking apparatus, and his account skates over the embarrassing details of the sequel to the 'joyful reunion.'" One can speculate as to how this sequel went, but Louis's letter to Baxter makes clear that he had hit rock bottom. Fanny evaded the subject when asked for news of the progress of her divorce, then confessed that she had not yet set a petition in motion. Her excuse was that a nervous breakdown had left her incapable of deciding anything. In despair Louis took himself off, after Fanny made it clear that his presence was now inconvenient. Any chance of a divorce called for discretion. Belle spoke of her mother's dealings with Louis, and his with her, as "almost coldly casual."

Miserable and discouraged, not knowing what to think or how to feel, he obeyed an instinct which always told him to walk away. "I have walked myself into my best thoughts, and I know of no thought so burdensome that one cannot walk away from it," wrote Kierkegaard. This had worked for Louis in the Cévennes, but now he was in no condition to hike anywhere. His first letter from Monterey to Baxter refers flatly to his "itch and a broken heart."

He hired a horse and pack and wandered off into the hills above Carmel, with no idea of the terrain or where he was heading. There was nothing in the least romantic about any of this, and his action seemed almost suicidal. Death wish or not, he might have believed, in the eternally hopeful part of himself, that he could physically walk out of his illness. But his emotional distress went with him. His news was nil, he told Baxter, and he knew nothing. With good reason, though he was hardly capable of rational thought, he wondered if he was being rejected. If so, why had Fanny sent the telegram that sparked his journey of six thousand miles?

Whatever was in her mind, it didn't prevent her from staying in touch with her admirers, Messrs. Lloyd and Reardon. Both were prosperous businessmen, and Louis was plainly penniless. By the way he spoke, he could easily be disinherited. With Louis wandering disconsolately in no-man's-land, Fanny explained his arrival in America by telling Reardon that her "literary friend from Scotland" had come on a lecture tour, adding casually that it was amusing to meet again the one person in the world who really cared for her. This was the kind of teasing she had gone in for in France in her letters to Reardon, the lawyer who would soon be handling her divorce, though advising against it.

Louis's trek into the Carmel hills, as he trailed his disappointment with Fanny, ended in disaster. He was quickly near death. Eighteen miles from Monterey he set up camp and then literally collapsed. For three days he staggered about in a daze, watering his horse and swallowing coffee. Delirious, he was being driven out of his mind by the sound of tree frogs and goat bells when two frontiersmen found him, taking him back to their Angora goat ranch. Captain Smith, a Mexican war veteran and bear hunter of seventy-two, and his partner Tom, an Indian, spent a night watching over the "real sick" stranger while his fever passed. Baxter, who provided news and a very limited supply of cash, heard that his distant friend was "pretty well dished," unable to walk and lying in an upper room nearly naked, with flies crawling over him and a clinking of goat bells in his ears. The bells meant that the goats were back and it would soon be time to eat. "The old hunter is doubtless now infusing tea, and Tom the Indian will come in with his gun in a few minutes." There were children at the ranch, and as soon as he was strong enough he taught them to read. Telling Colvin this in a letter he mentioned working at his notes of the nightmarish voyage over, eventually to be *The Amateur Emigrant.* He had written nothing like it before but hoped it would not be any the worse for that. As for his inner state, "I will not deny that I feel lonely today, but I do not fear to go on, for I am doing right." Clearly his moral code was still intact.

Certainly he had little idea of the turmoil his departure for America had created at home, though he must have guessed. His father was sending furious letters to Colvin about his son's behavior. It would be months before his mother entered his name in her diary. As a last resort Thomas Stevenson had the family doctor send Louis a telegram requesting his presence at home as a matter of urgency. Whether Thomas was seriously ill on his own account or as a result of "this sinful mad business" was not made clear. Struggling in the maelstrom he had generated, Louis told Henley, "All kinds of miseries here." Unable to refuse directly, he sent a telegram saying "Letter following." His father would be better or dead by the time he got home, and anyway, "I won't desert my wife." Fanny would not be his wife for some time to come, but there were signs of movement at last.

In a letter to Gosse he wondered if it was his fate to battle always and to cause pain to others. "Some people are so made, I fear, that their ahem brings down the avalanche; and step where they please they most always tread on other people's hearts. . . . I try to tell myself that I am indifferent to people's judgments, but it is partly a pretense. I give you my word of honor, Gosse, I am trying to behave well, and in some sort, which is as much as one can say, succeeding." As he regained some semblance of health and strength he recovered his belief in America as the land of the new day. A later poem, "In the States," hailed Whitman's new democracy:

> With half a heart I wander here
> As from an age gone by
> A brother—yet though young in years
> An elder brother I.
>
> You speak another tongue than mine
> Though both were English born
> I towards the night of time decline
> You mount into the morn. . . .

Things were moving because Sam Osbourne had finally agreed to a private divorce providing it was not rushed through with indecent haste. He was still hypocritically determined to save face. Nevertheless he agreed to vacate the Oakland cottage, and Fanny and her family moved to it in mid-October. By then Louis had crept back to Monterey to lie low. He was given lodgings by a Dr. Heintz and his wife in their old adobe inn, and was soon exercising his gift for making friends.

At midday he would take a meal at the restaurant of Jean Simoneau, an expatriate who longed to see France again and was happy to converse with such an enthusiastic Francophile. He befriended Crevole Bronson, editor of the local paper, the *Monterey Californian*, who took Louis on as a freelance as a way of paying him a two-dollars-a-week salary. With this and the credit extended by Simoneau, plus the meager supply of money from Baxter, he somehow got by. Then he hit more financial trouble. He was reduced to his last eighty pounds when Fanny heard that Sam was out of a job and could no longer support her and the family. This could have been pique. Why should he go on supporting his family with someone waiting in the shadows to step into his shoes? Louis wrote despairingly to Baxter that he was now faced with propping up "a wife, a sister-in-law, five cats, two dogs, three horses . . . and occasional descents of a son-in-law from boarding school."

Fanny's daughter Belle was now living with the painter Joe Strong, to whom she was engaged despite her mother's doubts. Fanny's sister Nellie was about to marry Adolfo Sanchez, a young saloon-keeper in Monterey. Their child would be called Louis, after Stevenson. In spite of the dire shortage of money, the hard-pressed Scot was getting to like Monterey, the little Spanish town of only three streets, with its sea-sand roadways and wooden boardwalks which ended suddenly, so that walking at night in the absence of street lights was hazardous. He joked to Henley that he marveled at the smallness of his world: "The population of Monterey is about that of a dissenting chapel on a wet Sunday in a strong church neighborhood." Restricting as this was, he appreciated the Mexican way of life, writing a little later of its attractively un-American character that "It is not strong enough to resist the influence of the flaunting caravanserai, and the poor, quaint, penniless native gentlemen of Monterey must perish, like a lower race, before the millionaire vulgarians of the Big Bonanza." Despite its small scale he was captivated by the air of seclusion behind adobe walls, the baked tiles, the floribunda, the singers with their guitars as night fell, their voices having "that high-pitched womanish alto which is so common among Mexican men, and which strikes on the unaccustomed ear as something not entirely human, but altogether sad."

After breakfast he made for the Alvarado Street post office to pick up his mail, and was soon sitting down to a noon lunch at Simoneau's in the company of a mixed bunch which included two Portuguese, a Mexican, an Italian, an Indian woman, a Swiss, and a German. Simoneau's crowd liked the unpretentious Scotsman, and one thing they all had in common was lack of money. To do Bronson a favor, Louis composed a broadsheet attacking an enemy of Bronson's: the narrow-minded local priest. As well as this he wrote fifteen articles in all for the *Monterey Californian*. His two-dollars-a-week salary was in fact being subsidized in a kindly conspiracy organized by Simoneau among the boarders of his French hotel.

He loved the wild coastline of Monterey and would go with Lloyd on jaunts into the pines, emerging to explore the beach with its sandpipers, seaweed, and half-buried whalebones, awed by the huge Pacific seas. One day he broke the news to the boy that he intended to marry his mother. It was a delicate undertaking, and perhaps he was fearful of the child's response. Lloyd remembered long afterward that he was struck dumb. "I walked on in a kind of stupefaction, with an uncontrollable impulse to cry—yet I did not cry—and was possessed of an agonizing feeling that I ought to speak, but I did not know how, nor what. . . . But all I know is that at last my hand crept into Luly's."

At his lodgings Louis completed "The Pavilion on the Links" and worked away at his voyage documentary and a novel, *A Vendetta in the West*, which Colvin believed he destroyed, possibly because the principal character was too closely based on Belle.

In London, Colvin was still receiving wild distraught letters from Stevenson senior. "For God's sake," Thomas wrote, "use your influence. Is it fair that we should be half murdered by his conduct? I am unable to write more. . . . I see nothing but destruction to himself as well as to all of us." When he spoke a little later of leaving Edinburgh to avoid the disgrace his son had brought down on their heads, Colvin began to think privately that the poor man was unhinged. This only tells us that he had no idea of what it was like to live in a Thomas Stevenson world, in an Edinburgh where the man was so well known, feeling himself to be the object of scandal, gossip, and mockery. His anguish was undoubtedly genuine, but who else in Edinburgh could have known what was going on? The point was that he imagined the whole world knew.

Colvin was now growing weary of acting as intermediary. He

spoke with Henley and Gosse of his exasperation with the whole business. None of them could see what Louis hoped to achieve by his exile, putting his inheritance at risk into the bargain. Thomas blamed in turn his dissolute nephew Bob, Herbert Spencer (the dangerous free-thinker), and his English friends in London for leading his son astray. He appealed to Colvin only because there was no one else he could turn to. He should never have weakly agreed to let Louis go off to live in London. What was it but a cesspit, bubbling and seething with prostitutes, theatres, atheists?

Henley tried the lever of disinheritance to persuade his friend to turn his back on this foolishness. He had also begun to realize that he was no longer benefiting from being shoulder to shoulder with a coming man. Louis, however, was too far down the road of his liberation to stop now, and he was starting to doubt the worth of his friends when it came to moral support. Only the loyal Baxter accepted his behavior without a word of criticism. Louis reported to Colvin, "With my parents, all looks dead black," and told Henley that "I am glad that they mean to disinherit me; you know, Henley, I always had moral doubts about inherited money and this clears me of that forever."

NEAR THE END of December 1879 he moved to San Francisco, to be closer to Fanny across the bay in Oakland. His spirits higher than they had been for months now that he could see an end to his quest, he was being tested continually by the discouragement of his friends, who were using various stratagems to get Louis away from "that woman." Henley, Fanny's enemy before he had even met her, would soon call her the "Bedlamite." Now he, Colvin, and Gosse combined to blind themselves to any merit in the work Louis was sending over in the hope of finding publishers. They either lapsed into silence or made tepid and negative comments. The belief that they knew best what was good for him was making them arrogant and secretive. Among themselves they said condescendingly that America would "never produce anything worth a damn." What are we going to do about Louis? was the question around which their discussions crystallized. They alone knew what was best for him, and sooner or later he would come to his senses. Henley thought their friend should be brought to see that "England and a quiet life are what he wants, and must have." This fatuous solution was so out of touch with Louis's feelings that he would have shaken his head in disbelief had he known of it.

When Colvin received *The Amateur Emigrant* he dismissed it out of hand as the result of poor artistic judgment. It was in two parts, and the second section, "Across the Plains," appeared four years later in *Longman's Magazine*. The complete work would have to wait for publication until after Louis's death. Reissued in a paperback in 1984, it comes over now as an extraordinary masterpiece of a work, a blow-by-blow travel book unlike anything else he would write. It is easy to see why Colvin, a critic of timid appetite who knew his Victorian readership, should so dislike this subtle and evocative account which is at the same time profoundly symbolic. For Colvin the squalor alone would have been too much. It was all too harsh and coarse and raw, above all a picture of flayed and shrieking nerves. Jonathan Raban, in his glowing introduction to the reissue, is fully aware of the way in which the book is wrenched, as it were, out of Stevenson's grasp by the very nature of the ordeal he experienced and only just survived. The lyrical ramble of *Travels with a Donkey*, with its whimsical and digressive touches, just would not work here. Victorians like Colvin and Henley would have been alarmed by the familiarity of Louis's encounters with workingmen, as if the class war did not exist. The specter of socialism had begun to haunt Victorian society. What did the classlessness of this author signify? In the book's finale, the vision of California with its vines and green landscape was dreamlike, "like meeting one's wife." The old Britain that Henley thought would be good for Louis was a tomb. "He comes to California as a bridegroom," writes Raban, who thought this book the best that Stevenson ever wrote. It is an opinion likely to infuriate ardent R.L.S. lovers.

While at Monterey, Louis had been seriously ill with pleurisy and malaria. He was also half starved, judging by his remark to Colvin: "I suppose if I ate two ounces of food a day for nearly two months it must have been the extreme outside; the rest was coffee, wine and soup." At some point before leaving for San Francisco he suddenly asked Colvin not to direct mail c/o Joe Strong in Monterey: "No more to Strong, difficulties about Belle having hurt me a good deal. More hell with that young lady." What had happened? As late as 1922 Katherine Osbourne said that in 1879 Belle approached Louis and proposed that he marry her instead of her mother. She was not then married to Joe Strong and wanted to avoid doing so. This has been ridiculed as vicious nonsense from an embittered woman by those who maintain that Belle was already married at the time. Not so, says McLynn, and goes on to speculate that this strange episode, or one very much like it, may well account for Louis's cryptic message, and explain the uneasy relationship that existed between him and Belle for the next ten years.

Why Fanny's sister Nellie had joined the family from Indiana is not clear, but she was there when Louis first arrived. She was about to marry Sanchez, and she was pressed into service as a "chaperone" whenever Louis visited Fanny at East Oakland. He dictated stories to her, told her that Francis Parkman was a favorite author of his, warned her off the profane Zola, and said he liked "Marching Through Georgia" but didn't care for "Home Sweet Home." While dictating he had a habit of walking rapidly up and down the room. Belle would become accustomed to it in Samoa. To prevent him from tiring himself, Nellie and Fanny hemmed him in with tables and chairs when he was too absorbed to notice.

In San Francisco he lodged with an Irish family, Mr. and Mrs. Carson, on Bush Street. Just before moving in, huddled in bed in Monterey to keep warm after being brought low yet again, he succumbed to self-pity, writing to Gosse that he thought his days were numbered. "But death is no bad friend; a few aches and gasps, and we are done."

On the move again, crossing the bay and responding as always to a change of scene, he forgot his despondency and weakness and thought how splendid the approaching city looked, how welcoming, how bright. It captivated him at once with its vibrancy and its mix of peoples.

> Choose a place on one of the huge throbbing ferry-boats, and when you are midway between the city and the suburb, look around. The air is fresh and salt, as if you were at sea. On the one hand is Oakland, gleaming white among its gardens. On the other, to seaward, hill after hill is crowded and crowned with the palaces of San Francisco; its long streets lie in regular bars of darkness, east and west, across the sparkling picture; a forest of masts bristles like bulrushes about its feet. . . . The town is essentially not Anglo-Saxon; still more essentially not American. . . . Here, on the contrary, are airs of Marseilles and of Pekin. The shops along the streets are like the consulates of different nations. The passers-by vary in features like the slides of a magic lantern. . . .

At the Carsons' boardinghouse he was as near destitute as he would ever be. Mrs. Carson, a kindly soul, waited while he scratched around for the rent and tried to survive on a ten-cent breakfast and a "copious" fifty-cent lunch. Between these two snacks he went back to his room and worked, writing an early version of *Prince Otto* and an essay on Thoreau. Mr. Carson would in due course appear as Speedy in *The Wrecker*. Mrs. Carson, taking pity on this alarming apparition who could just about stand upright, helped him occasionally with tidbits from her larder, and he showed his gratitude by chopping firewood for the household. Sometime after eight each morning he would emerge from his room smiling wanly and take breakfast in a coffeehouse in Powell Street. Lunch was at the Donadieu restaurant, where he treated himself to half a bottle of wine with his meal. In the afternoons he got his legs into motion and walked, his old remedy for feeling better and organizing his thoughts, sometimes making for the ferry to meet Fanny but otherwise simply walking for the satisfaction of it. Always the literary voyager, he traveled even when immobilized by ill health as he so often was, restlessly walking in his mind. Unable to afford medical help for his condition, he could at least walk, no matter how unsteadily.

He consoled himself with the thought that the divorce was at last progressing in spite of the opposition of both families and Sam's prevarication. Because Fanny felt obliged to go through the ritual of a family Christmas he was alone, writing miserably to Colvin on Boxing Day, "I am now writing to you in a café, waiting for some music to begin. For four days I have spoken to no one but my landlord or landlady or to restaurant waiters. This is not a gay way to spend Christmas is it?" He filled a notebook with seven pages of notes inspired by the stories of his landlord for a novel with the working title *The Adventures of John Carson*. In the evening he would be out for another roll and coffee at the café, then back in his room working until eleven. Battling gamely through this ghastly January he told Henley that he was faced by an "Alpine accumulation of ill news. . . . My spirits have risen *contra fortunam*. I will fight this out and conquer." He was now the miser of 608 Bush Street and would have walked half a mile, even with the ague, he told Colvin, for a brandy and soda. It took six weeks for an exchange of letters, and when he heard that Colvin had transferred a hundred pounds of his own money to a bank in San Francisco he went frantically searching for it, only to conclude that his friend must have dreamt it.

"The Osbourne" continued to frustrate and madden him. He seemed to be behaving honorably, causing Louis to hope that an early marriage was in the offing. Then he heard that he had reneged on his promise to return Fanny's dowry and make her a joint owner of the Oakland property. "His whole conduct is an undecipherable riddle," Louis confessed to Baxter. "But I suppose the truth is that he changes his mind and sometimes wants only money and sometimes both money and respect." He was baffled too by Osbourne's attempts to find out his address. To cap it all, Fanny, it turned out, wanted more time to win over her family in Indiana, who knew absolutely nothing about Stevenson. He wrote to Gosse that against all the odds he was hoping to come through. His people may have cast him off but "I do not think many wives are better loved than mine will be." His father was now a stranger to him. No one could know how this grieved him.

At home things were not as black as he feared. Attitudes were slowly if painfully changing. Thomas Stevenson wrote to his son on January 26, 1880, to say that he had misunderstood the situation, which Colvin had now clarified. He meant by this that he had no idea there was a divorce pending and a marriage to follow. By the time this letter reached him, Louis was again at death's door. His chronic decline followed directly after the illness of his landlady's four-year-old son Robbie, who had gone down with pneumonia. Louis identified with the little boy, nursed him through the night when it was touch and go, and felt he was sitting at his own bedside watching himself die. He wrote a distraught letter to Colvin: "Oh what he has suffered! It has really affected my health. O never, never any family for me! I am cured of that. . . ." The boy lived, but the stress and strain hastened Louis's most severe illness. He sweated profusely, coughed himself to exhaustion, and became a victim of the dreaded "Bluidy Jack" for the first of many times. He began to bleed from the lungs; his mouth filled with blood and he was unable to speak. A local doctor pronounced him in the final stages of galloping consumption. Fanny came over from Oakland and took him to a hotel, then to her own cottage in defiance of gossip so that she could care for him. He was on the brink for six weeks, unable to feel reprieved until April. "This is not the first time, nor will it be the last," he wrote prophetically, "that I have a friendly game with that gentleman."

Fanny certainly believed he had tuberculosis. Modern medical opinion is inclined to discount this and believe he suffered from another chest disease, bronchiectasis, which can occur in childhood after pneumonia or whooping cough. The malady produces persistent pulmonary hemorrhages and weight loss and in 1880 could easily have been mistaken for consumption. In this case it was malaria, aggravated by weak lungs and inadequate diet. Once diagnosed correctly it was cleared up with quinine.

Fanny must have written a panic-stricken letter to the Steven-

sons about their son's collapse, and in any case they were getting
alarming reports from his London friends. His penury was made
worse of course by Sam Osbourne's backsliding. Respectability was
the cry on all sides. As long as this was preserved, Louis could go to
the wall for all anyone cared. He applied to the *San Francisco Bulletin*
for work but there was nothing doing. A letter from his mother
sounded sorrowful but not unforgiving. Why didn't he let them
know the names of his friends in San Francisco? Two new friends were
Virgil and Dora Williams, Fanny's painter friends before she de-
camped for France. Through them he met Charles Warren Stoddard,
author of *Cruising in the South Seas*, a seminal work for Louis. It was
Stoddard who led him to the books of Herman Melville, another literary nomad.

It was good to cross over on the ferry to see the Williamses.
Their welcome was always warm, and though at times he still felt
feverish, the city where he had been incarcerated seemed to match his
mood, with its airy and rapid images. "The streets lie straight up and
down the hills, and straight across at right angles, these in sun, those
in shadow, a trenchant pattern of gloom and glare . . . the sea-air
singing in your ears, the chill and glitter, the changing aspects both
of things and people, the fresh sights at every corner of your walk . . .
steep descending streets . . . whiffs of alien speech, sailors singing on
shipboard . . . crowds brawling all day in the street before the Stock
Exchange—one brief impression follows and obliterates another. . . ."
He could have been describing the feverish contents of his own mind
as he waited for developments that did not happen, and braced himself for yet more difficulties and obstacles in the way of his desire.
Would he ever be clear of muddle, family objections, hysteria?

Out of the blue came a cable from his father: "Count on 250
pounds annually." The joyful news, with its unspoken blessing which
meant more to him than the money, was followed by a letter from his
parents saying they would receive Fanny in due course. All Thomas
asked was a decent interval between divorce and marriage, again for
respectability's sake. No matter: the nightmare was over. With the
divorce all but complete he could ignore prying eyes and sit openly in

the garden at Oakland while Fanny set about building him up with soups, eggs, cream, and fruit. He was now showing her his work for comment. Hopeful again, he attempted yet another novel called *What Was on the Slate*. It foundered like the others. He and Fanny damned it in unison as "too morbid, ugly and unkind; better starvation." Thanks to his father who had relented yet again he was not going to starve. America now had a different aspect, one that Scott Fizgerald would call "a willingness of the heart." He wrote proudly to Gosse, "I shall be married in May and then go to the mountains, a very withered bridegroom."

THE LONG FOUGHT-FOR MARRIAGE took place on May 19, 1880, in San Francisco at the home of the Reverend William Scott, a Scottish Presbyterian. Louis, not his father's son for nothing, had left Fanny the day before and now met his bride decently separate off the Oakland ferry. She and Louis rode in a cable car to their friends the Williamses. Dora Williams and the vicar's wife were the only witnesses. Still badly off, they could not afford gold, exchanging plain silver rings, peasant fashion. On the marriage certificate Fanny owned up to being forty but described herself as "widowed." The groom was said to be a citizen of "Edinboro." Louis gave his bride some specially composed verses to mark the occasion, and presented the Reverend Scott with a copy of his father's "defense" of Christianity.

His account of the marriage could hardly have been more realistic, describing it to P. G. Hamerton as "a sort of marriage *in extremis*." He was only a married man thanks to the lady "who married me when I was a mere complication of coughs and bones, much fitter for an emblem of mortality than a bridegroom." To Fanny's brother Jacob he made clear that he saw himself as being on probation. "I may very well never see next spring. . . . I am an author but I am not very likely to make my fortune in that business, where better even than I are glad to get their daily bread."

He was now a sober and responsible husband, and would remain one. Yet once in March, sick of his penny-pinching existence, a devil whispered in his ear, urging him to turn everything upside down. He spent money he could ill afford in a restaurant called Garcia's. He rubbed shoulders with some of the city's socialist leaders. One woman "who kept a brothel, I reckon, before she started socialist, particularly interests me. If I am right as to her early industry, you know she would be sure to adore me." Following this boast he added like a desperado, "When I die of consumption you can put that upon my tomb." No doubt he was feeling a pang of nostalgia for his "wild" youth, when he wore duck trousers and a black shirt, "a slithering loose flail of a fellow" who liked to sit with prostitutes and social dropouts in the taverns of Lothian Road. All his life he would speak up for prostitutes.

The long struggle to be married had been a visceral one. The fight for Fanny was at the same time a fight to overcome dark doubts. Fanny had gone back to Sam too many times for him to be completely sure of her. These two were far from being romantic lovers flying together to unite. Both had been tried and tested by the three and a half years they had known each other. She must have wondered if she was marrying a permanent invalid. He had been badly shaken by the coolness of his reception when he first arrived in Monterey, and her mysterious illnesses, depressions, and dizzy spells troubled him, as did the realization of mental instability in her family. He had made clear in an essay his reservations about marriage, though he did want to marry. The truth was that he did not feel strong enough to stand alone. Their relationship as it developed was based on a kind of mutual aid. She restored his belief in himself, and his talents, hopes, and ambitions rejuvenated her, introducing her to a world that enabled her to feel creative.

Her painting had not been serious, merely a way of escape. It could be said that her marriage conferred a kind of creativity on her by association, since she was now the intimate of a true practitioner, a gifted, willful artist whose example strengthened her determination to be a woman in her own right. They would live their own lives side by side, come what may.

Ever since childhood his illnesses had been like accomplices, often occurring when he was faced with problems that seemed insoluble. Now they bound him to a woman who knew how to appreciate his dependence on her. In exultant moments she would be tempted to think that it was she who had turned him into a real writer. Always claiming second sight, she said she knew she was marrying a genius "if he lives and works!" And it is true that she used her flair for organization to get him down to the writing of lucrative books. The anti-Fanny lobby in London had long ago decided that she had a sinister, smothering side and was out to take over his life. This picture of a talented aesthete given purpose and direction by a stern nurse-mother, without whom he would have caved in, leaves out the peculiar spell he cast, and one essential fact. There could be no more convincing evidence of the iron in his soul than his ability, time and time again, with death knocking on his door, to go on believing he had something important to say. Undoubtedly he owed Fanny a great deal, but in the end, self-expression being what it is, no one could help him but himself.

CHAPTER NINE

The Wolverine on
My Own Shoulders

T HE NEWLY MARRIED Stevensons went back on the ferry to Oakland to prepare and pack for their honeymoon. Fanny now had to think of the best place for a man with lung problems. Naturally the Bay Area with its sea fogs sweeping in from the Pacific was to be avoided. Louis fancied Shasta County in far northern California. Then the Williamses suggested the Napa Valley to the northeast, where they could squat in one of the abandoned miners' shacks for next to nothing. Fanny, with her experience of such settlements, thought this an excellent idea, and the mountain air would be good for Louis. The frail husband and his new wife boarded a train to Calistoga together with Lloyd and a setter spaniel called Chuchu. When Maggie heard of it and wondered at the wisdom of her invalid son living rough in the Silverado Hills, Fanny replied briskly: "Why, if you only knew how thankful I was to get there with him! I was told that nothing else would save his life, and I believe it was true. We could not afford to go to a 'mountain resort' place, and there was no other chance." Here, not for the first time, Fanny was being creative with the facts. No one had told her anything of the sort.

Louis was in a strangely light-headed frame of mind, not caring much where he went, only grateful to be free at last of his endless worries. He stopped writing anything except verses like "Not I," lighthearted stuff for his own amusement, or for Lloyd to print later at his boarding school. He would feel mad laughter rising up inside himself at the thought of his fate.

At Calistoga Hot Springs they stayed in a hotel, were initiated into the use of a telephone, and called in at a vineyard. Louis, seeing the area in a romantic light, "a land of stage-drivers and highway-men: a land, in that sense, like England a hundred years ago," had not yet been hit by the reality of the place. They went on by horse to Mount St. Helena. They were still very hard up and were told of a man named Hanson who could find them a shack high in the Silver-ado Hills. The Lakeport stage called daily at the Toll House nearby, so they would be in touch after a fashion with civilization. The book *The Silverado Squatters* gives the saga in full. They found themselves "in a world of wreck and rust, splinters and rolling gravel" among the ruins of a deserted mine. It seemed to mirror in some way the up-heaval they had come through. There was "a rough smack of resin in the air and a crystal purity." The tumbledown shack that was to be their honeymoon home had once been a miners' dormitory and office.

It consisted of three rooms, and was so plastered against the hill that one room was right atop of another, that the upper floor was more than twice as large as the lower, and that all three apartments must be entered from a different side and level. Not a window-sash remained. The door of the lower room was smashed, and one panel hung in splinters. We entered that, and found a fair amount of rub-bish: sand and gravel that had been sifted in there by the mountain winds . . . a table, a barrel, a plate rack on the wall. . . . The win-dow, sashless of course, was choked with the green and sweetly smelling foliage of a bay; and through a chink in the floor a spray of poison ivy had shot up. . . . It was my first care to cut away that poison oak, Fanny standing by at a respectful distance. . . .

The room immediately above could only be entered by a

plank propped against the threshold, along which the intruder must foot it gingerly. . . . In front, in the strong sunshine, the platform lay overstrewn with busy litter, as though the labors of the mine might begin again tomorrow in the morning.

For all his boyish delight in its possibilities for adventure, it was in truth a squalid, chaotic, and dangerous dump. Fanny, her erstwhile pioneering spirit aroused, attacked the piles of rubbish vigorously and tried to make the squat habitable. They traipsed back to the Toll House for tools and supplies and again Fanny set manfully to work, Louis being still in an enfeebled state and in any case useless with his hands. He was given the task of fetching water from a spring, and he chopped wood for the stove. Somehow a makeshift homestead was created in the midst of this shambles, "with beds made, the plates on the rack, the pail of bright water behind the door, the stove crackling in a corner . . . the table roughly made against a meal."

As a Scot he loved being in the mountains. With his essentially forgiving nature he even began to feel more kindly toward his faint-hearted friends in London. Soon, though, it all proved too much. After six days Fanny and Lloyd went down with mild diphtheria and they retreated, all three, to rent a cottage in Calistoga. Louis reported to his friends at home that "the first night I had a cramp and was quite worn out after it; the second day Fanny mashed her thumb while carpentering and had a nervous chill. . . ." When diphtheria struck he got her and Lloyd down in an open cart. This fiasco of back-woods life soon had him feeling homesick for Europe, though it was touch and go whether he would be strong enough to face traveling home that summer.

Reinforcements came up from San Francisco, Joe Strong, Belle, and Nellie arriving by stagecoach to lend the trio some assistance. The honeymooners clambered back up for one more session in their eyrie. Louis was in charge of the stove and made the morning coffee and porridge. Near the old forge was a clump of dwarf madronas, and under their shade he took books and tried to write. Looking ahead he gazed over a forest of redwoods. Beyond was the distant Napa Valley. Fanny, determined to coddle her charge, would carry down a rum punch sprinkled with cinnamon. The platform was scorching hot by day, but in the evening they were pleasantly cool, perched like birds on it, catching on the breeze the aromas of bay and nutmeg. Situated as they were hundreds of feet high, the night struck chill. Rattlesnakes were all around, "whizzing on every side like spinning wheels." Only after they had departed did they realize that the dump, precariously supported, could have gone sliding down the hill in an avalanche, taking the squatters with it.

BACK THEY WENT at the end of July to San Francisco and began to organize themselves for the enormous journey to Scotland. For Fanny this planning would include opening an astute correspondence with Maggie Stevenson to prepare the ground for her arrival. Presenting herself cleverly as the dutiful wife who knew what she was about, she wrote, "Taking care of Louis is, as you must know, very like angling for shy trout; one must understand when to pay out the line and exercise the greatest caution in drawing him in." This may have hit the right note, but did it make her sound like an unscrupulous woman who had hooked Maggie's beloved son? She went on at once to put herself in the inferior position. "Your fancy that I may be a business person is a sad mistake, I am no better in that respect than Louis, and he has gifts that compensate for any lack." And for good measure she added a little unctuously that "I fear it is only genius that is allowed to be stupid in ordinary things." She had her tongue firmly in her cheek. She too was a snob, which would not go amiss in the society she would soon be entering.

Determined to make the best possible impression, she overlooked nothing in this first approach. Apologizing for the photograph of herself which she enclosed, she said it flattered her, but alas she could get no other. "I do earnestly hope that you will like me, but that can only be for what I am to you after you know me, and I do not want you to be disappointed in the beginning in anything about me, even in so small a thing as my looks."

Nor did she neglect to ease the way for her errant husband, telling the Stevensons that "I believe his best medicine will be meeting with you and his father, for whom he pines like a child. I have had a sad time through it all, but it has been worse for you, I know." She took careful note of the religious household she was addressing. "Louis has come out of this illness a better man than he was before; not that I did not think him good always, but the atmosphere of the valley of the shadow is purifying to a true soul." She was out to disarm them in advance and succeeded even better than she could have hoped: her use of certain odd phrases would have added to their curiosity, and her thoughtfulness was undeniable. When it came to Louis's friends, all of them opposed to the marriage, it was a different matter entirely.

On the way at last, they traveled to New York via Chicago and embarked on the *City of Chester.* It was August. Louis had been away for twelve months and it felt like a lifetime. He had written heart-breakingly of a grueling sea voyage and an even worse train journey, recording it all with an absolute veracity that made it sound as if he were in hell. He had known the huge emptiness of mid-America, his eye "tortured by distance." Colvin and others had turned up their noses at this remarkable black book, and Louis was typically willing to give them the benefit of the doubt, putting it to one side. But literary matters were not at the forefront of his mind as they traveled first class all the way, paid for by his father. He had clung like a bit of wreckage to the rails of rear platforms and balanced on the roofs of railroad cars as he crossed the continent on the journey out. The contrast was bizarre.

So was the reunion ahead of him as he anticipated it. He had made his peace with his parents in letters, but what would they think of him face to face? He had skulked off like a fugitive without a word in an act of cowardice which had caused them great pain and shock. There they were, waiting to welcome a wife they had never met who was divorced, ten years older than their son, in their generosity willing to help him yet again and forgive him everything. Thank God they didn't know the full story of Fanny's past, of Sam Osbourne's shenanigans, or the fact that she was about to become a grandmother: Belle was now pregnant. Louis left no record of the train journey or the voyage over on the Royal Mail liner, which docked at Liverpool on August 17, 1880. He must have been daily preoccupied with how he was going to look his eager parents in the eye.

He need not have worried. He was becoming adept, writes Ian Bell, at moving from one world to another. It was the nature of his fate, which sometimes made him laugh in spite of himself, so absurd it seemed. Colvin, who had traveled up from London on the mail train overnight, went out in the tug and clambered up the ship's ladder to the deck as if determined to be the first to greet them.

Fanny's preliminary letters make her seem very confident. The truth was, as she admitted to her intimates, she lived in fear of this first meeting. The gentle mother she had got to know through correspondence was no threat, she felt sure, but Thomas's photograph put her in mind of a judge. Still, she could assume different roles, and the one she now chose was that of a respectable matron, with no resemblance to the adventuress they half expected. The one daring thing about her was her short-cut hair, but it was greying, and she looked decidedly staid. She lowered her gaze, which, when it was trained on you, was like "the sighting of a pistol," and she refrained from rolling and smoking cigarettes, something she liked to do as much as her husband.

At the hotel where the prodigals were taken for lunch, Lloyd put away his meal as if he were starving. Colvin stayed only long enough to gauge his friend's reception and report back. He thought "the old folks put a most brave and kind face on it indeed." About Fanny he was more caustic (though of course they had met already), telling Henley that Mrs. Stevenson, ten years older than the American, looked the fresher of the two women. He went on, "When I had him alone talking in the smoking-room it was quite exactly like old times; and it is clear enough that he likes his new state so far all right, and is at peace in it; but whether you and I will ever get reconciled to the little determined brown face and white teeth and grizzling (for that's what it's up to) hair, which we are to see beside him in future—that is another matter." Previously, meeting her for the first time in London, he had pronounced her "vivid, eager, devoted." The change of tone was perhaps for the benefit of Henley, already a foe in the making.

ONCE IN HERIOT ROW, which impressed her tremendously with its elegant rooms and handsome furniture, Fanny concentrated on pleasing the old man. Black stockings had become fashionable but she quickly sensed that he preferred white ones, and on they went. Maggie was won over at once, and though Fanny's liking for her father-in-law was at first diplomatic, it rapidly became genuine. They were surprisingly at ease with each other. He was shrewd enough to see that this mature woman of strong character would be likely to keep his impulsive son in check, and that it was probably due to her influence that relations between him and Louis were so wonderfully improved. Louis for his part was amazed by how completely his father was subjugated. Fanny was a good listener, like her husband, and this alone worked wonders. Soon Thomas was calling her "The Vandegrifter" and she retaliated with "Mr. Tommy" and "Uncle Tom," without ever descending to overfamiliarity. Thomas, she wrote to Dora Williams in San Francisco, was a lovely old person. He was much better looking

> than I fear Louis will ever be, and is hustled about, according to
> the humor of his wife and son, in the most amusing way; occasion-
> ally he comes in with twinkling eyes and reports a comic verse of
> his own making with infinite gusto . . . and he comes in with a
> sprig of heather in his hat looking so pert and wholesome. . . .

Partly forearmed with confidences from Louis but unusually perceptive at such short acquaintance, she was quick to see that

Thomas Stevenson could have been a greater man than he was. "One could almost see," she wrote, "the struggle between the creature of cramped hereditary conventions and environment, and the man nature had intended him to be." For all his quirky humor she saw him as a fundamentally tragic figure, unlike his wife, "who lived as a bird lives, for the very joy of it," with a natural gaiety that she had passed down to her son.

She was soon aware that Maggie Stevenson was a more complex creature, "much more like Louis." Her husband spoiled her like a baby, and Fanny saw that both of them had spoiled their son. Though she was working hard at being watchful and demure, Fanny's innate forcefulness did not escape Louis's Uncle George Balfour, who told his nephew, "I too married a besom [a broom] and have never regretted it." The servants were fascinated by the new addition to the family. A maid told her she spoke English very well for a foreigner. She may have been untroubled by her dark complexion until one day she overheard two servants gossiping about a Scot who was just back from Africa. "He's merrit a black woman," one said, and the other, in a mirror, gestured toward Fanny's back and put a warning finger to her lips.

Lloyd too was making a hit. "Mr. Tom and Aunt Maggie both liked him," Fanny wrote to Belle. Having a boy in the house again took them back to Louis's childhood. Walter Simpson gave the bride a young black Skye terrier for a wedding present. First called Wattie, his name changed to Woggs, Woggy, Wiggs, and finally Bogue over the course of the next six years. He was an irascible, ill-tempered creature who messed on carpets and snapped at waiters wherever they went.

The Victorian remedy for sufferers with weak lungs was mountain air, and Fanny, still eager to pander to Louis's parents, urged him to go with them on a short holiday to Blair Atholl and Strathpeffer. He went off obediently and then wished he hadn't. The Highlands were beautiful—he thought he might write a history of the Highlands—but he hated the hotel and the guests, venting his spleen in some verses on his "ghastly companions":

They had at first a human air
In coats and flannel underwear.
They rose and walked upon their feet
And filled their bellies full of meat.
They wiped their lips when they had done—
But they were ogres every one.

The weather was raw, and Louis's health was once again in decline. Back in Edinburgh the city's climate was no kinder. His gloomy prediction that Scotland would be the end of him was, he felt, as true now as when he wrote, "I must flee from Scotland. It is, for me, the mouth of the pit." Laid low with catarrh and weakness, he alarmed his doctor uncle, who saw his extreme thinness and the congestion in his lungs as sure symptoms of tuberculosis. He urgently recommended Davos-platz in southeastern Switzerland, the latest panacea for well-off consumptives.

They left for the south on October 7, luggage including a dog in one basket and a cat in another. In London they stayed extravagantly for a few days at the Grosvenor Hotel, accumulating expenses for which Thomas picked up the bill. They saw a number of publishers, and then, as word got round that their "gay beloved Stevenson" was in town and dying, many friends flocked round. Fanny, at first as eager to please as she had been at Heriot Row, soon saw that this was a very different scene. Instinct told her that she was making waves and that these friends of her husband were possessive, snobbish, and inclined to do him harm from sheer thoughtlessness. They came at all hours, stayed too long, and tired him out. Overnight she turned into a tough little watchdog, determined to keep guard over him. Edmund Gosse found her "a sort of savage nature in some ways . . . extraordinarily passionate and unlike everyone else in her violent feelings and unrestrained way of expressing them. . . ." Frieda Lawrence, another forceful and intrusive foreigner, would show the same angry resentment, a mixture of jealousy and insecurity, as she kept watch over her "genius," driving her husband's friends into opposing camps just as Fanny would do. "Marriage often puts old friends to the door," Louis had generalized in *Virginibus Puerisque,* and "the most masculine and direct of women will some day, to your dire surprise, draw out like a telescope into successive lengths of person-ation."

Unaware that he was on dangerous ground, Louis treated his friends Gosse, Henley, Lang, and Pollock to a lavish lunch at the Sav-ile, and the Burgundy flowed. Before long, the procession of callers to the hotel drove Fanny to write angrily to her mother-in-law, "If we do not soon get away from London I shall become an embittered woman. It is not good for my mind, or my body either, to sit smiling at Louis' friends until I feel like a hypocritical Cheshire cat, talking stiff noth-ings . . . and all the time furtively watching the clock and thirsting for their blood because they stay so late."

Already she had begun to see herself as the one indispensable person in her husband's life, whereas there was no one person, writes Jenni Calder, "with whom Louis felt he could share all aspects of his intimate life. This reinforces the sense that grows powerfully in his later years that the major dislocation in his life and career was that his art, his marriage, his love for friends, his parents could never coa-lesce."

Louis, never skimpy with money, was generous with his friends and extravagant in his tastes when he had the chance. The bill he and Fanny ran up at the Grosvenor alone came to forty-six pounds, a huge sum for those days. He was in a spendthrift mood in any case after a year of near starvation and terrible accommodations. So was Fanny, given a taste for bourgeois comfort in Edinburgh which would never leave her. Its significance for her had to do with the security it repre-sented rather than things in themselves. She was experiencing the fruits of prosperity for the first time.

The 250 pounds allowance promised by Thomas would soon be double that amount. The indulgent father was opening his check-book again before the trio had reached the Channel. In order to get as far as Paris, Louis had to claw back 10 pounds from the 50 he had loaned Colvin.

The Stevensons went on slowly in the direction of Davos, breaking the journey in Troyes, "in the midst of wind, rain, coughing and night sweats." The bridegroom, wrecked by his London orgy of excited talk, late nights, tobacco, and wine, his lungs full of fog, was fit for nothing but bed as they climbed aboard a final train through the mountains and then a diligence in the darkness over frozen roads to the Hotel Belvedere and the chalets of Davos. From the train he had gazed out at the vast bulk of mountains: "the Alps are all there: they beat everything to smash." Here was the famous setting of Thomas Mann's *The Magic Mountain.* In the hotel, with Fanny inspecting the rooms upstairs, the landlady said, "Your mother will be down soon." And it was true that Louis always looked boyish, with his skinny build and his spontaneous delight in new surroundings. The child in him was drawing steadily closer to young Lloyd, who was showing a flair for writing, and later described the Swiss resort as a small straggling town

> where nearly all the shops were kept by consumptives. It possessed a charity sanitorium and three large hotels, widely separated from one another, in which one could die quite comfortably . . . and its pine woods and its glorious winter sunshine were supposed to work wonders. For five months of the year—"the season"—it was buried in snow, and rimmed about with dazzling white peaks. Snow, snow, snow, icicled trees; a frozen little river; a sense of glinting and sparkling desolation—such was the place we had come to.

Louis, examined at the clinic of the famous Dr. Karl Ruedi, was ordered to restrict his smoking, to drink milk, eat meat, and not write more than two hours a day. In fact, unusual for him, he was scarcely writing at all. While there, however, he did manage to write an essay, "The Morality of the Profession of Letters," and yet again tried his hand at a novel, *The Squaw Man,* which petered out after three chapters. The nearness of death was hardly a spur to achieving anything. What was the point? Half the patients seemed to be having mad love affairs in the short time they had left. The whole place was feverish with gossip, wild jealousies, and people driven reckless to the point of gaiety by the knowledge that the dead were being discreetly removed. It was bizarre to live day by day in the rare air and blinding light of an Alpine winter and be stingingly alive yet ever conscious of "the wolverine on my own shoulders." Invalids marched up and down on the snowy roads, skated on the ice rinks, threw snowballs at each other, and tried to believe that their sunburned faces meant they were getting better. The sterility of it all soon got to him. So did the isolation, the weirdness of the altitude. Familiar faces disappeared, funeral after funeral took place, new invalids moved in.

Only a friendship with another literary man, the consumptive John Addington Symonds, made things bearable. Symonds, a distinguished Renaissance scholar, had already been at Davos for three years when Louis arrived. Talking for hours with the newcomer over the "dark Valtellina wine," the historian had doubts about Louis's intellectual powers. "The more I see of him," he wrote stuffily in a letter, "the less I find of solid mental stuff. He wants some years of study in tough subjects. After all a University education has some merits. One feels the want of it in men like him." Louis's caprices of humor and fantasy seemed lightweight and frivolous to Symonds.

At the hotel Louis was soon out of favor with the other guests. He felt out of step with them and behaved oddly. An imp in him felt impelled to provoke them. For instance, he allowed his "son" to address him as Louis. These were proper times. They didn't care for his long hair and were baffled by his wife, who spent her days lying on a couch because the altitude affected her heart. In the center of their room was an enormous porcelain stove "like a monument" which went from floor to ceiling.

The friendship between Symonds and Louis had shifting nuances as it developed. Symonds was married with four daughters but spoke disparagingly of the "illusion" of heterosexuality. His marriage existed for the sake of appearance, apparently with his wife's agreement. Louis confided in Symonds, told him about the romance of his pursuit of Fanny, and was aware of the other's preferences, which he no doubt knew already from his friends in London. Mrs. Symonds came to resent his long visits with her husband, and she and Fanny had taken a dislike to each other. Having anything to do with Symonds was, he told Gosse, "to adventure in a thorn bush." All the same he was glad to kill the dragging hours with him. He felt sorry for Symonds's wife but had little real sympathy for her, "moving daily with people whose talk she doesn't understand." When Chatwin recounted that Louis's sickbed sheets were stained with ink and blood and gravy he was repeating spiteful gossip spread later by the Symondses. Symonds, perhaps regretting the disclosure of his own bedroom arrangements, let Margot Asquith know that Louis slept with his back to the light and Mrs. Louis in the same bed with her face to it. Later, he dropped his Balliol condescension toward the man lacking a decent education and looked back on his Davos days with the "Shelley-like man" as among his happiest times.

Louis, hard up as usual, wrote to his parents that "your two letters and fifty quid are all duly received." He began sending his father long lists of books he wanted for a book he planned to write which he called *The Transformation of the Scottish Highlands.* The project never got off the ground, though the research came in handy when he came to write *Kidnapped.*

Colvin came to visit in January and was promptly bitten by Woggs when he stroked the irritable creature's fur the wrong way. After him, Mrs. Sitwell suddenly arrived with her eighteen-year-old son Bertie, who had been at Marlborough until forced to leave with galloping consumption. Fanny, upset at being reminded of the loss of her own son in Paris, did her best to comfort the distraught mother, and so did Louis. They were both anxious now at the thought of Lloyd and the risk he ran in a place like Davos, and sent him out of harm's way to a private school in Bournemouth. Again Thomas came forward to foot the bill. More expenses accumulated when Fanny, who had been ill, went off to Paris for a consultation.

Meanwhile poor Bertie was dying. Fanny returned just as the boy passed away in his mother's arms. Louis's poem "In Memoriam: F.A.S." begins:

Yet, O stricken heart, remember, O remember
  How of human days he lived the better part.
April came to bloom and never dim December
  Breathed its killing chills upon the head or heart. . . .

All that life contains of torture, toil and treason,
  Shame, dishonor, death, to him were but a name.
Here, a boy, he dwelt through all the singing season
  And ere the day of sorrow departed as he came.

One farcical episode lightened the atmosphere of gloom and sorrow, though no one thought it funny at the time. A young woman patient obsessed with religion kept pestering Lloyd with questions about his feelings for Jesus. Getting nowhere, she began passing notes on the subject to Louis in the dining room. Another guest, a young man, came to the conclusion that Louis was having an affair. Fanny had to be shown the notes before she was reassured.

Before the death of Bertie he had begun to come to terms with Davos. His health improved, to such an extent that he wrote, "I think there is no doubt, on the whole, that I should stay here." But what McLynn calls a Jack Sprat type of marriage was now developing, whereby a climate that suited him was anathema to her, and vice versa. Maggie Stevenson received a letter from her, wailing that living in Davos was like living in a well of desolation. One can understand her depression. She had fainting fits, and as an American divorcée she had no status among the hotel guests. Disagreeable letters came from America. Sam Osbourne, referred to by Louis as "that putrid windbag," seemed to think he had the right to meddle in Lloyd's future, though he had withdrawn all financial support. Fanny's old admirer John Lloyd wrote hotly that she had pulled the wool over his eyes by marrying Louis in secret. Perhaps as a way of occupying herself she had begun to take over part of her husband's personal correspondence. Was this from a desire to take control, as her critics have suggested, or a symptom of insecurity, as she sought to keep a foothold in a world where she seemed to be contributing nothing? The consequence of this access to his desk was, as her biographer points out, that "This sometimes altered the tone of his letters to and from his old friends, even the many letters which he himself penned."

Undermined finally by the death of the Sitwell boy, they decided to leave, and in April 1881 started to wend their way homeward, pulled by nostalgia first of all to Barbizon, scene of their carefree days, and then to St. Germain-en-Laye. Louis bought an antique watch that Fanny had fancied, spending their last sou on it. "Now we'll starve," Fanny said. Back at the hotel he plunged his hand into the pocket of an old coat and came up with an uncashed check he had somehow overlooked.

A few days later their money did run out. The landlord of the Hotel du Pavillon Henry IV became nastily suspicious of Louis's appearance, and when they asked for time to pay he insulted them. The trouble, according to Fanny, was Louis's red flannel shirt. A large money order arrived from Scotland and totally confused their host, who now thought he was dealing with "the eccentric son of a wealthy British nobleman."

THEY WERE on the move again. As always, Louis's spirits revived. Uneasy about a return to Scotland for a reunion with his parents, he had put in a request for "a house, not an inn, at least not an hotel; a burn without reach; heather and a fir or two." After their stay at the Belvedere in Davos they had had their fill of hotels. Springtime too rejuvenated him. He had fought through another deadly winter and was still alive and kicking. The mountain sarcophagus of Davos had not claimed him. Though he had no way of knowing, the "succession of defeats" he had suffered with novels was about to come to an end. 1881 would be his breakout year as a writer.

The traveling Stevensons joined Thomas and Maggie at a small farmhouse called Kinnaird Cottage above Pitlochry in the Vale of Atholl. The nearest hamlet was Moulin. There was a glen behind, and then the great rising purple-brown moor, which had a honey scent.

The cottage was conveniently split into two flats. Its austerity appealed to his parents, if not to Fanny with her newly acquired bourgeois inclinations. It had no bath and was lit by oil lamps. Quaint it may have been, but its charm was lost on her. In the two months they were there, Thomas went to and from his office in Edinburgh. Lloyd would join them a little later. It was the beginning of June and could have been autumn, with cold rains and penetrating winds. Fanny wandered out bravely with her mother-in-law, both armed with umbrellas. More often than not they came back drenched. Louis, nervous of venturing out, was left staring into the fire. The only books in the place were two large volumes of the life of Voltaire, which his parents considered unsuitable for Sabbath reading.

To pass the time he and Fanny wrote stories to read to each other in a sort of collaboration, their first. The idea was to put together a joint venture of eight tales. Fanny wrote well but was inclined to be facile. Her liking for Gothic horror, encouraged in childhood by her grandmother, was similar in origin to the fondness for the ghoulish inspired by Louis's nurse Cummy. Both enjoyed what he called "Crawlers." Soon he was at work in earnest. In quick succession he turned out "The Merry Men," "The Body Snatcher," and that dark fable "Thrawn Janet," written in broad Scots, which Henry James came to call a masterpiece. One might call them experiments, suiting his temperament so well that they led eventually to *Dr. Jekyll* and made him famous. In an excited letter to Henley he called "The Merry Men" "a fantastic sonata about the sea and wrecks." He was already sensing a breakthrough, calling it "my first real shoot at a story, an odd thing, sir, but I believe my own, though there is a little of Scott in it." In other words he was edging closer to finding his own voice. And he was dabbling in the use of doubles. "The Body Snatcher" was derived from the life of Robert Knox, the recipient of bodies provided for dissection by the infamous Burke and Hare. A later story, "Markheim," has a murderer for a hero whose conscience is undermined by a devil, tempting him to further crime before revealing himself as an angel in disguise.

Maggie kept to her ritual of staying in bed until nearly noon. In the afternoon she and Fanny would take the dog for a walk. Once when Louis went too they encountered a Highlander beating his own dog. Louis protested and was told, "It's not your dog." Answering as his father would have done, Louis said, "No, but it's God's dog and I'm not going to see you ill-use it."

Reading "Thrawn Janet" aloud one evening scared them both. The light of their one candle flickered, the shadows in the corners menaced, the rain drove down on the roof close to their heads, the brawling wind shook the windows in their frames, and "By the time the tale was finished my husband had fairly frightened himself, and we crept down the stairs hand in hand like two scared children." Not to be outdone, Fanny wrote a horror story called "The Shadow on the Bed," sending it to Henley for his magazine.

Fanny's screams during one of these spooky readings so alarmed Mrs. Sim, the widowed owner of the cottage who did the family's cooking, that she came knocking on their door. And one day when Fanny was out sketching a mountain she had an experience that confirmed beyond doubt her belief in the powers of second sight. Something made her feel giddy, and she staggered to the road just as a tree uprooted itself and fell where she had been standing.

Louis's temporary preoccupation with horror had to do with the use he could make of such tales as frameworks for moral and topographical exploration. His feeling for the malevolent power of the sea, influenced to some extent by his first reading of Melville, appears in "The Merry Men," as does his fear of the sound of the wind at night, whirling him back to the terrible nights of his childhood. His nightmares would always have a gale blowing gigantically through them, tearing at everything as it came to snatch at him.

Cooped up by the atrocious summer weather at Kinnaird Cottage, he came up with a crazy scheme to get himself elected to a chair at Edinburgh University. The professorship of history and constitutional law would have demanded only three months of lecturing each summer, and he saw it as an easy way to earn a living and go somewhere warm in the winters. Amazingly his father backed him to the hilt, completely ignoring his son's dubious university record and short-lived career as an advocate. Using his standing and connections he set to work to gather testimonials from all and sundry. Men of letters, judges, professors, and ministers were canvased by father and son in a concerted effort. The prize, a stipend of 250 pounds, dangled before Louis alluringly. The university, unimpressed by his squad of backers, held the customary election. Louis received 9 votes to the winner's 82. He went back to more practical ways of raising money, one of which was an imaginative biography of Jean Cavalier, the Protestant leader of the Camisards in the Cévennes. This got no further than the opening paragraph. Fanny for one was glad that her husband had not been given the university chair. The last thing she wanted, she told her friend Dora Williams, was to end up a professor's wife.

Louis caught a cold, dangerous for him. He began to spit blood and was soon unable to speak because of chest pains. The doctor advised a move to Braemar. "Bluidy Jack" was calling the tune again. His mother's diary entries were monotonous: "Weather wet. . . . Bad weather. . . . Still wet. . . . Afraid to go out. . . . Pouring rain." They hoped for milder days, but the rain and wind refused to let up. By the end of July the ménage was installed in another cottage near the road to Balmoral. Queen Victoria was seen driving past in an open carriage. Gosse had been up to Kinnaird Cottage and proposed a return visit to Braemar. Louis told him, "If you had an uncle who was a sea captain and went to the North Pole you had better bring his outfit."

Thomas Stevenson could now come more often, and this was another snag. Father and son, with the best intentions in the world, rapidly got on each other's nerves at close quarters. Thomas, unable to refrain from nagging, thought Louis smoked too much, and objected vehemently to *The Amateur Emigrant,* which he thought altogether unworthy of his son. He went further. "I am quite satisfied that one of the great causes of your condition is just what occasioned the same state in Alan [his depressed brother]—a total want of business habits." Before long Louis was confiding to Colvin, "I am in a great hurry to leave this hell of a place."

Yet in spite of awful weather, parental objections, an atmosphere of "personal quarrel," being ill, he remained in curiously good spirits and eager to work. For no apparent reason he felt a new surge of confidence. His mother had Kate Greenaway's children's book with her, and Louis, picking it up idly, thought he could do as well. In no time he had produced fourteen of the verses that would make up *A Child's Garden of Verses*. Then one day, dabbling with watercolor and ink, he made the map of an island. Lloyd later claimed wrongly that it had been his work. Certainly though, the twelve-year-old boy was the touchstone at hand to gauge the appetite of a young audience. And though he had counted on one boy for an audience when the tale began to unwind and catch fire, he had two. His father was so keen for it to go on that he came up with the idea of the apple barrel, where Jim Hawkins hid and overheard John Silver's treacherous plotting. Thomas had recognized something akin to his own imagination, "for it was his own kind of picturesque." Gosse, visiting with Colvin, was captivated both by Stevenson's shamanlike reading and the exciting narrative itself.

Treasure Island began with the map. Writing later of "My First Book," Stevenson realized that it was most of the plot. Beyond doubt this was the engendering catalyst. It was like "a fat dragon standing up"; it contained harbors "that pleased me like sonnets." Before he knew it, poring over his imaginary map, the future characters of the book began swarming out. He snatched up some paper and was writing out a list of chapters which seemed to write themselves. "On a chill September morning, by the cheek of a brisk fire, and the rain drumming on the window, I began *The Sea Cook,* for that was the original title." Owning up to the work of others he didn't forget his father, who contributed, as well as the apple barrel idea, the inventory of Billy Bones's chest. He acknowledged a debt to Washington Irving's *Tales of a Traveller,* to *Robinson Crusoe,* and someone, playing the game of influences, told him that the stockade came from *Masterman Ready.* Not that he cared. An artist in full flow plunders as if by right, and the book flowed effortlessly, and he with it. He picked up whatever he fancied like a magpie. Whatever he made use of, he knew the story would still be his. Maybe he found the skeleton in Poe, but what of it? No one, he remarked happily, "can hope to have a monopoly of skeletons or make a corner in talking birds." Something out of Fenimore Cooper's *The Sea Lions* may have found its way in there. It all worked. He admitted to Colvin in 1884 that the book "came out" of Charles Kingsley's *At Last,* from which he had lifted the Dead Man's Chest, and that he owed something to a *History of Notorious Pirates,* borrowed from Henley in August. Johnson's *Buccaneers* was dipped into, and his own recollections of canoeing and a cruise through the Western Isles in a fifteen-ton schooner yacht made up the rest of his material. He should have made the *Hispaniola* a brig but was unable to describe handling one. Then he had an idea for John Silver, "from which I promised myself funds of entertainment." He was recalling Henley with his one foot, his "maimed strength and masterfulness." He would take this admired friend, deprive him "of all his finer qualities and higher graces of temperament," and leave him with "only his strength and courage and his geniality, and try to express these in terms of a raw tarpaulin."

In his article "My First Book," published in the year he died, he made clear at the outset that what he meant by first book was his first novel. Until he was thirty-one a succession of failed attempts lay behind him. He mentioned a string of these "defeats," including one of the earliest, a bulky historical romance entitled *The Pentland Rising* that was devoid of merit. He wrote *A Vendetta in the West* and abandoned it when he was twenty-nine. Why did he have this mania to write novels? "Men are born with various manias: from my earliest childhood it was mine to make a plaything of imaginary series of events; and as soon as I was able to write I became a good friend to the papermakers." Some attempts had nearly gone the distance, and then stopped "inexorably, like a schoolboy's watch." At thirty-one he was building a literary reputation, but the problem of the novel remained unsolved. The puzzle had vexed him for years. What was so difficult about it? Anybody, he thought, could write a short story, even if it was a bad one, but not everyone could write even a bad novel. Why was this?

> It is the length that kills. The accepted novelist may take his novel up and put it down, spend days upon it in vain, and write not any more than he makes haste to blot. Not so the beginner. Human nature has certain rights; instinct—the instinct of self-preservation—forbids that any man (cheered and supported by consciousness of no previous victory) should endure the miseries of unsuccessful literary toil beyond a period to be measured in weeks. There must be something for hope to feed upon. . . . I remember I used to look, in those days, upon every three-volume novel with a sort of veneration. . . .

What was seen in Stevenson's day as a boy's adventure story is now seen very differently in our own time. Significances have been discerned by academics and gathered in psychoanalytical studies in such quantity that the novelist would be struck dumb in astonishment, or more likely doubled up with hysterical laughter, if he could read them now. Most are pure speculation. Chatwin, for all his bias, did see that Stevenson was in essence an autobiographical writer who "kept a tight rein on the confessional," and the hints are there throughout his stories for anyone who wishes to take them up. Ian Bell finds it hard to speak of *Treasure Island* except in terms of Stevenson's life. Louis had just recovered from a chaotic year of disruption, setting sail for the unknown and making himself virtually fatherless in the process. The hero of *Treasure Island* is fatherless, and even at the outset he finds himself in a nightmare world which grows progressively more terrifying when he is at sea. In the opening pages he meets an old sea dog in the inn kept by his father who was soon "far gone in a decline." The old sailor tells him to look out for a seafaring man with one leg of whom he is obviously afraid. The boy's imagination turns this expected one-legged stranger into a figure that haunts his dreams as terrifyingly as Magwitch in *Great Expectations*:

On stormy nights, when the wind shook the four corners of the house, and the surf roared along the cove and up the cliffs, I would see him in a thousand forms, and with a thousand diabolical expressions. Now the leg would be cut off at the knee, now at the hip: now he was a monstrous kind of creature who had never had but one leg and that in the middle of his body. To see him leap and run and pursue me over hedge and ditch was the worst of nightmares.

Stevenson was entangled with his father emotionally and financially for as long as his father lived. Here was a rival he could never supplant, on whom he depended absolutely for the support of himself and Fanny. He spoke once of his feelings of bitter exclusion because of his mother's love for Thomas, and was both excited and horrified by the sight of his father stripped naked on the beach at North Berwick. But Jim Hawkins's rampaging one-legged figure was based on Henley, his surrogate father.

We are on surer ground when we consider the moral complexities inherent in this swift-moving adventure story. Most of Stevenson's work is preoccupied with moral ambiguities. *Treasure Island* raises a host of unanswerable questions for the modern reader. Were islands paradises or prisons? Did the Shakespearean chaos involved in the pursuit of treasure, the intrigue, betrayal, and passion swirling like a whirlpool mean that the universe was a brutal Darwinian one, with no justice, no love? Was there a God looking down on all this, and was He good or vengeful? Did the dream of getting rich motivate the "good" characters as well as the villains? Long John Silver appears as now strong, now weak, and never to be trusted. If he was evil, why was he allowed to escape? Is the whole tale a pretext for the rehabilitation of a boy in disgrace as he struggles against male authority figures? No one in 1881 had any inkling of its power to endure as a fable which contains all these things.

In fifteen days he wrote fifteen chapters, reading it to his family in the evenings as he went, to the delight of his stepson in particular. His father too was entranced by it, and it brought them closer together than they had ever been. The writer's voice put a spell on many who heard him read, Fanny finding it "extraordinarily thrilling and sympathetic." Alexander Japp, another visitor to Braemar, spoke of its "wonderful power of inflection and variation." Only Fanny cast doubt on the enterprise, believing her husband was wasting his talent, though it was nice to see him in close consultation with his father and her son, "like three lads playing pirates." Louis, more and more certain that he was on to something, wrote full of confidence to Henley, saying,

> If this don't fetch the kids, why, they have gone rotten since my day. Will you be surprised to hear that it is about Buccaneers, that it begins in the "Admiral Benbow" public house on the Devon coast, that it's all about a map, and a treasure, and a mutiny, and a derelict ship, and a fine old Squire Trelawney . . . and a doctor, and another doctor, and a sea-cook with one leg, and a sea-song with the chorus "Yo-ho-ho and a bottle of rum." . . . Buccaneers without oaths—bricks without straw. But youth and the fond parent have to be consulted.

Henley was disgruntled, for once lining up with Fanny. He wanted his friend to concentrate on plays, but Louis saw "some coin" in this island story of subterfuge and escape. His inspiration dried up after fifteen days, when he was nearly halfway there. He must have wondered if the old pattern of "defeat" was to continue. This time, however, he had ample encouragement. Gosse came again, this time accompanied by Alexander Japp, with whom Louis had been corresponding about Thoreau. Listening enthralled to Louis's readings, Gosse thought that his friend James Henderson, editor of *Young Folks* magazine, might take on a novel of pirates and hidden treasure as a serial. He carried the completed chapters off in his luggage. Henderson accepted the tale but wanted the title *The Sea Cook* changed to *Treasure Island.* Louis would have called it anything for the chance of earning some quick money. It began serialization in October under the pseudonym of "Captain George North." His snobbish friends in London didn't think he should demean himself by stooping to pot-boilers, and reacted sniffily to Henley, who was quick to pass on their disapproval. The newly fledged novelist gave them short shrift: "I will swallow no more of that gruel. Let them write their damn masterpieces for themselves and let me alone." To emphasize his impatience he signed himself "the infuriated victim of his early books." Those days, he announced triumphantly, were over. Now he would follow his own nose.

He was paid for the serial at space rates, earning thirty-five pounds instead of the fifty he had expected. No matter: "Yo-heave ho!" When the novel came out in book form, a step opposed by Fanny who still regarded it as "tedious," he was amazed to be offered "a hundred jingling, tingling, golden-minted quid."

CHAPTER TEN

Flutes of Silence

L OUIS HAD TOLD GOSSE before he first came to stay, "You will like my wife because she likes cats." It would be the first of her fallings-out with her husband's friends. He had tried to patronize her, she complained to Dora Williams. "Mr. Gosse and I are at daggers drawn." Gosse described his initial visit in a book, the sleet falling outside, the howling wind, Louis's cold and his loss of voice obliging him to stay in bed. He sat up to play chess with his guest. Gosse remembered his dark flashing eyes and ruffled hair. If he felt tired he would rap on the board with his knuckles, and Gosse and Fanny "would arrange his writing materials on the bed."

On September 23 the party gave up on the weather and fled to Edinburgh. It was time in any case for Louis to escape the northern winter and return to the icy cage of Davos. After a brief interlude in Heriot Row, he and Fanny made for London. Lloyd was still with them: to keep him in boarding school was more than they could afford. They packed the unfinished *Treasure Island* and took it with them, together with a toy theatre for the boy and a large box of watercolors for him to paint the sets.

They called at Weybridge en route to London, paying a return visit to the novelist George Meredith. When *The Egoist* appeared in

1879 Louis was convinced that the character of Sir Willoughby Pat-
terne resembled himself. "No, my dear fellow," Meredith said, "he is
all of us." While at Weybridge he added a few more short chapters to
his novel before drying up again. Setting course for Davos, they had
already decided against more hotel life. Louis had misgivings about
going at all but could see no alternative, and Fanny hated the very
thought of it. Lloyd, in his *Intimate Portrait* of his late stepfather,
wrote of what seemed to him in retrospect the cruel delusion of the
invalid in the Alps who seemed to be recapturing "a sort of intermittent youth, with periods of lassitude."

> You wake every morning, see the gold upon the snow-peaks, be-
> come filled with courage, and bless God for your prolonged exis-
> tence. Is it a return to youth, or is it a congestion of the brain? It is
> a sort of congestion, perhaps, that leads the invalid, when all goes
> well, to face the new day with such a bubbling cheerfulness. But,
> on the other hand, the peculiar blessedness of boyhood may itself
> be but a symptom of the same complaint, for the two effects are
> strangely similar. . . .

Louis, at any rate, was keen to settle down somewhere and work,
and was looking forward to taking up again his friendship with
Symonds. In London, on the way through, he had experienced one of
those comic misunderstandings that kept happening to him over
the years. Calling to see the editor of *Young Folks* he had alarmed the
clerks with his scruffy appearance; they had to be convinced that he
was one of their authors and not a tramp off the streets.

This time they rented the Chalet am Stein at Davos, a rather
bleak, very small wooden house perched on the mountainside. It was
expensive, but at least they could escape the hothouse gossip always
simmering at the Belvedere. After twice stalling in his efforts to finish *Treasure Island* he was anxious to apply himself to the task, not to
mention overcoming his fear. What if the novel had died on him? It
had happened often enough before. The early installments had been
printed already in *Young Folks*. One October morning he sat down in
bright sun to find out the truth, awful or not, "and behold! it flowed

like small talk." And went on flowing. He bent to the work, producing pages at the rate he had set himself, a chapter a day, and was almost sorry to finish.

Altogether, in the six months of his second stay at Davos he wrote 35,000 words. He worked on his Silverado journals and made a vivid narrative of it. He did some research for a biography of Hazlitt, then discovered that he disliked the man. He produced some of the essays that were collected in *Talk and Talkers*. He made progress with *Prince Otto* and would still be rewriting it after five versions. Bernard Shaw said perversely that it was one of the best pieces of literature produced in a decade, though everyone else found it a complete failure. David Daiches, a fine critic, refers to it as "the strangely coy Ruritanian romance that shows Louis's bohemianism, precocity and moralism in artful but unsatisfactory combination." The sick author worked tremendously hard on it, unwilling to give up, admitting to Henley that it was pitched "pretty high and stilted." While he was engaged on it he felt positive, but he was too honest not to say that "some parts are false, and much of the rest is thin." He wrote "A Gossip on Romance" which went into *Longman's Magazine,* defining the importance for him of a sense of the spirit of place. For instance, the old Hawes Inn at the Queen's Ferry, standing apart from the town in a climate of its own, "half inland, half marine," seemed to suggest some story which expressed the meaning of that inn. The story is there in an early chapter of *Kidnapped.*

On April 1, 1882, he wrote to Alexander Japp that his miserable carcass was holding together wonderfully, but before that it had been a tale of woe that went on unwinding like a bad dream. He and Fanny had been married for eighteen months, and in an essay he put the best gloss on it he could: "Marriage is one long conversation, checkered by disputes. . . . But in the intervals, almost unconsciously and with no desire to shine, the whole material of life is turned over, ideas are struck out and shared, the two persons more and more adapt their notions one to suit the other, and in the process of time, without sound of trumpet, they conduct each other into new worlds of thought."

The truth was that the intervals of respite and thankfulness were few and far between. November and December were terrible. Things went badly and got worse. Fighting off ill health was like fighting a war, and who could be blamed? In early November, Symonds wrote to his historian friend Horatio Brown that he had gone into the Stevensons' chalet to find Louis lying in bed looking ghastly with his purple cheekbones, yellow cheeks, and bloodless lips, in a fever, without appetite. The dog was "squealing," Mrs. Stevenson doing her best to cope.

In November the outlook was so black that it was almost comic. Louis wrote to Baxter giving him the awful picture. He and Fanny were ill in bed together, there was a sick nurse coming and going, and outside the door the dog howled miserably with an abscess in its ear. Louis was swigging away at chloral from a flask because his cough was such a torment to them both. The next week he felt better, and now inevitably Fanny became very ill. Louis wrote worriedly to Mrs. Sitwell that he suspected "drain poisoning." She had diarrhea, stabbing pains, spotted throat, "and I know not what." A doctor advised a rest cure and consultations in Zurich and Berne. Lloyd refused to be parted from her and went along as well. It seems she had passed a gallstone. Left alone, Louis sank in his solitude to a nostalgic longing for the old glory days of his youth in Edinburgh, when he and Baxter lived on hope and laughter. Alas, that "lamplit fairyland" was now far behind him. "O for ten Edinburgh minutes—sixpence between us, and the ever glorious Lothian Road, or dear mysterious Leith Walk!"

HE WAS IN TOUCH with Baxter on the subject of other people's difficulties. His cousin Katherine de Mattos was living alone and reduced to poverty. Bob Stevenson was newly married, and Walter Simpson had, he feared, married badly. He had a poor opinion of Lady Simpson: "A lady of title will not rest (and at present is not resting by any means) till she has cleared every manjack of her husband's friends out of the boutique." McLynn sees this as ironic in view of the tension between Fanny and Henley, but although she was keen to lever her husband out of the orbit of literary London it would be hard to accuse her of the clean sweep Louis saw as Lady Simpson's intention.

On Christmas Day he traveled down to Berne to fetch Fanny and Lloyd. He didn't care for solitude so much now: the result, he supposed, of marriage. The dichotomy between solitude and company was a problem for him, as it is for any serious artist. "Nothing can be done without solitude," said Picasso, and like him, Stevenson always needed to be with people. Yet solitude was at times an absolute necessity for the work he had to do.

They drove for seven hours up the steep snow channels in an open sleigh, freezing and silent. Louis tried to lift their spirits by singing, until Lloyd said, meaning to please, that he was the only one with courage, and Louis was overcome with a sense of shame.

As soon as Christmas was over the couple took to their beds. According to Symonds they stayed inside their chalet from the first of January to the beginning of March. Fanny recovered a little, then had a relapse. If either of them succeeded in being well it would be the dog's turn to be ill. "I wish to God I or anybody knew what was the matter with my wife," he cried out in a letter, obviously at the end of his tether. "I will not write much more for I should fear to say what I really felt." But what else could he have said? They were neither of them saints, and they were closeted together for twenty-four hours a day. It could be that he found her illnesses harder to bear than his own.

By now Symonds had developed a real liking for Louis, blaming himself for not being more outgoing before. He seemed genuinely concerned in his reports on Louis's condition. He had heard that Dr. Ruedi was finding it hard to decide between a diagnosis of consumption and erosion of the lungs. In Symonds's opinion his Scottish friend was certainly not going to die yet. As a veteran of Davos who had developed techniques of his own for survival, he doubted whether Stevenson had "the sort of toughness or instinctive energy of self-control, the faculty which I possess of lying still when I feel my center of vitality attacked." Then he would be confounded by his friend's ability to suddenly recover, against the odds. But he still thought the man's refusal to accept the life of an invalid was a mistake, though he did have "a serenity of soul about what is called comfort." The trouble was that he had the restless mind of a bohemian and "never did any systematic open-air cure, or systematic anything." Horatio Brown agreed with much of this. Louis had literally to break down before he would take to his bed. Instead of filling his lungs with fresh air he sat up writing, he drank wine and smoked, and he talked incessantly. Sometimes Brown got the impression that "there was nothing of him in the room but his bright eyes moving about, and his voice."

The alternation of his illnesses with Fanny's would become one of the patterns of his life. The start of a power struggle could be read into it, unacknowledged by either of them. Stresses were bound to put a strain on any relationship, given the dire circumstances of an environment given over to sickness and death. Hints of serious rifts were beginning to appear in his confidences to Bob. Rows flared up, he fell into "the blackness of low spirits," and comments were sometimes barbed, often drunken. Fanny's character would seem to be at variance, suggests Malcolm Elwin, with the picture sometimes painted of the stoical nurse devotedly tending the querulous consumptive. And Louis in his worst moments was beginning to wonder, when no word reached him from the outside world, if he had been abandoned. In March he sent a letter to Colvin that was half accusation, half plea: "I brought home with me from my bad times in America two strains of unsoundness of mind, the first a perpetual fear that I can do no more work—the second, a perpetual fear that my friends have quarreled with me. I struggle as hard as I know against both, but a judicious postcard would sometimes save me the expense of the second."

By April his health was showing signs of improvement. He and Lloyd were like two playmates, having fun with the toy theatre, with the boy's hand printing outfit, and with the deployment of tin soldiers in Louis's war games, lying in ambush in the hills of cushions, advancing through the woods around the legs of chairs.

Then they heard the whistling of birds: they had won through again. Snow was melting, flood water rushing down the few streets, the steep meadows around the chalet white now with crocuses instead of snow. Fanny sat writing to her mother-in-law one day while Louis sang beside her. "I do not care for the music, but it makes me feel so happy to see him so well," she wrote. They were ready to migrate. Dr. Ruedi gave his reluctant blessing provided they went south.

They toyed with the idea first of all of basing themselves in Normandy, which would be near his publishers in London. Instead they went direct to London and were met by his parents. In the few days they were there they met Bob and his new wife, visited Katherine de Mattos in Surrey, and then paid another visit to George Meredith. Though Louis was not in *The Egoist* as he thought, he was soon to appear in Meredith's *The Amazing Marriage* as the character Gower Woodseer.

They went north to spend a month in Edinburgh, and then to Stobo Manse in Peebleshire. The plan to spend the summer there quickly misfired. Louis coughed up blood after two weeks, went on a flying visit to London to see Sir Andrew Clark, the doctor who had first ordered him south, and on his recommendation went farther north to Kingussie on Speyside. They settled into a cottage, again for the summer of 1882, and he worked at his short story "The Treasure of Franchard." Harassed by more requests from Belle in California, who seemed to see it as her right to be subsidized by her stepfather in spite of having a husband, he was suddenly felled by a second hemorrhage. It was autumn, when the retreat usually sounded. In London again to consult Sir Andrew Clark, who was no devotee of Davos, he was advised to go south. Fanny, not too well herself after packing Lloyd off to his boarding school in Bournemouth, stayed behind to be cosseted at Heriot Row while Louis, having recruited Bob as his traveling companion, made for the south of France to find somewhere suitable to rent.

It was like old times. *New Arabian Nights* had appeared in August and was fairly well received. Prince Florizel, another Ruritanian hero, is the protagonist in this book of linked stories. He took along his unfinished "Treasure of Franchard," which drew on his recollections of Grez and his time there with Bob.

On the way south he suffered a dreadful hemorrhage which must have scared Bob half to death. They broke the journey at Montpelier and were literally stranded there. Another bout of bleeding found him reduced to sitting in a Dr. Caisso's waiting room, trying to make conversation with the locals.

As soon as he was well enough to travel, Bob returned to England and Louis went on alone in the direction of Marseilles, intending to search there. His letter to Fanny shows him at his most divided and dejected, wanting her and not wanting her: "At least it's only half of me that wants you, and I don't like to think of your coming back and not finding me better than when we parted. That is why I would rather be miserable than send for you." It disgusted him to think that he lacked courage. Marriage had made him soft, he thought. Sinking lower still into self-pity, he wrote: "I do not ask you to love me any more. I am too much trouble. . . . You cannot put up with such a man. In one way I see you act on these principles, for I hear from you very rarely. . . ."

He was casting himself at her feet and at the same time accusing her of not staying in touch. Was she still ill? Pleading abjectly for a word, he admitted that he had "wearied awful for you. But you will never understand that bit of my character." On the contrary, she understood very well his need of her. He rallied again, enclosing some comic doggerel illustrated with pen drawings.

Where is my wife? Where is my Wogg?
I am alone and life's a bog.

His drawing showed a fat woman and a woefully thin man running to each other with open arms, followed by

The fat and lean
Shall then convene.

They did have a sense of humor in common, and how necessary she found it, though Louis's had such a zany streak that she was often lost, and he would instead fire off pages of it to Baxter. By mid-October they were reunited, and house-hunting began in earnest. "The wreck was towed into port yesterday evening," Louis informed his mother. They had moved into a roomy house called Campagne Defli, in the dry Midi uplands to the east of Marseilles. Really it was in a suburb of the city. Things looked hopeful at last. The rent was low, Fanny sent for the heavy luggage, and servants were found in short order for cleaning and renovating. She fell out with the maids almost at once, as she often did. Short on tact, she did manage to write consolingly to Louis's friend Baxter—his unofficial agent— whose small child had just died. "I know too well," she wrote feelingly, "that there is nothing to be said. I thought once that I could not lose my child and live: and sorrow seemed impossible to bear. . . ."

Things began to go wrong with the discovery that their dream villa was infested with insect life. They were in a region where the mistral blew for a third of every year. Fanny, unwell again, began to speak of bad omens. A fever epidemic in Marseilles which she took to be typhus convinced her that they should get out. Louis had got himself entangled in an invitation to William Dean Howells which he felt obliged to withdraw after learning of Howells's views on divorce. He wrote stiffly, "It will be my sincere disappointment to find that you cannot be my guest. I shall bear up, however: for I assure you I desire to know no one who considers himself holier than my wife."

Leaving the house at St. Marcel, with a situation looking out over woods and cliffs that he found most attractive, as was the rent of only forty-eight pounds a year, was hard to accept. He took refuge in more doggerel:

> Campagne De-fli:
> O me!
> Campagne De-bug:
> There comes the tug!
> Campagne De-mosquito

It's eneuch to gar me greet, O!
Campagne De-louse:
O God damn the house!

He was dispatched to Nice out of harm's way while Fanny stayed behind to pack up. Her maids would not have been dismayed to see her go. After moving in she was perched on a ladder banging in a nail for a picture and one maid, thinking she knew no French, whispered to her companion, *"Elle est folle."* She brandished her hammer at them, cried *"Pas folle. Beaucoup d'intelligence!"* and then ruined her retort by falling off the ladder.

Money was expected from Colvin, and as soon as that arrived she went off to meet and collect Lloyd, due in Marseilles for Christmas. All at once everything became nightmarish. Somehow she lost contact with Louis and went searching for him in near hysteria, believing him to be the victim of a plague. A letter had gone astray and he was in fact waiting calmly for her in the Nice hotel. Cables had been sent by Fanny to his friends in London, canceled by more cables when it turned out he was not dead or dying as she had feared. The comedy of errors confirmed the prejudices against her. Colvin wrote furiously to Baxter, "I will never let myself be frightened by that maniac partner of his again, and she may cry wolf till she is hoarse." One biographer, usually prepared to give Fanny the benefit of the doubt, has called her version of events "retrospective falsification."

The hostility gathering around her name in England centered on one heinous crime: she had stolen their Louis. Clucking disapproval like hens, they still hoped he would see the error of his ways and return. What could he see in that uncouth, blunt, suspicious woman? Her chief enemy was Henley, whom she instinctively distrusted, though open warfare had not yet broken out between them. The muttering of the others was largely wishful thinking. Rumors circulated to the effect that she had Creole blood, that she was a lunatic, ignorant as a savage, that Louis was being dragged down and driven mad against his will. If Fanny was being demonized it was partly her own fault, or the result of her persecution complex.

In all this the complicity of their darling friend was overlooked. Maddening though she sometimes was, the truth was that Louis could not live without her. Her hit-and-miss nursing was one thing, but she held him together with her determination to be the most important person in his life. She was undoubtedly the most necessary, whether he liked it or not. This was her compensation for the hell in which she found herself, shackled to a chronically sick man. Her endlessly recurring maladies were perhaps protests from within against an intolerably cruel fate.

UNKNOWN TO HIM, these were to be his last years in Europe. It took him until early February to wriggle out of the Campagne Delfi lease. "Hooray!" he wrote jubilantly to his parents. "Got rid of the house." Finally they escaped hotel life and moved into a cottage they had found in the small inland town of Hyères. It was no more than a chalet, designed for the Paris Exhibition of 1878 and called La Solitude. He had fond memories of that exhibition, where he had had a brief sinecure as Fleeming Jenkin's secretary and slipped away whenever he could to be with Fanny.

At the end of March Colvin came on a visit and they had secured the services of a local French girl, Valentine Roch, whose father worked on the railways. Given Fanny's problems with servants she was a real find. Louis was enraptured with the house, telling Mrs. Sitwell in a letter that it was "the loveliest house you ever saw, with a garden like a fairy story and a view like a classical landscape." In fact it was rather poky, with three small rooms on the ground floor and four above. Valentine Roch would be with them for six years, a tribute to her patience and tolerance, not to mention her good humor. Intelligent and charming, she was a better nurse than Fanny when the occasion demanded, and it soon would.

He got down to work, finishing *The Silverado Squatters,* which had dragged on for some time, working on *Prince Otto* and starting *The Black Arrow,* another yarn meant for a serial in *Young Folks.* His poems *A Child's Garden of Verses,* called at first *Penny Whistles,* was almost ready for the press. He wrote full of optimism and high spirits to Mrs. Sitwell that he was poised to make a fortune, though "it has not begun yet." But a streak of rapacity had begun to reveal itself in his character, he told her, "the greed of the protuberant guttler. Well, doubtless when the hour strikes we must all guttle and protube. But it comes hard on one who was always so willow-slender and careless as the daisies." He would be sixteen months here and survive onslaughts of sickness that brought him close to death, but he would say later that he had never been as happy anywhere as during his time at La Solitude, with its fragrant garden in the evenings and its "flutes of silence." It was where he and Fanny could retreat and "feel like people."

The Black Arrow was an attempt to repeat the success he felt he had achieved with *Treasure Island.* It didn't work, though it has remained in print. The themes of pirates and treasure are there again and the novel is awash with evil, but the tale is unrelievedly black, Dick Skelton's men massacred, his ship broken on the rocks in a world given over to chaos, with no light anywhere. The hero is more Hamlet-like than Jim Hawkins ever was. Set historically in the fifteenth century, it is clogged with archaic language. His novels set in the eighteenth century always seemed to give him the freedom he needed. *The Black Arrow* plays with dualities and has an explicit "double," a foretaste of his use of the device in *Dr. Jekyll and Mr. Hyde.* The young readers of *Young Folks* seem to have preferred it to *Treasure Island,* possibly because there was more gore. Fanny hated it, and Louis, who knew he had been trying to write a potboiler, dismissed it as "tushery."

In mid-May he went down with flu, and as always the complications brought him close to death. Valentine Roch nursed him to great effect, but Fanny's bossiness led her to hand in her notice. Then she caught flu herself and was looked after by a caring Fanny. Gratefully she decided to stay on. Louis was soon fond of her, calling her Joe when she was happy and Thomasina when she had a fit of the sulks, usually brought on by Fanny. His poem "Ne Sit Ancillae Tibi

Amor Pudori" ("Don't Be Ashamed of Your Love for a Maid")
may have been addressed to Valentine as part of a playful flirtation.
On the other hand it could be merely imaginary, or about some other
maid:

> There's just a twinkle in your eye
> That seems to say I might, if I
> Were only bold enough to try
> An arm about your waist.
>
> I hear, too, as you come and go,
> That pretty nervous laugh, you know;
> And then your cap is always so
> Coquettishly displaced. . . .
>
> O graceful housemaid, full and fair,
> I love your shy imperial air,
> And always loiter on the stair
> When you are going by.
>
> A strict reserve by fates demand;
> But, when to let you pass I stand,
> Sometimes by chance I touch your hand
> And sometimes catch your eye.

THE DEATH OF Louis's old university friend James Ferrier in September 1883 was a cruel blow. This charismatic son of the philosophy
professor had charmed him utterly at university. Now he had gone
under, wrecked by drink and tuberculosis. Louis had lost his first
friend. It brought home to him even more than his own teetering on
the brink the "trade winds" of death that blew around everyone. "Up
to now I had rather thought of him as a mere personal enemy of my
own; but now that I see him hunting after my friends he looks altogether darker."

He was now reading widely, ambivalent as ever about Dickens

and with little time for Balzac. His objections to Balzac show us how intent he was on crystallizing his own aims and methods. The Frenchman was, he believed, a man

> who never found his method. An inarticulate Shakespeare, smothered under forcible-feeding detail. It is astonishing to the ripe mind how bad he is, how untrue, how tedious; and of course, when he surrendered to his temperament, how good and powerful. And yet never plain or clear. He could not consent to be dull, and thus became so. He would leave nothing undeveloped, and thus drowned out of sight of land amid the multitude of crying and incongruous details.

Most telling was his conclusion in the letter he wrote to Bob: "There is but one art, to omit! O if I knew how to omit I would ask no other knowledge. A man who knew how to omit would make an Iliad of a daily paper."

By December he was able to report progress at last on the financial front. The year had yielded an income of 465 pounds. Then he scored a triumph with *Prince Otto. Longman's Magazine* was about to serialize it and, wonder of wonders, asked him how much he wanted. Egged on by Fanny, he asked for 250 pounds. He was about to halve this amount when *Longman's* cabled its agreement.

Thomas had written to Fanny to say that he was seeking more humility in his life, and Louis, perhaps feeling in the ascendancy now that he was in funds, weighed in with a little sermon of his own. "What you say about yourself I was glad to hear; a little decent resignation is not only becoming in a Christian, but is likely to be excellent for the health of a Stevenson. To fret and fume is undistinguished, suicidally foolish and theologically unpardonable. . . . We are the foam of a wave, and to preserve a proper equanimity is not merely the first part of submission to God, but the chief of possible kindnesses to those about us."

Sam Osbourne, as intrusive as ever, had now got it into his head that Lloyd should learn metallurgy and chemistry in order to become a mining engineer in the States. He had married again, to a Rebecca

Paul, "Paulie," and proposed coming with her to Europe so that Lloyd could join them on a holiday in the south of France. Reporting on this new wife, Sam's sister Cynthia wrote, "He and Aunt Paulie visited our house soon after their marriage. I have heard Mama say that it seemed that he chose a wife as much like Fanny as he could find. There was a strong resemblance between them. But while Aunt Paulie was sweeter, she lacked the keen-mindedness of Aunt Fan."

Lloyd was now digging in his heels when plans were made for his welfare, objecting to anything that didn't appeal to him. Because he was unhappy about going back to his boarding school in Bournemouth, Louis was again his tutor as he had been at Davos. His closeness to the boy prompts Richard Aldington, an unreliable if lively commentator, to some absurd speculation. "Stevenson," he declared, "was not a homosexual, but he had played about so much with women in his youth that he could not give himself entirely to a woman, and kept some of the best of himself for men. . . . There are times when one stands a little aghast at suspecting that he really loved Lloyd more than Fanny." Aldington needed his hypothesis of a youthful playboy Stevenson to account for a disability that had no basis in fact.

To be sure, he knew those fluctuations of the heart that occur in most marriages, those moments of misogyny when men and women seem natural enemies and the relation between the sexes becomes outright war, and that resentment a man feels at his dependence on a woman who is nevertheless indispensable. And Fanny was undoubtedly becoming more and more insistent on having her views on his books considered. Disagreement flared up, it seems, over the fate of a half-drafted novel entitled *The Travelling Companion,* with a setting in Italy and a prostitute as protagonist. Colvin recalled a publisher being shown it and labeling it a work of genius but improper, just as Ford Madox Hueffer would shy away from Lawrence's *The Trespasser,* calling it "a rotten work of genius." Fanny agreed with the verdict, and it could well have been this that goaded a man who lived for his work to tell Henley in a letter, "I sleep upon my art for a pillow; I waken in my art; I am unready for death, because I hate to leave it. I love my wife, I do not know how much, nor can, nor shall, unless I lost her; but while I can conceive of being widowed, I refuse the offering of life without my art."

1884 STARTED with high hopes. Was he really about to achieve financial independence from his father? Henley and Baxter came on a visit, which got off to a bad start. Louis had footed the bill for Henley's expenses: after all he was acting as his friend's literary intermediary in London. Fanny had no time for these considerations and was finding it hard to swallow her dislike, faced with Henley's habits of hard drinking and raucous shouts of laughter. The three men went off on an outing to Nice, spending a couple of days there. Inevitably Louis caught a cold. His friends left for England and at once Louis collapsed with an infection of the lungs and kidneys which had him stranded in Nice at the Pension Louis Rose. Fanny rushed there, and the old battle to save him began once more.

Any denigration of Fanny—and there is a great deal—should take account of the horrors she endured during these attacks. His hemorrhages soaked clothes and sheets. She had to cope alone with the physical demands of nursing a helpless man as well as withstanding the anxiety and mental strain, knowing she was totally responsible. To control these horrible rushes of blood that went everywhere and threatened to choke him, she had to be ready at any hour to give him doses of ergotine. Doctors had to be called, parents contacted. Misunderstandings and second opinions would sometimes drive her frantic. And he was no docile patient. She had to lift and turn Louis herself, and sometimes carry him when he had to relieve himself. Indignities such as this infuriated him. He would be light-headed and difficult, refusing to use a commode, fussy about what he ate, and short-tempered with her because he loathed to be so helpless. Badly in need of male assistance, she cabled frantically to Simpson, who made some excuse. An appeal to Bob brought him to Nice, though not before Louis's fight to stay alive reached a crucial stage. Fanny was sending daily bulletins to all and sundry. Doctors contradicted each other. One said the patient was sure to die, but a British physician believed that Louis could live to be seventy if he survived beyond forty.

The extraordinary thing about him was his resilience. Once over this ordeal, he went back to the chalet and was condemned to lie in bed with his right arm strapped to his side and forbidden to talk for fear of fresh hemorrhages. An attack of ophthalmia, possibly caused by the dust swirling up in the evil-smelling lanes of Hyères, left him too blind to read. He recovered slowly and seemed his old self for a while, then in May came his worst bout of illness yet. The bleeding went on and on. Sciatica struck. He was back in bed with his arm strapped, his eyes bandaged, too exhausted to talk. A note he scrawled in pencil to Fanny read: "Don't be frightened—if this is death, it is an easy one." Even allowing for the instinctive theatricality that he shared with many Victorians, it was as if he had access to a private source of strength at such moments. After a month in bed, buried in silence, never moving without being lifted, he felt "devilish like being dead."

Not until June did he feel genuinely on the road to recovery, with Fanny able to write, "His courage is wonderful. I never saw anything like it." To his mother she wrote her most cheerful words for months: "I am not very good at letter writing since I have been doing blind men's eyes, but here is a note to say that the blind man is doing very well, and I consider the blindness a real providence. Since he has been unable to read or do anything at all a wonderful change has come over his health, spirits and temper, all for the better."

Even when he could see normally he was now so often confined to bed that he made this his place of work. He wrote there with his powers of concentration and his attention to detail undiminished, and corrected proofs there as well as dealing with his flow of correspondence. He had been given up for dead so often that his innate stoicism had become defiance, and illness did nothing to dim his consummate mastery of the language. Again one is reminded of Lawrence, though in his case the refusal to admit defeat would be fueled by sheer rage. And Louis was still deeply affected by the death of his friend Ferrier. When he wrote to Walter Ferrier's sister Coggie, "he could not see for crying." Part of the pain he felt was grief for his own lost youth and their times of rapture together, "sharing that weatherbeaten Fergussonian youth, looking forward through the clouds to the sunburst: and now clean gone from my path."

As soon as he regained sufficient strength he started work on *Kidnapped,* more a long short story by Victorian standards than a novel. He had chosen his moment of history well, five years after the Jacobite defeat at Culloden. Some have seen it as the nearest he came to Scott, but the multi-charactered canvas was not for him, and though he was tempted now and then to try, his remarks on Balzac show that it was not. The control and irony of the narrative and the deft balancing of David Balfour and Alan Breck make this book one of his best. Just to take it on showed what a fighter he was, when much of the time he was forced to watch Fanny playing patience, and described himself in a letter to Colvin as "a bloodspitting, superannuated son of a bedpost." How he managed to crack jokes in the pitiful state he was often in is a subject for wonder.

Fanny was now a subscriber to the medical journal *The Lancet,* which did nothing for her peace of mind when she heard rumors of a case of cholera in the slum quarter of Hyères. In fact this was a yearly occurrence in the town, but Fanny panicked. It was confirmation of her suspicion that the Midi was a bad place for Louis. She rushed to consult doctors, and they agreed he could be moved, providing it was slowly. The word was not in her vocabulary: when she was overcome with fear she moved at lightning speed. In no time they were out and on the road to Royat. Louis, in spite of having been so deathly sick, saw this period as one of his most productive and was ambivalent about leaving. But he was in no condition to withstand his wife's will, and in any case the nomad in him was alive as ever and clapping its hands. Already he was putting behind him the maladies that had overwhelmed him one after the other in that tiny house until he was near to entering heaven's door. Always susceptible, like habitual wanderers everywhere, to the omens and encounters of the open road, he was liberated by movement and by his escape from that dreadful coffinlike bed. "Oh highway," exclaimed Whitman, "you express me better than I can myself." On his highway Louis experienced the same sense of rewriting himself, no longer dwindling into "a kind of valley of the shadow picnic." He was sick of being blurred, "dim, dowie and damnable." At Royat, a health resort, he was already feeling better.

CHAPTER ELEVEN

A Steam Press Called
the Vandegrifter

F ROM ROYAT they went on by slow stages to England. They had arranged a reunion with his parents at Richmond-on-Thames, where they stayed a few days. This was close enough to town for Fanny to attend the first night of *Deacon Brodie,* on which Louis and Henley had collaborated in London and Scotland in 1878. It was fairly well received and earned them next to nothing. All it did so far as Henley and Fanny were concerned was encourage them to believe that plays could bring them fame and money. A consultation with doctors at Richmond gave the Stevensons a cautious all-clear to live in the south of England. They decided on Bournemouth because Lloyd was at boarding school there. It would be Louis's address for his last three years in Europe.

In Bournemouth they rented Bonallie Towers, a furnished house in the leafy Brankstone Park area of the town. Louis coughed his way through the autumn and winter and managed to stay on his feet and out of bed. Lloyd, who had now expressed a wish to be a lighthouse engineer, departed to Heriot Row to be tutored by Thomas in preparation for college. The globe-trotting Stevensons were left on their own with Valentine.

Bob arrived, their first visitor, quickly followed by the red-bearded, crutch-swinging Henley, brimming with ideas for plays to make them rich. Fanny soon saw a role for herself in these playwriting projects, putting forward suggestions and lying awake at night rehearsing lines in her head. Her iron will was turning her into her husband's manager and the chief guardian of his well-being, unwelcoming to those of his friends who came carrying colds or kept him up drinking and talking late into the night, like Henley. Compromised to some extent by her dreams of financial security, living as she did with a husband who often believed he would die soon, she tried hard at first to put up with the company of a man she had always taken for an enemy. She nicknamed him Buffalo William, after Buffalo Bill Cody, and told him wittily in a letter after one fraught visit, "You know we love you in spite of your many faults, so try to bear with our few."

The first two months at Bournemouth were given over to the writing of plays with Henley under the watchful eyes of Fanny. They came up with the wretched *Admiral Guinea,* in which Blind Pew from *Treasure Island* makes another appearance. Louis was quick to see that it was terrible, and after reading it again told Henley it was "vomitable in many parts." After this came *Beau Austin,* dashed off in four days but with no takers in London until 1890. In January they wrote *Macaire,* a melodramatic farce built around the eponymous hero, a master of disguise. The collaborators approached Beerbohm Tree with this one, only to be told that they knew nothing of stagecraft. Henley did at least know more than Louis, and believed he knew in which direction the modern drama was heading. He wrote, "The Shakespeare of tomorrow will take for his hero not Othello but Iago. . . . In fifty years the Deacon, if we had done it, might be a great work. We are syphilized to the core, and don't know it. Zola is our popular eruption, as Balzac was our primary sore. Presently we shall get to our tertiarism, and the Ugly will be as the Beautiful."

By now Louis was becoming bored with the whole fiasco of

playwriting, telling Henley that in his opinion the stage was only a lottery. He had embraced the dream of wealth as a means of escaping his solitary work: now he wanted his solitude back. Lloyd, looking back, saw it as a time when his stepfather lost the "last flicker of his youth" in Bournemouth, together with any belief that he might be a popular dramatist.

All at once they had a real farce on their hands. Fanny's attempt to accept Henley as a friend failed utterly. She accused him of pushing her husband into more illness: he was spitting blood again. As for Henley, he refused to go on collaborating with Louis if it meant working with both of them, when in his view she was not qualified to participate. What is more, he told her baldly that the pretense of their friendship was at an end. "I think, Mrs. Louis," he wrote to her, "that we'd better give up corresponding on any save the commonest subjects." Louis must have turned with relief to the writing of a Christmas story commissioned by the *Pall Mall Gazette.* In the event, he couldn't deliver. He offered them *The Body Snatcher,* a piece well below his best. They took it, but much to Henley's disgust Louis refused the original forty pounds proposed, accepting a lesser sum.

After a Christmas of sickness when he and Fanny were both ill in bed, they had startling news. Thomas was ailing now at sixty-six, vague in his mind and frequently depressed. Fanny had been confiding in him and Maggie for years with her anxieties about money, giving him an edited version of Belle and Joe Strong's continual demands for funds. They had now moved to Honolulu, where Joe was supposed to be too ill to work. Fanny, evidently suspicious, had written to her friend Dora Williams, "Do please try and find out if Joe Strong is really ill." Now, in the New Year, Thomas decided to buy her a house, "a wedding present." He even added five hundred pounds for them to furnish it. It was a desperate ploy to keep his son fastened in Britain during his last years. The villa, originally "Sea View," was sited on the Westbourne cliffs. They moved in that Easter and Louis renamed it "Skerryvore" to please his father. He had a ship's bell installed in the garden.

Later he would see himself as trapped there "like a weevil in a biscuit." At the time he did his best to like it, choking down his loathing of the respectability it signified for him, a taxpayer in a villa surrounded by villas. Peter Ackroyd, writing of Ruskin, remarks that the best Victorians hated and despised nineteenth-century civilization as well as the whole gamut of "Victorian values" and the belief in progress that went with them.

The villa's previous owner was a retired naval captain, and this may have consoled him. It was all spick-and-span, so typical of an old sailor. The irony would not have been lost on him—the wanderer anchored, "the quiet life" advised by his friends an accomplished fact. Would he be able to stick to it? Was he, as he told Colvin, just a "beastly householder" waiting for the vicar to call? Had his cursed sickness brought him to this?

Fanny loved it. She had never been so snug. Who could blame her for wanting her own front door, her own title deeds? She wrote gaily to Dora Williams, "We have just moved into our lovely house. . . . It is very comfortable to know that we have a home really and truly and will no more be like Noah's dove, flying about with an olive branch." The yellow-brick villa with a blue slate roof, its walls clad in ivy, had an acre of land around it that sloped steeply to the south, its lawns coming to a halt at the edge of a narrow ravine called Alum Chine. Laurel and rhododendron grew thickly on the slopes together with pine and heather, so that Louis if he tried hard could remind himself of Scotland.

Down below them was a busy stream. Fanny, who had been a keen gardener in Oakland and again at Hyères, and would come into her own on Samoa, immediately had plans for a "delicious" garden, a dovecote and a kennel, and even a studio for her to paint in when she felt inclined. When they were rich enough—from playwriting—she would have a horse again, "if I am not too fat by that time." There was a stable and outhouses to the rear. She was now a middle-aged woman of forty-four, inclined to be dumpy, which gave her stance an immovable look when she confronted visitors and those fiends disguised as friends, as she called them. Soon she was energetically planting fruit trees, roses, tiger lilies, and hydrangeas, and creating a kitchen garden, experimenting with Indian corn and tomatoes. She had plans for benches along "a seductive little labyrinth" of paths, steps, and arbors where Louis could write out of doors with a board on his knee. After all, this was more or less the English Riviera.

They were still unpacking their possessions when their first un-expected callers rang the bell, or tried to. The bell was out of order. Adelaide Boodle, a syrupy-sweet girl with literary aspirations, had persuaded her mother to meet this Scots oddity whom the locals had begun to call "the Squire." They waited stranded on the threshold, and then the timid mother began to cry. Afterward Louis called their front porch "The Pool of Tears." When Valentine came to the rescue she should have said it was an inconvenient time, but she let them in. There was Louis in his velvet jacket and flowing red tie, Fanny in a painting robe. They perched on packing cases and sat the Boodles down on the only two chairs. Adelaide, determined to remember everything, gazed on a writer who was "just an animated bundle of shawls and wraps, with long, thin hair and burning eyes." She had in-tended to be worshipful and she was, and became a willing runner of errands for them both. Rarely allowed past Fanny to sit with her idol, she noted everything down and later wrote a little book about her hosts. She was a witness to occasional blazing rows, "when the casual looker-on might have felt it his duty to shout for the police," up-heavals that calmed down as suddenly as they had erupted. She called as often as she dared and was one of the few people who genuinely ad-mired Fanny, who was quick to see she was no threat. Skerryvore be-came her shrine. It was one of the few buildings in the resort to be destroyed by the Luftwaffe in World War II.

In the summer of 1885 Fanny made a flying visit to France to settle matters at Hyères. Valentine was installed in Louis's room in her capacity as nurse while her mistress was away, and gossips con-cocted an affair from the arrangement, helped by Henley who saw it as a way of embarrassing Fanny. Most authorities dismiss it as non-sense. Louis was always fond of Valentine, and she had great respect and admiration for him, as she testified in later life: "From him I learned that life is not for self if we want happiness—and that it is only in service that we fulfill our destiny."

The elderly and the recuperating were as much in evidence then as they are now in Bournemouth, and the Stevensons' main friends locally were two elderly couples: Sir Percy Shelley and his wife (the poet's son and daughter-in-law) and Sir Henry and Lady Taylor. Sir Henry, late of the Foreign Office, made Louis a present of a South American poncho, dark red and quickly spotted with ink, which he afterward wore everywhere, even sitting up in bed, until the day he died. Fanny, who always had aspirations to be something in society, now came into her own as the mistress of Skerryvore. Louis was now a "name," attracting callers in increasing numbers. Often they would find their way barred by the fierce little American woman who saw it as her duty to protect her husband from people likely to tire him.

THE PAINTER John Singer Sargent had come down when they were still at Bonallie Tower, commissioned by a wealthy Boston couple to paint a portrait of Louis. These rich fans were a sure sign that he had arrived, even if the money was not flowing. Both hosts liked Sargent but disliked the painting, which Louis thought made him look weird and "pretty," the representation of "a large-eyed, chicken-boned, slightly contorted poet." Nothing could have made his spectral, emaciated figure look well. Sargent came down again in the summer of 1885, and this time Louis liked what he produced. The artist had got his subject to walk about in his own dining room in his velveteen jacket, twisting his moustache. This brilliant portrait of Stevenson, "the pale, agitated narcissist" of Chatwin's tart description, is now famous. But Fanny had overplayed her hand as a muse, telling Sargent coyly that she was "but a cipher under the shadow." That was how he showed her, looking like a ghost in a shadowy corner, dressed in an Indian sari for color and with one small brown foot poking out dimly. It was a witty touch and she wryly saw the joke. From this portrait came the myth that she used to attend dinner parties in London without shoes or stockings.

The respectability and dullness of his time in Bournemouth was "jarring to every feeling he possessed," as Lloyd was to put it, but Louis's stoicism saw him through, though he felt bound to mock himself as a man of property in letters to friends and in some wry verse:

> *My house,* I say. But hark to the sunny doves
> That make my roof the arena of their loves,
> That gyre about the gable all day long
> And fill the chimney with their murmurous song;
> *Our house,* they say; and *mine,* the cat declares,
> And spreads his golden fleece upon the chairs:
> And *mine,* the dog, and rises stiff with wrath
> If any alien foot profane the path.

It was in this year, 1885, that the unlikely friendship with Henry James began and developed. James had met the Scot in 1879 and was unimpressed by the bohemian minus a shirt collar who seemed a poseur, if an inoffensive one. Louis for his part looked on James as a fastidious snob who had turned his back on America. Then he read an article by James in *Longman's* in the autumn of 1884 on the art of fiction, which praised *Treasure Island* as a delightful story. Louis replied, in a piece called "A Humble Remonstrance," finding something perjorative about James's theory that art should oppose life, and on the term "the art of narrative." Huysmans, at the time belonging to the Zola camp, had said dismissively, "A story-teller is a gentleman who, not knowing how to write, pretentiously recites twaddle." James had spoken of art as being in competition with life, but in Louis's view this was wrong. Life, he insisted, was

> monstrous, infinite, illogical, abrupt and poignant; a work of art, in comparison, is neat, finite, self-contained, rational, flowing and emasculate. . . . The real art that dealt with life directly was that of the first men who told their stories round the savage camp fire.

Our art is occupied, not so much in making stories true as in making them typical. . . .

James wrote generously in praise of Louis's point of view and conceded that they did indeed share a great deal, notably a concern for prose style. He saluted Louis as a writer whose style "floats pearls and diamonds." Their friendship was under way. He was invited to Skerryvore, took his invalid sister there, and before long had his own big armchair allocated to him. It was the chair in which Louis sat for his portrait.

James was unique in getting immediately into Fanny's good books. They were fellow Americans, after all. He took her side when his new friends were burdened by the Stevenson parents in the autumn. The ordeal went on for three weeks. Thomas was by this time in steady decline, with Maggie fussing around him as well as her son in near hysteria. To cap it all they left Louis the legacy of an influenza cold, so Fanny reported indignantly to Colvin. "If Louis dies it will be murder." Nevertheless she took her husband to task for his unkind treatment of his unhappy father on one occasion. She waded into him with "a dreadful overhauling of my conduct as a son the other night," Louis wrote to his father, "and my wife stripped me of my illusions and made me admit I had been a detestable bad one. Of one thing in particular she convinced me in my own eyes: I mean, a most unkind reticence. . . ." Assuring the stricken father of his love he signed himself "Ever your bad son." After hot quarrels with Fanny he would now and then mutter against her in confidences to a man whom he knew agreed with him. He shared a nickname for Fanny with Henley, and wrote once, "I got my little finger into a steam press called the Vandegrifter (patent) and my whole body and soul had to go through after it. I came out as limp as a lady's novel, but the Vandegrifter suffered in the process and is fairly knocked about." Fishing for sympathy and sure of getting it, he added woefully, "I am what *she has made me*, the embers of the once gay R.L.S." Was this the truth? If so, why did he let it happen? The truth, of course, was altogether more complex. Patrick O'Brien writes that on the whole creative men have more sensibility than they have sense, and it is rare to find them happy. In a world that "has so much to distress even a common mind they pay a high price for their keener perceptions."

Adelaide Boodle thought there was something heroic about Fanny. Perhaps indomitable was the better word. If he resented his dependence on her at times, she was often out of patience with these droves of callers who came only to see him. How many of them saw her as a person in her own right? Did they realize that he was there only because of her vigils, the care she had lavished on him, the horrors she had faced?

Adelaide Boodle had come wildly hoping for some help with her own writing, though it took several visits before she dared mention it. Fanny told her sadly that Lou-us, as she called him, was always busy, but in any case his criticism would probably break the girl's heart. As it happened she wrote a little herself and was an experienced critic of Louis's work. Could she help? They had cozy literary sessions together, and then one day Fanny announced that she was working for dear life at a story of her own which was due off in the post to New York by the next mail. She hoped to raise money for a friend (probably Belle) who was expecting a child. The story, "Miss Pringle's Neighbors," appeared eventually in *Scribner's* magazine.

Fanny was not exactly planning to make a literary career for herself, but it made sense, she began to think, to collaborate with her husband on something. Was there anyone who knew more about the workings of his imagination? It would not have been difficult to persuade herself that—having sat in on so many of his creations as a critical listener and adviser—in reality they had always been working together. And it was true that she had been a source of encouragement and strength to him through those hideous months in the Midi, when he had more than once lost his way and wanted to die. A collaboration would be nothing new.

They worked together on a longish story called *The Dynamiters.* Louis's hatred of Gladstone may have triggered the idea. The story took a serious subject, the Fenian bombers agitating for Home Rule in Ireland, and wove a rather absurd fantasy around it. Chesterton, a staunch admirer of Stevenson and one of his shrewdest critics, saw the ludicrous element in the tale which made the whole thing untenable. "It is really impossible," he wrote, "to use a story in which everything is ridiculous to prove that certain particular Fenians or anarchist agitators are ridiculous."

As well as the brew of anarchy, murder, and intrigue there was a *femme fatale,* Clara Luxmore, who bore a passing resemblance to Fanny. As they worked away with their heads together, Louis's words in *Virginibus Puerisque* may have entered his head: "Certainly, if I could help it, I would never marry a wife who wrote. The practice of letters is miserably harassing to the mind, and after an hour or two's work, all the more human portion of the author is extinct." He was echoing, if unknowingly, Tolstoy's lament that the best part of himself went into the inkpot.

Harnessed to Fanny he had produced a detective story, one which anticipated Conan Doyle and influenced Jack London's *The Star Rover.* The modern detective is given almost heroic stature, someone who plucks out the clue from the thousands that surround and swamp us: "This clue, which the whole town beholds without comprehension, swift as a cat he leaps upon it, and makes it his, follows it up with craft and passion, and from one trifling circumstance divines a world." And Symonds in Davos, puzzled by the intensity of Louis's detestation of Gladstone, received an outburst which laid bare the extent of his self-disgust: "But why should I blame Gladstone, when I too am a bourgeois? when I have held my peace? Because I am skeptic: i.e., a Bourgeois. We believe in nothing, Symonds; you don't and I don't. . . ."

The little book appeared in May 1885, with the name Fanny Vandegrift Stevenson alongside that of her husband. At the time of publication another Fenian bomb exploded, giving the book some free publicity. *The Dynamiters* quickly went into two reprints. The reviewers passed over the collaboration with little or no comment, though one critic did wonder whether Louis's collaborator was his sister. Smarting at this, Fanny wrote to her mother-in-law, "I thought in the beginning that I shouldn't mind being Louis' scapegoat, but it is hard to be treated like a comma, and a superfluous one at that."

Death was soon knocking on the door at Skerryvore, first with news of the passing away of Fleeming Jenkin, and then of Fanny's friend Virgil Williams in San Francisco. In Stevenson's short life there was always death to be reckoned with. Thomas would be next, weakening daily, his mind wandering. When he came to stay he obviously saw his son as a small boy again. He kissed Louis goodnight at bedtime and said, "You'll see me in the morning, dearie." Fanny thought it was like seeing a mother with a young child.

Word came from Belle, now settled in Honolulu with her painter husband and child, that her father had disappeared and was presumed dead. Most people thought it was suicide, though ugly rumors circulated to the effect that Sam Osbourne had been mugged and murdered. The papers speculated that he may have deserted his wife Paulie and run off with a young girl from his office, in which case the disappearance may have been one of his stunts to avoid his debtors. A small pile of clothing was found later on the beach, too worn by exposure to be positively identified. The wife, left destitute and in debt, badly needed help. Louis was soon giving Lloyd money to send on to her. "I believe, in spite of everything," Fanny confided to Colvin, "that Louis feels a sort of joy in knowing that the boy now belongs to him entirely. Please tell nobody. . . ." From now on the boy's first name, Sam, was dropped and he became known to everyone as Lloyd.

THE WRITING OF *The Strange Case of Dr. Jekyll and Mr. Hyde* in this darkening year seems curiously appropriate. Frank McLynn comments that Louis worked well when he was ill or miserable. In this respect, at any rate, Bournemouth was beneficial. There is no doubt that he tried stoically to accept something that he deeply disliked. What had he done but joined the enemy? Not only that, but he had agreed to the arrangement meekly, like a lamb. Was this house-proud wife with her suburban villa who plainly exulted in her new role the free spirit he had met in France? "No insanity," wrote Chesterton of R.L.S. at Bournemouth "is so interesting to the psychologist as the shock of Stevenson going sane . . . his revolt into respectability." He was a trapped man who in black moments called himself "the hermit of Skerryvore." His wife seemed to be turning into an English-woman—her American accent was disappearing. He had to admire her passionate enthusiasm for this new role which she relished so much, but it set them against each other. He confessed to Henry James that he and his wife had fallen out, with Fanny calling her caged husband "a canary-bird," an insult too far. Later "it was discov-ered that there were two dead combatants upon the field, each slain by the arrow of truth, and we tenderly carried off each other's corpses. Here is a little comedy for Henry James to write! The beauty was that each thought the other quite unscathed at first. But we had dealt shrewd stabs." He signed off, "The Tragic Woman and the Flimsy Man."

In August they visited Thomas Hardy in Dorset, staying overnight in a hotel in Exeter where Louis fell ill and hemorrhaged. They were stranded there until mid-September. Fanny, hauling her husband in and out of bed when he was half out of his head with fever, may have been sworn at, as happened at Hyères. The specter of Davos with its deathly mountains loomed again as a grim possibility. Fanny fought this off with a charge of defeatism. Back at Skerryvore she retreated to her own bed before being called out by yet another hemorrhage—thankfully not as severe as the one at Exeter.

Before *Jekyll and Hyde* burst out of the darkness of Louis's misery he revised "Markheim," a short tale which was just as black, where a murderer is brought face to face with a visitor who is in fact his dou-ble. Louis had said to Symonds that he thought *Crime and Punishment* "easily the greatest book I have read in ten years." "Markheim" uses the ambiguous nature of evil in the murderer's tormented mind to convey the idea that no clear division between good and bad is possi-ble, and no salvation either:

Do I say that I follow sins? I follow virtues also; they differ not by the thickness of a nail, they are both scythes for the reaping angel of Death. Evil . . . consists not in action but in character. The bad man is dear to me; not the bad act, whose fruits, if we could follow them far enough down the hurtling cataract of the ages, might yet be found more blessed than those of the rarest virtues.

THE GENESIS OF *Jekyll and Hyde* plunges us straight into Louis's dream world. He had long ago talked of "Brownies," those imps in the underworld of his sleep who "manage man's internal theatre." He had been tormented by nightmares as a child, but these forces were benign. He claimed they did half his work for him while he was fast asleep, and "in all likelihood do the rest for me as well, when I am wide awake and fondly suppose I do it for myself."

The model for *Jekyll and Hyde* was Deacon Brodie, the subject of Louis and Henley's botched melodrama based on him. Fanny recalled a bookcase and chest of drawers in Louis's Heriot Row nursery, supposedly made by the eighteenth-century cabinetmaker. Cummy, with her lurid imagination, had poured stories into her nursling's receptive mind concerning Brodie and those pieces of furniture.

For Louis, work was always a refuge. If, as he believed, this went on even in sleep, one can understand his frustration when he was interrupted in it by Fanny who thought in the small hours of one morning that he was in the throes of a nightmare. "Why did you wake me?" he asked angrily. "I was dreaming a fine bogey tale."

Lloyd was another witness to what happened next. His stepfather came down preoccupied to lunch, hurried through his meal, and mentioned that he was having great success with a story that had come to him in a dream. He wanted to be left alone to finish it, even if the house caught fire. For the next three days everyone went around on tiptoe. Lloyd, passing Louis's door, saw him hard at work filling page after page as he sat up in bed, never pausing for a minute. At the end of three days of this hectic scribbling he announced that he was finished. Lloyd and Fanny were called to hear him read aloud from the rough draft. When he came to the end there was an extraordinary scene. Lloyd was riveted, bowled over by the tale. To his amazement his mother was carping when he had expected her to be wildly enthusiastic. Surely this was her kind of "crawler"? Instead she vehemently attacked the tale. Lloyd was "thunderstruck at her backwardness." She insisted that Louis had missed the point entirely. Instead of writing an allegory he had merely written a story that was no more than a splendid bit of sensationalism, when it should have been a masterpiece.

Lloyd had never seen his stepfather so furious. His eyes glared, his voice shook as he shouted Fanny down in a rage of bitterness. The stepson was so unnerved that he slipped away. Coming in later he found his mother sitting alone, "pale and desolate" in front of the fire.

Louis's bell rang and Fanny went up to him. He sat up in bed with a thermometer in his mouth and pointed at a pile of ashes in the hearth. "You're right!" he told her. He set about rewriting the novel from the beginning. He slaved away as hard as before for another three days. The strange thing was that the sustained effort seemed to refresh him, as if he somehow gathered strength from it. According to Lloyd he looked better than he had been for months.

This time Fanny fully approved of the new version. He revised and polished for another six weeks and dispatched the manuscript to Longman's. The rest is publishing history. Forty thousand copies were sold in Britain in the first six months from January 1886. By the end of the century, writes Stevenson's first biographer, 250,000 had been sold in the United States. People who did not normally read fiction gobbled it up, priests quoted from it in pulpits. There were stage versions, articles, translations.

Frank McLynn dismisses as absurd the suggestion, put about by Nellie Sanchez, Lloyd, and by Fanny herself, that Louis burned his first draft because he had missed the point of the allegory until alerted by Fanny. The idea of a critic as perceptive as Louis overlooking something so obvious is, he says, laughable, and believes that

Fanny panicked when she was confronted by the adult sexuality her husband had allowed himself to present. The "disgraceful pleasures" indulged in by Jekyll may indeed have been specified, as well as the connection between sex and sadism. None of this can be more than speculation, since the original manuscript no longer exists.

The territory of duality that would always preoccupy Louis had been depicted in a different way by two fellow countrymen who preceded him—Burns in "Holy Willie's Prayer," and James Hogg's *Memoirs of a Justified Sinner.* Chesterton was the first to see that the story of Jekyll and Hyde which was apparently happening in London was in reality taking place in Edinburgh. Mr. Utterson the lawyer was, noted Chesterton, an unmistakably Scottish lawyer. More to the point, Louis had grown up in a city split down the middle. Slums abut the houses of the rich to this day. Louis knew very well that respectable citizens slipped over from New Town to the brothels of the Old, just as he knew how Calvinism preached of a world divided between the chosen and the damned. In the play written by Louis and Henley, Brodie refers to his nighttime self as "my maniac brother who has slipped his chain."

Chesterton, with his love of paradox, saw that there was a sense in which Puritanism was expressed even more in Hyde than in Jekyll. "The sense of the sudden stink of evil, the immediate invitation to step into stark filth" was not only implied by the embarrassed and furtive vices of Jekyll, it was "the tragedy of a Puritan town." In his 1927 book on Stevenson, Chesterton pointed out that the story concerns one man, not two. They were not even twin brothers, but like father and son. "After all, Jekyll created Hyde; Hyde would never have created Jekyll." The message of the story, went on Chesterton, was that a man cannot cut himself off from his conscience. When Jekyll tries to amputate himself from Hyde, both parts die.

How is it that a theme which has become so banal for a modern reader should still grip the imagination? Duality has long been a commonplace. Some people are supposed to possess multiple personalities. We have reached the end of a century of human horror, of mass slaughter on an unprecedented scale. Who could deny that the world is morally bankrupt? Our newspapers are filled with murders, armed robberies, atrocities of all kinds, like our films and television. Serial killers are served up for entertainment, along with an ever-popular fare of scandal and betrayal. Documentaries exposing the "truth" turn us into voyeurs. A handyman in Colombia confesses to the rape, torture, and beheading of 140 children: the item rates four lines in a "quality" Sunday paper. What we call modern culture is an underworld, says Isaac Singer in a posthumous work.

Stevenson was convinced that his novel was negligible precisely because it was successful. In his disillusionment he wrote to Gosse in 1886:

> Let us tell each other mad stories of the bestiality of the beast whom we feed. What he likes is the newspaper: and to me the press is the mouth of a sewer, where lying is professed as from a university chair, and everything prurient and ignoble, and essentially dull, finds its abode and pulpit. I do not like mankind; but men, and not all of these—and fewer women. As for respecting the race, and above all that fatuous rabble of burgesses called "the public," God save me from such irreligion—that way lies disgrace and dishonor. There must be something wrong with me or I would not be popular.

Again and again in letters he tried to make his position clear. But what was it? Where did he stand in this brown swirling fog that Hyde seemed to emit from his squat, apelike body, the brown color of which had filled his childhood nightmares? *Jekyll and Hyde* implicated him in ways he did not fully understand. Fanny had once said lightheartedly that Louis looked like an angel in one photograph and a devil in another. Was he a dual man himself? As a writer he was unique in drawing inspiration directly from dreams without resorting to drugs, though we should remember that he dosed frequently on medicines such as tincture of opium, a common practice among Victorians. Jacobite plotting that went into his stories had come to him in dreams. As a student he once began to dream in sequence.

If art can be said to issue from conflict, we do not have far to look to find conflict in this unhappy period of his life. One should not assume that the dream world delivered up all its contents, willing though he was to be a channel for it. The imps working in his unconscious sometimes played games with him. He would be left floundering in ambiguity, feeling he had been given clues to some loss of direction in himself. "I have a genius for morality and no talent for it," he had told Fleeming Jenkin years before. Psychiatrists and academics have had a field day uncovering layers of possible meaning in the murk of *Jekyll and Hyde.* Jungians think that if Fanny did veto the original draft because it contained "a true female figure," this would account for the turn toward chaos rather than order in the narrative. Chesterton had taken note of the fact that just as Jekyll had created Hyde, Hyde could be seen as his son. Given the conflict between Louis and his father, wasn't the slaying of Sir Danvers Carew by Hyde "disguised parricide"? Hadn't Thomas once accused his son of bringing ruin and disgrace on his house? And so on.

Frank McLynn observes that Stevenson "moved the problem of evil in mankind on to a new plane." He was not dealing with a case of unleashed libido "but of the heart of darkness in the heart of human beings that would produce the death camps in the twentieth century." Aware of the confusion he had created in some minds, Louis wrote to John Paul Bocock to protest that Hyde

> was not, Great Gods! a mere voluptuary. There is no harm in voluptuaries: and none, with my hand on my heart and in the sight of God, none—no harm whatsoever in what prurient fools call "immorality." The harm was in Jekyll because he was a hypocrite—not because he was fond of women. . . . The hypocrite let out the beast of Hyde—who is no more sexual than another, but who is the essence of cruelty and malice and selfishness and cowardice, and these are diabolic in man—not this poor wish to love a woman that they make such a cry about.

In a profound sense what he had written was a terrible monster of a book, which went counter to current optimism and the Victorian belief in human perfectability. Symonds was one disturbed reader who found the moral chaos at the heart of the book hard to take. For him it was dreadful in its "shutting out of hope." Poe was water compared to this abyss down which he was being forced to look. He complimented Louis on one of his finest achievements but confessed that "it has left such a deeply painful impression on my heart that I do not know how I am ever going to turn to it again. The fact is that, viewed as allegory, it touches one too deeply. Most of us at some epoch of our lives have been on the verge of developing a Mr. Hyde."

This was so honest that Louis responded at once. "*Jekyll* is a dreadful thing, I own, but the only thing I feel dreadful about is that damned old business of the war of the members. This time it came out; I hope it will stay in, in future."

THE BOOK WAS ISSUED as a shilling paperback, to the consternation of his friends. Louis turned back in some relief to *Kidnapped*, which he had begun "partly as a lark, partly as a potboiler" and then laid aside. It ran along easily, always a good sign, full of confidence and clarity in spite of complaints about "bloodie jackery," about losing his spectacles and suffering with itching eyeballs. The first-person narrative still reads freshly today, from its opening pages with David Balfour setting out for Cramond, coming to the top of a hill and seeing the country fall away before him to the sea, "and in the midst of this descent, on a long ridge, the city of Edinburgh smoking like a kiln. There was a flag upon the castle, and ships lying anchored in the firth . . . and both brought my country heart into my mouth." He intended to bring the adventures of David and Alan Breck to a close in this volume, but ran out of steam. Colvin advised him to continue the story in a sequel, which six years later became *Catriona*. Big books were never Louis's forte, and perhaps this was just as well.

Kidnapped shows Louis at his finest as a novelist, opposing what he saw as the two halves of himself, the Covenanter and the Jacobite, in another probing of duality which never halts the flow of adventure. It is in a sense a repudiation of the passivity in himself, the feeling, as

McLynn puts it, "that skepticism was always another name for cowardice."

His parents had rented a house in Bournemouth now that Thomas's mind was faltering. With Fanny in Bath to consult a doctor, it was left to Louis to take his father on an outing to the Hydropathic Institute at Matlock. It was spring, but they reached Derbyshire in a flurry of snow. The stay was soon nightmarish as well as boring. "I have no plans," he told Fanny, "but to keep my father in patience for as long as I can and then streak for home like a swallow." Looking after a disruptive Thomas, after years of past enmity, was hardly likely to show Louis in a good light. There were bouts of "Hyde" over breakfast to face, which he tried to deal with by not speaking, or by treating it as a joke, but the confused man was hard to manage. Adding to Louis's impatience was his eagerness to get back to *Kidnapped* and finish it—he had left it in the middle. Then he had plans to write a memoir of Fleeming Jenkin. Miss Boodle would come round for instructions from the Master, finding him before a roaring fire wrapped in his dark red poncho, books sliding from his lap onto the floor. He was teaching her by the "sedulous ape" method he had used himself when starting to write. The "little brown deer," as Fanny called her, went on to become a primary school teacher and then a missionary in the Far East.

Though there was little to laugh about in 1886, the opportunity for a little levity was provided by a brainwave of Louis's, aimed at restoring harmony in the household. Valentine was still with them, but Fanny had trouble with female servants in general. So why not a man? Louis wrote chirpily to Colvin, "We have a butler! He doesn't buttle, but the point of the thing is the style. When Fanny gardens, he stands over her and looks genteel. He opens the door, and I am told waits at the table. Well, what's the odds. I shall have it on my tomb—"He ran a butler." The situation was comic enough to call for light verse.

He may have been this or that,
A drunkard or a guttler;

He may have been bald and fat—
At least he kept a butler.

He may have sprung from ill or well,
From emperor or sutler:
He may be burning now in Hell—
On earth he kept a butler.

Early in May 1887 they heard that Thomas Stevenson was dying. Louis and Fanny got there in time, but only to sit unrecognized beside the old man's armchair—Thomas refused to get into his bed. He died the following day. Louis had caught one of his dangerous colds and was ordered by his doctor-uncle not to attend the funeral. He was there at Heriot Row to shake hands with the mourners. He could find few words to say. His poem "The Last Sight" consists of six lines. Finding it hard to come to terms with the "dread changeling," knowing nobody that Thomas had become, he wrote to Colvin, "He will begin to return to us in the course of time, as he was and as we loved him."

The couple stayed with the widow till the end of May. Louis was too sick to leave the house. His uncle Dr. George Balfour recommended the high dry air of Colorado, since the two had been considering a return to America. Even the mild climate of Bournemouth had done him no good. Lloyd, back in Skerryvore waiting for them to come back, had two contrasting letters, one from his mother saying heartbrokenly that England was ended for Louis and they had to leave almost at once for Colorado. The letter from his stepfather was by contrast "almost jubilant. . . . He was plainly glad to be off, and the sooner the better."

AT THE END of World War I a tubercular young writer from the industrial north Midlands was getting ready to depart for Italy: the dream of being a wanderer surfaced again in his imagination. D. H. Lawrence wrote to his friend Gertler that his ideal now was to be houseless, to have a caravan and a horse and move on forever, and never have a neighbor, in some sort of free, lawless life like a gypsy. It was March, with snow falling thickly. His frail body was still upright, having survived the killer flu epidemic of 1918–1919. He ended a letter to Katherine Mansfield with the wistful, "I wish it was spring for us all."

Thirty-two years earlier, his "predecessor and herald," as Aldington puts it, was in a remarkably similar mood. He liked to see himself in spirit as belonging to a long line of vagabonds. Scots had been departing from Edinburgh to all corners of the earth for generations. The person once seen by Lloyd as a happy-go-lucky bohemian, who had talked of touring France in a caravan, was now a sober and preoccupied man. His father was dead: the ties to the past were gone. The endless "battle-battle" that had torn his sick body emotionally as well as physically, shattering his father and grieving his mother, had brought him to the brink of a departure that was nothing like his flight to America to rejoin Fanny. Here was his life's Great Divide. He would not see Britain again. He would have liked to move cleanly and swiftly, as if by doing so he could shed his old self with its guilts and regrets like an old skin and begin again. For him, this was what the itch to travel was all about. He was out on a new track.

He received three thousand pounds under his father's will, and his writings were starting to generate money. The open cab taking them from Heriot Row to Waverly Station, where as a youth he had hung over the bridge longing to get out of gaunt, soot-blackened Edinburgh, was spotted by Flora Masson. She saw the man and woman sitting together in an open cab piled high with a jumble of luggage. As it passed, a thin figure she recognized stood up and waved a wide-brimmed hat at the professor's daughter. "Goodbye!" he called out. "Goodbye!"

CHAPTER TWELVE

The Purity of Forests

*L*OUIS, a grown-up, responsible adult at last, was concerned for his mother. How could he as the only child go off blithely and leave her to fend for herself? She was comfortably off, but that was hardly the point. Her husband had doted on her. But her son need not have worried: as sometimes happens, the husband's death had somehow transformed her. Deeply though she grieved, she was suddenly tougher, calmer, more confident. She astonished everyone, including herself, by electing to go with them if they would have her. Fanny, perhaps surprisingly, had no trouble accommodating herself to this arrangement. The two had always got on.

At fifty-eight, small and dumpy, Maggie could have been mistaken for Queen Victoria, dressed in a black dress and white starched widow's cap with two long streamers. "Louis and Lloyd have longed for adventure," she wrote in her prim diary, now discovering a curious longing for it in herself.

When they set sail aboard the *SS Ludgate Hill* they were a group of five: Louis, Fanny, Lloyd, Valentine Roch, and the indefatigable widow. Gosse, meeting Louis in London the day before, found him smartly dressed "instead of looking like a Lascar out of employment, as he generally does." Fanny, always the organizer, had shopped around for a cheap passage to New York and located a tramp freighter with good passenger cabins. Henry James sent a case of champagne as a remedy for seasickness. They sailed from Tilbury on August 17. At Le Havre, Fanny was in a state of indignation and shock: the shipping firm had neglected to tell her that they would be taking on a cargo of stallions, cows, apes, and matches. In no time the ship smelled like a zoo. At night the pandemonium was hard to take.

Louis loved it all. Fanny's Bournemouth nest had felt like a tomb to him. It was a rough crossing, but he gloried in the storms too. Again his mother surprised everyone by demonstrating that she had sea legs. She even managed a hammock. Fanny was extremely seasick, Lloyd and Valentine less severely so, and Louis was finding out yet again that "The sea voyage proves that the sea agrees very heartily with me. . . ." Why, he exclaimed to Colvin when they had reached New York, had he allowed himself to rot so long on land? There was nothing like being at sea. "O it was lovely on our stable-ship, chock full of stallions. . . . I made a friend of a baboon whose embraces have pretty near cost me a coat." Later he told Bob, "I had literally forgotten what happiness was, and the full mind, full of external and physical things, not of cares and labors and not about a fellow's behavior. My heart literally sang." His imagination followed suit, spinning out dreams of future travels, to Japan, Algiers, Australia. He spent the voyage wandering around the ship in all weathers, offering Henry James's champagne to ill passengers. Regaining the physical world even to this extent made him hungry for more.

He reached New York to discover that he was a celebrity. *Jekyll and Hyde* had done it. Even before landing the Stevensons heard that the boarding pilot was nicknamed "Hyde" and his partner "Jekyll." Reporters swarmed aboard the moment they docked, wanting his opinion on everything. When he talked, nobody was listening. The scandal of copyright and pirate editions was on his mind, as it had been when Dickens came. He spoke up for Henry James and avoided politics. "America is . . . a fine place to eat in, and great place for kindness, but what a silly thing is popularity!" he wrote to Henry James. In the same vein he told Colvin of his "idiotic" reception. "If

Jesus Christ came they would make less fuss." He admitted to liking the "interviewer lads" for their humor and for ignoring anything he asked them to ignore. Yes, he liked the lads.

Will Low came up the gangplank to welcome them, and those rich Bostonians who had commissioned the Sargent portrait, the Fairchilds, whisked them all off to a suite at the Victoria Hotel as their guests. They pushed through another eight reporters to reach their carriage. If Louis recalled his experience on first landing as an emigrant he must have thought he was on another planet.

A stage version of *Jekyll* was about to make a hit in New York. Fanny and Maggie went to see it, but not the author. Publishers began queuing up to make offers so dizzying that he was frightened out of his wits. Fan mail came in by the sackload. Giving in to *Scribner's* magazine for the sake of some peace, he agreed to accept $3,500 for twelve articles a year, though he found these sums demoralizing. They transferred to the Fairchild mansion at Newport, and even there press attention did not let up. A sculptor, Augustus Saint-Gaudens, had been engaged to make a medallion of Stevenson. The image of him sitting up in bed writing and smoking, his red poncho around his shoulders, caught him exactly. He spent twelve days on Rhode Island, much of the time in bed. Autumn had arrived: it was time to move. Colorado was now seen as too far to travel for a man exhausted by New York, and its resorts at 5,000 feet too high for Fanny's liking. She had no intention of repeating the Davos experience under another name.

Someone suggested the Adirondack Mountains in upper New York State as being a fine place for the lungs. Fanny and Lloyd went ahead to investigate, traveling by riverboat and train, loving the red and gold fire of the early October trees. Loon Lake was the end of the railroad line, and they pressed on by buggy for another twenty miles to Saranac Lake. They were six hundred feet high in the pine forests of the Adirondack wilderness, close to the Canadian border. A Dr. Trudeau, once a consumptive himself, had established a remote sanatorium at a logging and trapping village. Fanny, ever the fixer, went searching for suitable accommodation. A local guide and trapper named Baker agreed to rent half of his frame house as separate living quarters for the Stevenson ménage. Crudely built, it had green shutters and a veranda around it, and was all on one floor. Lifted up on a wooded ridge over the river, it looked down on the cluster of log cabins and frame houses ten minutes' walk away. Fanny cabled her approval to Louis and his mother and then rolled up her sleeves. In these situations she came into her own, putting her experience as a single parent to work: she had not forgotten what she had learned the hard way in the mining camps of Nevada.

By the time the others came she had got everything as shipshape as it would ever be, even caulking the doors and windows against the cold, "as one caulks a boat." When Maggie Stevenson arrived at Saranac with her convalescent, there was Fanny in command in a petticoat and jacket, busy cooking dinner. The only food available seemed to be venison and bread. A boy came up every morning with drinking water from a distant spring. Water for washing was hauled up from the river by their landlord. Louis took one look and approved of everything. It was Silverado revisited, a camp life with a spartan regime that made him feel invigorated, as adventures always did.

Dr. Edward Trudeau took his new patient on, examined him, and declared that Louis's disease was in remission. His diagnosis of genuine consumption would be challenged later by those who questioned the nature of Louis's pulmonary illness. The writer promised to follow Trudeau's strict orders, though his promises to doctors were soon forgotten, as Ruedi had discovered at Davos, and he refused outright to give up smoking. Also he soon came to hate Trudeau's laboratory tests with guinea pigs, and there was something boorish and dictatorial about his manner that Louis disliked. At Hunter's Home, as the Stevensons had renamed their rooms, he settled down to work, wrapping himself up to pace the veranda while he composed, something he would always do when on his feet. He tackled the first of the twelve monthly articles for *Scribner's* because the thought of a deadline preyed on his mind. He told Henry James that he could hear the bell of Lloyd's typewriter making an agreeable sound in the next room as the youth banged out "the early chapters of a humorous romance." And he could hear Valentine busy at the kitchen stove. Fanny, after making sure that her charge was in a fit state to be left, had gone off to visit her mother in Indiana.

The "humorous romance" was *The Wrong Box*, first called *A Game of Bluff*, a collaboration between Louis and his stepson. Lloyd had dropped out of university and now had ambitions to be a writer, apprenticing himself to his stepfather as a stage in the process. This oddity of a tale, which Louis thought "incredibly silly" but quite funny, hinged on a trust fund and a corpse in a barrel that kept disappearing and turning up again. The first draft had yet another title, *The Finsbury Tontine*, and went through a great deal of rewriting. In the end, according to Lloyd, neither knew who had written any given passage. The enterprise could have been sanctioned by Louis to encourage the boy, who was then nineteen and suffering with poor eyesight. His proud mother applauded when it was read out at a family gathering one evening.

Fanny returned to Saranac by way of Montreal. In the city she had been on a shopping spree, buying a supply of garments so that everyone could withstand the approaching winter: coats and robes and rugs of buffalo hide, fur caps with earmuffs, and snowshoes, all made by the Canadian Indians. At the Bakers' the cold was already ferocious, so severe that the water froze when Valentine tried to wash the floors.

It grew steadily colder. Soon it was dangerous to touch metal for fear of being stuck. Lloyd and Fanny ventured out with three pairs of gloves each. Days now had a pattern. Louis would be off for a walk in Canadian moccasins with his nearsighted stepson, or to skate on the pond a little. He lay down until six, when the family gathered for their main meal. There were talks and readings aloud by the fire, or they played cards. Or Louis and Lloyd amused themselves piping duets on pennywhistles. Bedtime was early for everyone, with a hot soapstone to help keep warm.

An exciting event was the arrival of a parcel from William Archer, who had sent a novel called *Cashel Byron's Profession* by his friend Bernard Shaw. Louis wrote in thanks, "I have read your friend's book with singular relish. . . . It is full of promise, but I should like to know his age. It is *horrid fun*. All I ask is more of it (I say, Archer, my God, what women!)."

Fanny was delighted to be told by Henry James that he admired the "elegance" of her letters, but she would have been less pleased if she could have seen his letter to Owen Wister, author of *The Virginian*. Sending him a note of introduction to Louis he told Wister, "You will find him a young, unique, dishevelled, undressed, lovable fellow. There is a fresh, youthful, complacent Scotch mother, a poor sightless (or almost so) American stepson, and a strange California wife, 15 years older than Louis himself, but almost as interesting. If you like the gulch and the canyon you will like *her*. . . ."

But she had a fan in Sam McClure of the *New York World*, who would be important to Stevenson's future career in America. McClure, a Scots expatriate, had a reckless streak, and when he paid a visit to Saranac and was told by Louis of his dream of fitting up a yacht for a half-year's cruise, he said, "That's easy. If you get a yacht and take long sea voyages and write about them, stories of adventure and so forth, I'll pay all the expenses." Back in New York he did search for a suitable yacht, but in vain.

Long after meeting Fanny in their frozen camp McClure paid tribute to her qualities. So far as he could see she had the kind of imagination that expressed itself in living. "She always lived with great intensity, had come more into contact with the real world than Stevenson had done at the time when they met, had tried more kinds of life, known more kinds of people. When he married her he married a woman rich in knowledge of life and the world." More especially, "She had the kind of pluck that Stevenson particularly admired. . . . A woman who was rigid in small matters of domestic economy, who insisted on a planned and ordered life, would have worried Stevenson terribly. . . ." Naturally he had no knowledge of Fanny in her Bournemouth heaven, but as a tribute to her adaptability it is worth citing. The irony is that Saranac was proving too much for her.

Still the temperature dropped. Amazingly, Louis had rarely been in better health. From the time he left England he was to go sixteen months without a hemorrhage. His rise, as we have seen, was often the signal for Fanny to decline. As at Davos, she complained of the altitude, which made her suffer from breathlessness. She disappeared for long absences, visiting her cousin in Philadelphia and neglecting to write to her mother. A worried Louis had to maintain contact on her behalf. Maggie, on the other hand, was impressing everyone with her staying power. Will Low thought her courageous and unassuming: "She had a keen sense of humor, and her conversation, without any pretense of brilliancy, for one of her most charming traits was a modest assumption of surprise that she should be the mother of so brilliant a son, was always interesting." Louis did his best to make light of his wife's wanderings, writing to Coggie Ferrier that he was unhappy about her going alone, but she was "better anywhere than here—a bleak, blackguard, beggarly climate, of which I can say no good except that it suits me and some others of the same or similar persuasions whom (by all rights) it ought to kill." In himself he was "compared with last year in Bournemouth an angel of joy." To another correspondent he explained why—apart from being forbidden by the doctor to travel—he found it impossible to go with Fanny: "I myself dread, worse than almost any other imaginable peril . . . the American railroad car. . . . Ah, if it were only an ocean to cross, it would be a matter of small thought to me—and great pleasure. But . . . I fear the railroad car as abjectly as I do an earwig, and, on the whole, on better grounds."

SAM MCCLURE had provisionally bought *The Black Arrow* for American publication in syndicated form, but Louis felt obligated to delay agreement until Fanny's return from a trip to New York and again to Philadelphia, where she met Whitman and was "disenchanted." Back again from an absence of nearly two months "on her own devices" she was in the same uncommunicative mood as when she had been away. *The Black Arrow* was a book she had vehemently disliked and evidently still did. To make amends for going against her judgment he dedicated it to her, thanking her with sly humor for her "unsleeping watchfulness and admirable pertinacity." It was surely right and proper, he went on, that he should place her name on the flyleaf "of the only book of mine that you have never read—and never will read."

Something about the Adirondacks inspired him to start work on *The Master of Ballantrae*, "a story conceived long before on the moors between Pitlochry and Strathairdle, conceived in Highland rain, in the blend of the smell of heather and bog-plants, and with a mind full of the Athole correspondence and the Memoirs of the Chevalier de Johnstone." Surrounded by similar scenery, pacing the narrow veranda in his thick buffalo-skin coat, Indian boots, and astrakhan hat which made him look (he hoped) like a Polar explorer, the icy air stinging his nose, he let the story of the 1745 rising unwind in his head one night toward the end of 1887. He was on to something good and knew it. His novel was tragedy: two sons, good and evil, involved with the same woman. It was yet another study in duality. The elder, evil brother is "an incubus," supposedly killed at Culloden, who turns up like a Heathcliff to bleed the family of money. As always with Stevenson it is the ambiguity of evil that is being explored. Like Heathcliff his demon is deeply divided. The narrator addresses this aspect of him directly when he says: "You could not have been so bad a man if you had not all the machinery of a good one." Louis, as if struggling with the devil himself, wrote to Colvin, "The Master is all I know of evil." Flawed in its ending, it is nevertheless a masterly work by a novelist coming into his own. He put it to one side when the first excitement died and finished it later in Hawaii. Writing to Will Low in May 1889 he announced, "I have at length finished *The Master*: it has been a sore cross to me, but now he is buried . . . his soul, if there is any hell to go to, gone to hell." He had avoided plunging too deeply into the heroine's character because, he explained, "I am always afraid of my women, who are not admired in my home circle."

One stimulus that had helped to set *Ballantrae* going, as he stood that dark night in the freezing air "sweet with purity of forests," was Marryat's *The Phantom Ship*. He had just finished his third or fourth rereading of it. Again, in a spirit of emulation, he felt the urge to write a big book, something he had not yet managed to do. He wanted to create a story of the sea and the land, of savagery and civilization that was an epic, and to treat it "in the same elliptic method" as the Marryat he admired. And as always when he wrote his Scottish novels he was turning in his spirit toward home.

He didn't doubt the book's worth, plunging on for five and a half chapters at top speed before being distracted. Henley would call it "grimy" and Louis said no, it was grim. Black it certainly was. When he finished it he called it a tragedy, telling Colvin that it "contains more human worth than anything of mine but *Kidnapped*." Always attentive to his dreams, he remarked when he was hard at work on the book that "I never knew time to elapse in dreams . . . dreams are merely novels, they are made with every sort of literary trick: and a word stands for a year, if it is the right year."

By the end of January the temperature had sunk to a brutal forty below zero. His buffalo coat welded itself to the kitchen floor. Valentine woke up one morning to find her handkerchief in a hard frozen lump under her pillow. The ink froze. Food had to be thawed. Snow was piled high at the back of the house.

As well as his work on the novel he took up the essay form in order to produce material for *Scribner's*. In rapid succession he wrote "Random Memories," "A Chapter on Dreams," "A Christmas Sermon," and his most ambitious, "Pulvis et Umbra," which appeared in *Scribner's* magazine in April 1888. In a cosmological vision he pictured the earth "loaded with predatory life, and more drenched in blood, both animal and vegetable, than every mutinied ship," a planet scudding through space with unimaginable speed, turning one cheek and then the other to "the reverberations of a blazing world ninety million miles away." He saw man, "this hair-crowned bubble of the dust," as a bundle of contradictions living "in his isle of terror and under the imminent hand of death."

Preoccupied or absentminded, he fell into a publishing muddle when Sam McClure, on one of his visits to Saranac, heard of a proposed sequel to *Kidnapped* and promptly offered Louis $8,000 for the serial rights. The bemused author agreed, overlooking the fact that his contract with Scribner included all American rights. He friend and legal agent Charles Baxter was given the job of smoothing *Scribner's* down and apologizing to McClure.

On a visit to London later, Sam McClure was taken aback by the amount of hostility and jealousy he found swirling around any mention of Stevenson's name among the Savile Club set and what Fanny called the "Shepherd's Bush gang." Henley, he thought, was the one most afflicted by this resentment of Stevenson's American success. This was ominous in view of a letter from Henley dated March 9, 1888, which would have devastating consequences for Louis.

ALL AT ONCE the Saranac world thawed. The spring came in with a rush, like a spring in Russia. Eaves dripped, icicles shrank, the snow melted. Fanny, never happy there, took off like a bird on March 26, 1888, to visit her friends in the blessed warmth of California. She was still withdrawn, leaving a depressed Louis to write to Mrs. Vandegrift that her daughter was heading for San Francisco. He was again anxious about her traveling alone but the doctor had vetoed any such journey for him, he told his mother-in-law.

Belle came over from Honolulu to spend time with her mother. She and her husband Joe Strong had been sponging on Louis for years unashamedly. They had gone to Hawaii in 1882 with Louis's help, ostensibly to further Joe's career. He was an artist who found art useful as a means of avoiding work. Throughout most of the rest of Louis's life he would be there, holding out his hand like a child. When they sailed into Honolulu for the first time he said, "I can't paint here—it's in primary colors."

Belle had brought her son Austin, described by Fanny as "a little, little child, very ugly, very delicate, and most affectionate and touching." The Stevensons left behind in Saranac were to rejoin her later in New York. Meanwhile they were left with packing. "Tell

Valentine not to work too hard," wrote her mistress as an after-thought.

The Saranac party left for New York on April 13. Louis, relieved that his wife was at least in touch again, wrote to ask her to look for a yacht to charter while she was in San Francisco. It was no more than a thought. In New York he enjoyed sitting on a bench under trees just coming into leaf in Washington Square, striking up conversations with children and once talking to Mark Twain, who—like everyone else—remembered the Scottish writer's eyes. Louis was uneasy away from Fanny, his power supply, and though Saranac had done wonders for his health in spite of the harsh winter, he was glad to get away from Dr. Trudeau's regime and the feeling of claustrophobia he emanated.

Quickly wearied by New York, he begged his friend Will Low, "Will, get me out of this." Low's solution was a white colonial inn on the Manasquan River in New Jersey. The party settled in comfortably. Louis did little but rest. He tried and failed to write, so he sailed a round-bottomed catboat with Lloyd, and had one or two visitors. Saint-Gaudens came. On his eighth wedding anniversary he was on the other side of the continent from Fanny, experiencing no obvious difficulties but, with his peace about to be destroyed, feeling uneasily in limbo.

The next news he had from her was bad. Taken ill while visiting friends, she had discovered a frightening growth in her throat. An operation was necessary. To make matters worse he had received a letter from London which made him more furious and despairing than he had ever been. It tore into him, leaving him empty and sick. The "great literary quarrel" dissected by scholars was under way.

At this distance the dispute with Henley seems even more trivial and absurd now than it was then, but it is clear that the fallout from it ripped to pieces his illusions of comradeship with his old friend. From the start Louis was in an invidious position. The truth was that Henley had been spoiling for a fight for years. He seized his chance with carefully disguised indecent glee. Fanny, his enemy, that "semi-educated" woman who dominated his old friend and kept him to herself, burying him in "the bloody country of dollars and spew," suddenly played into his hands.

Quarrels are hardly ever what they seem. Below their froth and nonsense there can run an undercurrent of something deadly that has been rankling for years. All at once the lava is out and burning. The aftermath of this eruption would be with the two men for years, the damage repaired at last after a fashion, only to end with something far worse when Louis was in his grave. The rancor had in fact only gone underground, and would come boiling out again in due course, unstoppable.

It all began innocently enough with a conversation at Henley's house a year or so earlier. Bob's sister, Katherine de Mattos, was there, an intelligent and cultivated young woman who was being helped by Henley to write. Her marriage had failed and she was on the rocks financially. Louis's ailing father had asked his son to subsidize her, as well as Bob, and he was trying to do so. Katherine had written a story about a poetic young fellow who meets a girl on a train. The girl turns out to be an escaped inmate from a madhouse. Fanny, in her self-assumed role of literary critic, decided that the story needed something, and suggested making the girl a nixie or water sprite. Feeling as she did in touch with the supernatural, this idea seemed an obvious improvement. It didn't to Katherine, who wanted her story to remain hers.

Henley did his best to place the manuscript with magazines, with no success. The subject came up again at Skerryvore, when Louis's cousin was visiting. Why, Fanny asked, didn't Katherine give her the subject to rewrite, since she could get nowhere with it? Clearly Katherine was reluctant, as everyone could see except the forceful Fanny. Nevertheless she handed over the manuscript. Fanny's rewritten version went with her to Canada, and "The Nixie" duly appeared in *Scribner's* magazine, credited to Fanny Van de Grift Stevenson. The Stevenson name had worked its magic. In the same issue was "Beggars," one of Louis's monthly articles.

The row that broke out and the ugly charge of plagiarism implied throughout could have been avoided if Fanny had published her story as a collaboration, or at least offered Katherine half her fee. That she did neither her biographer puts down to a hunger for recognition. This was her third published story. Was she harboring a desire to be a full-fledged literary lady in her own right?

If so, it was about to go horribly wrong. Henley's letter arrived. Cunningly disguising his malice he began with "Dear Boy," heading it *Private and Confidential*. He had read the magazine and "The Nixie" with amazement.

> It's Katherine's; surely it's Katherine's? The situation, the environment, the principal figure—*voyons*! There are even reminiscences of phrases and imagery, parallel incidents—*Que sais-je?* . . . I think it has lost as much (at least) as it has gained; and why there wasn't a double signature is what I've not been able to understand.

He was tired, "damn tired," and wished he had the wings of a dove, "a soiled dove even," so that he could fly off somewhere and rest. Then came his plea, which not only put the onus on his "dear boy" to pass judgment on his own wife, but shattered Louis's faith in a man he had trusted for so many years.

> Don't show this to anybody, and when you write, don't do more than note it in a general way. By the time you *do* write, you will have forgotten all about it, no doubt. But if you haven't, deal vaguely with my malady. . . .

He ended on a loving note, which must have induced nausea in the appalled Louis. He forgave his friend for living so far away, "for you have loved me much. Let us go on so to the end. Forgive this babble, and take care of yourself and burn this letter."

Louis took days to pull himself together sufficiently to write a coherent reply. The letter he was told to destroy had branded him like a hot iron. Not only had he been asked to accuse his wife of plagiarism, but he was being drawn into a vile conspiracy of silence against her. Was Henley mad as well as wicked? Did he really suppose Louis would let this slander stand?

He had taken issue with Henley before, but never like this, with its invitation to concealment. He had loaned him money on numerous occasions when he could ill afford it, for old times' sake. When Henley's dissolute brother Teddy had toured the States in 1887 with *Deacon Brodie*, getting drunk in Philadelphia and ending in New York trying to batten on Louis for his hotel bill, Louis had written angrily to Baxter of "The drunken whoreson bugger and bully living himself in the best hotels, and smashing inoffensive strangers in the bar! It is too sickening. . . . The violence of this letter comes from my helplessness. . . . In the meantime I add another twenty pounds to W. E.'s credit."

Fanny, about to go under the surgeon's knife in the West, was, he thanked God, ignorant of this calumny. He was never going to show her Henley's poisonous letter, though sooner or later he would have to put her in the picture. He went cold at the thought of her fury if she learned about it from other sources. Finally he felt calm enough to reply to the man he had always regarded as his staunchest comrade and ally. He drafted several attempts to refute the slanderous charge. He wrote:

My dear Henley,
I write with indescribable difficulty; and if not with perfect temper, you are to remember how very rarely a husband is expected to receive such accusations against his wife. I can only direct you to write to Katherine and ask her to remind you of that part of the business which took place in your presence and which you seem to have forgotten: she will doubtless add particulars which you may not have heard. . . .

He had imagined that his revulsion would have made it impossible to say much, but these things have a momentum of their own. Once he had started he found it hard to stop.

When you have refreshed your mind as to the facts, you will, I know, withdraw what you said to me; but I must go further and remind you, if you have spoken of this to others, a proper explanation and retraction of what you shall have said or implied to any person so addressed, will be necessary.

The lawyer of his legal studies had taken over. But he was above all a gentleman and a friend, and he drew back from the dead sea of this litigious language to add that "it is hard to think that anyone—and least of all my friend—should have been so careless of dealing agony. . . . You will pardon me if I can find no form of signature; I pray God such a blank will not be of long endurance." He signed stiffly in full, "Robert Louis Stevenson."

When Fanny did get wind of it, as she was bound to do, she wrote to Louis in a near frenzy to tell him that she had no intention of putting up with any of this idiocy. She was ill in bed, though the growth had not proved malignant. Alarmed, for all her rage, she decided on a friendly overture to Mrs. de Mattos, asking in the most reasonable way for Katherine's backing in this distasteful matter. If she would simply verify that she had handed the story over freely, that would be that.

Meanwhile, in what was developing into a war dance, Katherine wrote to Louis in New Jersey to say that "Mr. Henley's very natural but unfortunate letter was written without my wish or knowledge." Henley had a perfect right to be astonished, she thought, but what he chose to say had nothing to do with her. She affected a tone of superiority and distaste, ending "I trust this matter is not making you feel as ill as all of us." Later she withdrew from the row completely, rightly smelling "deviltry in the air."

Louis was stunned by her neutral stance. Where did this leave him? The loyal Baxter, drawn in to pour oil on the dispute, was told gratefully by Louis, "God bless you for your letter. . . . Suppose that I am insane and have dreamed all that I seem to remember, and that my wife has shamefully stolen a story from my cousin, was this the class of matter that a friend would write me? . . . And such an accusation—a theft of money and of reputation?" What he would never understand or forget was Henley's willingness "to seethe up" against him and his wife, and his heartless willingness to wound.

*

WAS THE VILLAIN of the piece Fanny or Henley? A sniveling letter came from Henley at last, concerned with his own feelings and little else. He made a false apology for having spoken "without a full sense of the regard that was due to you" but managed to avoid completely the little matter of having insulted his friend's wife. Her name, around which the whole storm revolved, was nowhere in sight.

Louis was not deceived. He wrote in disgust to Baxter, "I fear that I have come to the end with Henley; the lord knows if I have not tried to be a friend to him. . . . There is not one of that crew that I have not helped in every kind of strait. . . . If this be friendship, I am not robust enough to bear it. If it be want of tact, it is strangely like want of heart." He closed melodramatically, "I wish I had died at Hyères."

By this time Fanny was hotly in correspondence with all and sundry, intent on gaining allies. Louis, caught in the crossfire, stoutly defended his wife's honor. But Fanny suspected him of wavering. "I hope you are not worried about those people in England," she wrote bitterly. "I have cast it out of my mind only in so far as it affects you." The incident was already going the rounds of "those people" in the London clubs and elsewhere, many of whom had felt the rough edge of Fanny's tongue. Poor Baxter was the recipient of Fanny's final word on her husband's so-called friends: "As it is, they have nearly, perhaps quite, murdered Louis. It is hard for me to keep on living. . . . If I cannot, I leave my curse upon the murderers and the slanderers. . . . If it so happens that I must go back to perfidious Albion, I shall learn to be false. While they eat their bread from my hand—and oh, they will do that—I shall smile, and wish it were poison and might wither their bodies as they have my heart."

The malediction did have a certain ring to it. Fanny was nothing if not headlong; and Louis stayed on her side, even though he had not wanted her to take Katherine's damned manuscript, and his instinct was always for reconciliation where possible. They had been through too much awfulness together for him to be disloyal. Fanny's sister Nellie wrote of her in extenuation, "But as she loved, so he hated, and as she endowed her friends with all the virtues, so she could see no good at all in an enemy. . . ." But she did, according to her sister, suffer badly from fits of remorse after lashing out in one of her paranoid attacks. Subsiding, she would quote a favorite saying of hers: "To know all is to forgive all."

A codicil to his will which Louis sent to Baxter arranged for an annuity to be provided for Katherine's child. At the same time he asked his friend to devise some means of making Henley a small allowance—in view of his dire straits—which could be ascribed to "anybody but me."

In a moment of exasperation he wrote to Fanny in San Francisco that he envied "you flimsy people who rage up so easily in hate," before hastily canceling the word "flimsy." All he wanted was to wash his hands of the whole wretched business with "these hobgoblin figures, once my friends, for just now." He had been unable to work or to think of anything else. The breach with Henley was never completely healed. Their crippled friendship limped on until the day in 1890 when W. E., in Edinburgh to edit the *Scots Magazine*, neglected to call on Maggie Stevenson when she returned briefly from the Pacific. That, for Louis, was the ultimate snub on the family name.

Seven years after Louis's death, the snakelike Henley would strike again. The chance for him to mount his extraordinary splenetic attack came when he was given the official life of Stevenson by Graham Balfour to review for the *Pall Mall Gazette*. In no position to judge anyone, he castigated Balfour for presenting "this Seraph in Chocolate, this barley-sugar effigy of a real man" who was not "my old, riotous, intrepid, scornful Stevenson at all." He followed this lament for the Stevenson who went to America and never came back with a bitter condemnation of Louis as a writer and a man, whose style was "so perfectly achieved that the achievement gets obvious." The Stevenson he knew, he went on patronizingly, was an excellent fellow, "But he was of his essence what the French call *personnel*. He was, that is, incessantly and passionately interested in Stevenson. He could not be in the same room with a mirror but he must invite its confidences every time he passed it." Now he was able to unleash in a flood the anger he had stored up for years. Stevenson's vanity was such that "the smallest of his discoveries, his trivial apprehensions, were all by way of being revelations, and as revelations must be thrust upon the world; he was never so much in earnest, never so well pleased . . . never so irresistible, as when he wrote about himself."

He hurried on to recall, with feigned affection, the unmarried and irresponsible Louis, "the friend, the comrade, the *charmeur*." This was the dig in the eye for Fanny, the stealer of his "dear boy." Fanny, who did not need lessons on how to hate, thought he was drunk when he wrote it. The bitterness and ferocity of his debunking has only been equaled and indeed surpassed by Bruce Chatwin, who poured scorn on a figure he considered second-rate as a person and a writer. What makes Henley's "exposure" unique is that it comes from a supposed friend.

PART III

CHAPTER THIRTEEN

Get Out Your Big Atlas

LOUIS FRETTED in New Jersey, unable to settle or to get free of Henley's treachery in his mind. His instinct was to retreat into his privacy and shun the importunities of so-called friends. None of this would withstand long his desire to be with people. *The Master of Ballantrae* was stalled. For something to occupy himself he tinkered with revisions of *The Wrong Box*. His Hamlet-like crisis would only have deepened had he got wind of Henley's latest act of malice, spreading the word that Bob was the superior talent of the two cousins if only he could find the ambition and the will to work.

Will Low recalled in his memoirs that a telegram was brought in one day in May when they were at lunch. It was for Louis. He read it, then asked his mother to read it aloud. It said: "Can secure splendid seagoing schooner-yacht for seven hundred and fifty a month with most comfortable accommodation for six aft and six forward. Can be ready for sea in ten days. Reply immediately. Fanny."

Here was the impressive side of the woman Sam McClure saw as a splendid mate for Louis. The sea would never be her element, but she was determined to lift Louis out of his dejection. He scribbled a reply and handed it to the messenger boy: "Blessed girl, take the yacht and expect us in ten days."

Turning his back on Henley's chattering, petty world with relish, he thought of the "great affair" of an adventure as an interlude. There was no question in his mind of a final destination, though he had often dreamt of an ocean cruise, and specifically of the Pacific. It had begun as far back as 1875, when he heard his father's New Zealand visitor talk of Samoa. He told Will Low of his love for the Pacific in the days when he was at Monterey, "and perhaps now it will love me a little." But the rover in him had been born in childhood, as his dream of travel "when I'm a man" testifies:

> I should like to rise and go
> Where the golden apples grow;
> Where below another sky
> Parrot islands anchored lie,
> And, watched by cockatoos and goats,
> Lonely Crusoes building boats. . . .

The party made up of Louis, Lloyd, Maggie, and Valentine left for New York, took a train to Chicago, and then were stranded in Chicago for eight hours. Days later they reached Salt Lake City and then traveled west on a train that gave them nosebleeds because of the altitude. Fanny, anticipating the effect of such a grueling journey on her husband, met them at Sacramento. It was June 7. In San Francisco Louis went straight to bed at the Occidental Hotel and stayed there, under doctor's orders: hardly an auspicious start, but he had seen the Pacific. Only time would tell if it would be sufficient to wash away all the bitterness in his spirit.

Fanny took charge of everything. It was the seesaw again which always seemed to operate: with him weakened, she became strong and capable. How low he had sunk in spirits can be seen from his last letter to Charles Baxter while still at Manasquan. He had just received Fanny's news, been buoyed up by it, and then lapsed again into bitter regret. He swung about wildly between morbidity and hope, seeing this latest venture as a desperate gamble. "It will be best for all, I daresay," he moaned, "if the *Casco* [the schooner] goes down with me." The Henley business "has been my headstone; I will never be reconciled to life." He very rarely talked blackly like this when Fanny was there to bolster him. "I cannot say I think I act harshly. I am trying to do the best for all. The Lord knows there is in my soul this morning no hatred and no anger; a very weary disappointment, a dread of the future, and a doubt of all. . . ." Finally he seemed to rally, to shake himself into a different mood. "Well, I mean to beat the crowd. I *will* have a good time on the *Casco*; it means a hard heart. Well, harden it, O Lord! And let's be done."

Again it was the thought of life on the move that caught him up and challenged him, changed him, before he even reached the Pacific and looked on the open sea. A born traveler, he was about to be an astonishing one, an explorer even, about to leave America behind as he had left Europe. Yet he began with no expectations, no great hopes. In the opening paragraph of *In the South Seas* he would recapture his mood:

> For nearly ten years my health had been declining and for some while before I set forth upon my voyage, I believed I was come to the afterpiece of my life, and had only the nurse and the undertaker to expect. It was suggested that I should try the South Seas, and I was not unwilling to visit like a ghost, and be carried like a bale, among scenes that had attracted me in youth and health.

In the event the Pacific would transform him miraculously. In the words of Verlaine describing Rimbaud he would be "The man with footsoles of wind," though he was no Rimbaud. "I want to live!" he told his friend Will Low.

The *Casco* was a fast and graceful two-masted schooner-yacht of seventy tons, ninety-five feet long, with lofty masts, white sails and decks, and gleaming brasswork. It sat, Graham Balfour wrote, "like a bird upon the water," and that's how the photographs show it. Its owner, a wealthy man by the name of Merrit, doubted the wisdom of letting the crank he had read about in the papers look after his vessel. Stevenson had money but seemed clearly eccentric. Before Dr. Merrit agreed to the deal he saw Louis personally and was surprised to find that the odd-looking writer was "a plain, sensible man that knows what he's talking about just as well as I do." Louis always did well in interviews.

The owner did insist that he appoint his own skipper, Captain A. H. Otis. He told his captain in confidence that he might have to bury Stevenson at sea, he was in such poor shape, and should stow the proper equipment to do so. Otis, before he consented to the berth, insisted on talking to the "literary cove" himself, a man so ignorant of the Pacific that he intended to take his old mother with him. Louis, well versed in nautical language, made his usual favorable impression. They argued over the route, with Otis pointing out that all the great voyagers had gone west rather than east to the Galápagos as Louis wanted. He gave way but talked Otis into heading for the Marquesas first. Though Otis may not have thought so, this charterer was well acquainted with the "murderous innocence" of the sea, no stranger either to what Yeats would call the "haystack and roof-levelling wind / Bred on the Atlantic." The Pacific, he would soon discover, bred winds of equal ferocity. In the enormous "fetches" of the unleashed Pacific, McLynn tells us, a storm could build up a wave to a hundred feet. Alain Gerbault, the single-handed yachtsman and a fan of Stevenson, was following R.L.S.'s route in the 1920s and survived a sea with waves he estimated as 120 feet high.

The voyage was being financed by two thousand pounds out of the three thousand Louis had inherited from his father. On the eve of departure he was still talking to Baxter in terms of a gamble. "If I cannot get my health back (more or less) 'tis madness; but of course there is hope. . . . If this business fails to set me up, well, two thousand pounds is gone, and I know I can't get better." In a farewell letter to Henry James his mood was brighter. "It seems too good to be true, and is a very good way of getting through the green-sickness of maturity, which, with all its accompanying ills, is now declaring itself in my mind and life."

Preparations were going ahead at a furious pace. Fanny and Lloyd raced about, laying in seven months of supplies for their party and the crew, eleven in all, not forgetting scores of small gifts for the islanders they would encounter. Lloyd was the proud owner of a new camera. Belle, reunited with her brother after such a long interval, was full of admiration for this twenty-year-old stranger, six feet tall, lean and intellectual-looking with his spectacles. He sounded more English than American. As for her mother, with her short wiry hair and determined jaw, never without a cigarette, she looked the typical American liberated woman of the day and puts one in mind of Jack London's horse-riding Charmian, another tomboyish female, bred in the big outdoors, who went sailing through Polynesia in the *Snark* in 1907.

Fanny had met in San Francisco the woman Sam Osbourne had abandoned. Paulie, once pretty, was now deaf, lonely, and very poor. The story goes that she had wept in front of Fanny, saying, "You were right about that man and I was wrong." Fanny helped her with some money, but she was preoccupied with thoughts of her recent operation and whether she would need to see her doctor again, and with worries about Belle, whose marriage to Joe Strong seemed on the rocks.

On June 28, 1888, the tug *Pelican* towed the *Casco* through the Golden Gate out of San Francisco Bay and into the vast Pacific. Here was the start of that "pure dispassionate adventure" Louis had yearned for since reading of the great explorers in his youth. Belle had got the tug to deliver a farewell note, and Fanny answered it in haste, urging her sad daughter to "Get away as soon as you can, my dear. There is nothing else you can do, and the sooner you go the better. . . ." She had advised against the marriage from the outset, to no avail. Ferryboats in the bay whistled in salute as Captain Otis yelled out an order and the white sails unfurled and caught the ocean winds. Standing on deck, Louis was betrayed back to his childhood, to a desire he had had and then written as a verse for children:

> If I could find a higher tree,
> Farther and farther I should see,
> To where the grown-up river slips
> Into the sea among the ships. . . .

*

THE *Casco* was undermanned and its crew were an odd mixture of nationalities. Two Swedes, a Russian, and a Finn made up the deckhands. The steward-cook was Chinese, who for some reason wished to be known as Japanese. Valentine served as cabin boy. The skipper, unpopular at first with his passengers, and vice versa, inspired the character Nares in *The Wrecker*.

The three women, Fanny, Maggie, and Valentine, were accommodated comfortably in a cabin with a skylight and four portholes, a table screwed to the floor, sofas, and bunks. A small cabin leading off was Lloyd's, and another door opened on a large cabin occupied by Louis.

The first days out were rough on the stomachs of all the Stevenson party. Fanny, Lloyd, and Valentine, stricken with nausea, lay in their bunks too sick to move for three days. Only the seafaring Stevensons, mother and son, were up and about after two. The ship held a course south southwest toward the Marquesas. The climate grew warmer by the day, the sky pure blue. Louis and Lloyd stripped to undershirt and trousers. This was the life! When Fanny and Valentine emerged on deck they were wearing Mother Hubbards or *holuku*, ordered on Belle's advice from Chinatown in San Francisco. Underneath this loose flowing waistless gown they wore a chemise called a *muumuu*. Fanny was delighted with this outfit because she could dispense with a corset. Maggie Stevenson held off for a few days, wearing boots without stockings, which was daring enough. All the others were now barefoot. In her diary Maggie noted, "We are all painfully burned by the sun."

Captain Otis, his patience tried by Fanny making a nuisance of herself, chattering to the man at the wheel, said at last in exasperation, "Don't talk to him today, Mrs. Stevenson, I want him to steer." When someone asked him what he would do if old Mrs. Stevenson were swept overboard he said dryly, "Put it in the log." But he gradually warmed to them all, at any rate as far as his laconic manner would allow, and even changed his mind about the intrepid Fanny, who improved the daily menu by harassing the cook. The old lady won his admiration with her skill at whist, and the Scot whose *Treasure Island* he had little time for seemed a decent sort, levelheaded and reliable. Fanny went on struggling with seasickness, and this continued for their next two years of cruising. All the same she did her bit, mending the clothes of the crew and spooning medicine into them as well as improving the cooking.

Louis rose at dawn to write, or to read Hardy's *The Woodlanders*, and to watch the pilot birds, admiring the way they winged after their wake "stalwartly day after day with no more considerable hope than now and then a piece of orange peel and now and then a pot of floating grease." The Pacific was tremendous, its faint curdle of cloud above, the ship making that slithering slide and rise, that motion of freedom Louis loved. It was liberty, this surging pulsation with all one's cares left behind at the stern. The soul in him, that he had thought extinct after the recent insanity, was not dead after all: the wind and the ocean took it, as it took the ship in its giant cradling swells. But he was no fool when it came to seas; he knew its dangers, its strange prowling storms that pounced out of nowhere. Halfway to the Marquesas they were perilously close to hurricane weather, and "every day for a week or so . . . we have had from three to four squalls. Sailing a ship, even in these so-called fine weather latitudes, may be compared to walking the tightrope."

The women were in the captain's bad books again because his warning to keep the deadlights closed had been forgotten. Suddenly a squall hit them from a cloud, falling "like an armed man upon the *Casco*" before she could be brought to the wind. In a flash the wind spilled out of her sails and the wheelhouse was under water. In the cabins the occupants were flung about and piled up on each other, a waterfall of sea pouring into the cockpit and through the open deadlights. It took ages to dry out the cabins. Then, magically, it was as if only an amazingly calm sea had ever existed, the ladder of square sails above them, white and eager, the ship nimble and palpitating like a quick animal. At the end of each day they went on with their sunset ritual, assembling on deck for that great spectacle of the day, the sunset, the night coming on with its "brilliant phosphorescent water, the air mild." After darkness fell they played cards, taking care to douse the lamps in time for the cabins to cool down before bed.

These were experiences too valuable to waste, and in *The Wrecker* Louis recaptured the vagaries of life at sea, not forgetting Otis and his "rusty humors." The narrator noticed one day that the schooner looked oddly small, the crew standing about silently, eyeing the weather. The Otis-like captain

> Nares . . . afforded me no shadow of a morning salutation. He, too, seemed to observe the behavior of the ship with an intent and anxious scrutiny. What I liked still less, Johnson himself was at the wheel, which he spun busily, often with a visible effort; and as the seas ranged up behind us, black and imminent, he kept casting behind him eyes of animal swiftness, and drawing in his neck between his shoulders, like a man dodging a blow. From these signs I gathered that all was not exactly for the best; and I would have given a good handful of dollars for a plain answer to the questions which I dared not put.

The long sea-gallop of the ship went on for a month in the winy warm sun, with Louis in remarkably good health, as if the triumphant riding of the sea had dimmed his mind and was mending him physically and emotionally as nothing else had done. At five in the morning on July 28 Fanny heard her husband's thrilling cry of "Land!" The pale looming island ahead of them was Nuku Hiva, one of the French-owned Marquesas, the scene of Melville's *Typee*. Louis was perhaps more curious than anyone to experience this first landing on the island with its pricking hills. The first chapter of *In the South Seas* has a wistful description of that never-to-be-repeated first experience. "The first love, the first sunrise, the first South Sea island, are memories apart and touched with a virginity of sense," he wrote. Yet when he came to land he was half reluctant to leave the vast element of the sea, which had washed him so clean of cares like a great mother, so that he was free of the bickering pettiness of past times.

Lawrence, wonderfully illuminating on Melville, calls the Pacific the oldest of oceans. What did he mean? Simply that for him the Pacific was an ocean that had been dreaming with its peoples for thousands of years, and was still trancelike.

Melville, who thought there was something bestial and ugly about his white man's civilization, hailed Nuku Hiva as a sort of Eden. The savages were cannibalistic, but there was "not a single instance of natural deformity." Jack London, repeating Stevenson's voyage in his boat the *Snark* in 1907, found the valley of *Typee* "the abode of death," plagued with white man's diseases, smallpox, tuberculosis, venereal disease and "South Sea elephantiasis."

THE *Casco* dropped anchor in Anaho Bay. Anaho was no more than a group of grass huts and a number of stores around the bay. The party would be there six weeks. A German trader, Regler, the only white man, came out in a canoe with the chief, a fine specimen, tattooed across the face with blue stripes, wearing immaculate linen, who took a delight in shaking hands. A boat followed bearing half a dozen islanders and a cargo of coconuts, oranges, bananas, and baskets for sale. Old Mrs. Stevenson was intrigued, writing in her diary that the natives were "in every state of undress," and yet it didn't seem to matter—they were all tattooed in exquisite patterns. "It really looked quite as if they were wearing open-work silk tights." The chief, Captain Otis, Louis, and Lloyd went ashore. To the islanders the vessel symbolized wealth, and they were not mistaken, though in the belief that Louis was the owner they called him Ona. The ladies were left to cope as best they could with fourteen female natives who came swarming over the *Casco*'s side, led by the chief's wife. Excited by the yacht's luxurious fittings, they posed before the full-length mirror and felt the quality of the drapes. One beauty yanked up her *holuku* and experienced with her bare backside the sensuous feel of the crimson velvet cushions. She then planted kisses on the portrait of Queen Victoria and a framed photograph of Andrew Lang.

Louis, who as always had done his homework, went around on foot and by pony exploring the hinterland, alert to the changes ushered in by colonialization. Three powers, British, American, and German, were currently engaged in exploiting Polynesia among them. From the beginning he identified with the natives in their struggles and drew comparisons between their plight and the history of his own homeland:

> Not much beyond a century has passed since the Scottish Highlanders and islanders were in the same convulsive and transitory states as the Marquesans of today. In both cases an alien authority enforced, the clans disarmed, the chiefs deposed, new customs introduced, and chiefly that fashion of regarding money as the means and object of existence. . . . In one the cherished practice of tattooing, in the other a cherished costume proscribed. . . . The grumbling, the secret ferments, the fears and resentment, the alarms and sudden councils of Marquesan chiefs reminded me continually of the days of Lovat and Struan. . . .

By now he looked wonderfully well, walking vigorously about and deeply tanned. The sun flooded its energy into him. Fanny shared his fascination with everything he saw and noted. In his journal he observed, as the Marquesans sat observing him, that "the eyes of all Polynesians are large, luminous and melting; they are like the eyes of animals and some Italians." These islands were blessedly free of mosquitoes and knew nothing of malaria and other diseases spread by insects. But they had been decimated by smallpox and consequently feared ghosts, since the dead were legion. This catastrophe had lowered their spirits and induced a general fatalism, which they expressed as "The coral waxes, the palm grows, and man departs." Physically they were splendid specimens, the males six feet tall, not given to fat, graceful and swift in movement.

Fanny, glad to be on dry land, evidently found the sight of her mother-in-law hilarious as Maggie took a moonlight stroll on the beach in the company of a gentleman "dressed in a single handkerchief." The old lady was now going around barefoot like the others, and though in photographs of her in the South Seas she is always wearing her widow's cap and looking stiffly proper, she said in a memoir later that she only snatched it up when someone aimed a camera at her. Presbyterian or not, she wondered about the validity of missionary work when the natives seemed content. Their forefathers may have recently celebrated the sacrament of cannibalism, but they could not have been more gentle and generous with their white visitors. "I chose these isles as having the most beastly population, and they are far better and more civilized than we," Louis wrote to Colvin. He would never be mad with hatred of the civilized world like Melville, who had found his savage hosts lovable compared to the ravening wolves of his white brothers on an American whaleship and a man-of-war, but he did feel increasingly "untrue" to civilization, saddened by the dignity of the old chiefs with their rapidly dwindling and culturally confused people. "I know one chief Ko-o-amus, a great cannibal in his day, who ate his enemies even as he walked home from killing 'em, and he is a perfect gentleman. . . ." Gentlemanly manners went a long way with Stevenson.

THE VOYAGE AHEAD to the Tuamotus, in the direction of Tahiti (or Taiti as Louis always wrote it), was a difficult and dangerous one for the *Casco*, as they made first for Hiva-Oa, a distance of ninety miles. Picking their way through islands, some of them uncharted, could be hazardous. Knowing this, Otis took on a pilot and first mate, Golz, and got rid of his drunken cook. His replacement was a real find. Ah Fu had been shipped to the Marquesas as a Chinese bond-boy, along with coolie laborers destined for the plantations. He stayed with the Stevensons for two years, became devoted to Fanny, and was happy to be taught by her.

The *Casco* was considered unsuitable for perilous sailing, though Captain Otis refused later to admit it. They were lost for a day and a night on the run to Hiva-Oa, and woke up one morning at sunrise to see the yacht heading straight for an atoll which, according to the charts, shouldn't have been there. At the same time a vicious squall hit them, washing over the side a consignment of pigs and sheep bought by Louis as gifts. The next forty hours were the most miserable he and his party had known. "We were swung and tossed together all that time like shot in a stage thunderbox. The mate was thrown down and had his head cut open. The captain was sick on deck; the cook sick in the galley. Of all our party only two sat down to dinner. I was one. I own that I felt wretchedly. . . ."

He joined in with the hard-pressed crew, saying later that it was either the risk of a hemorrhage or the certainty of drowning. Anchoring off Hiva-Oa he set off on August 26 riding with a French lay missionary, Michel Blanc, to explore this twenty-two-mile-long island. He came on a lush valley, Atunoa, which Paul Gauguin would find in 1901 at the end of his life. He made the acquaintance of a Marquesan woman whose lover had been a whaling man, and saw a Marquesan maiden bathing modestly in a stream, "in a goyle between the two stepping-stones; and it amused me to see with what alacrity and real alarm she bounded on her many-colored underclothes."

At some point during this voyage to Hiva-Oa with its threat of disaster he experienced an epiphany, swerving back "like a flash of lightning" to his student days in Drummond Street and Rutherford's bar, the one they called the "pump," and it came to him how pathetic his youthful self had been, now he was nearly forty, and how the past came with him everywhere, as it always would, like a touchstone. "And when I remember all I hoped and feared as I picked about Rutherford's in the rain and the east wind; how I feared I should make a mere shipwreck, and yet timidly hoped not; how I feared I should never have a friend, far less a wife, and yet passionately hoped I might; how I hoped (if I did not take to drink) I should possibly write one little book." How much he had written since those days, how narrowly he had escaped a whole variety of shipwrecks! He wished he could inscribe the change on a brass plate and have it fixed to the corner of that dreary little street "for all students to read, poor devils, when their hearts are down."

In a very different mood he wrote like the real adventurer of his dreams to Colvin, telling him to "Get out your big atlas, and imagine a straight line from San Francisco to Anaho, and then imagine a day's sail on 12 August round the eastern end of the island to Tai-o-hae. . . ." How he loved reeling out these extraordinary names. At Tahiti, he promised himself and Colvin, he would cease sailing and do some necessary work ashore. He had filled 130 pages of a diary already: "I did not dream there were such places or such races." He was writing from the lagoon of Fakarava, the main coral atoll of the Tuamotus. The lagoon was huge and calm, like an inland sea. They had dropped anchor opposite the French Residency.

It was soon stiflingly hot on the *Casco*. They rented a primitive little cottage on the horseshoe-shaped island which stretched for eighty miles but was only a few hundred feet wide. The land was so low in the water that Fanny felt unsafe. Recently in a storm the whole strip of coral had been swept by waves.

It was good all the same to stretch one's legs and have space. For once Louis registered some disillusionment with the absurdly named Pacific ("aw-haw-haw"), declaring to Baxter that the sea could be a terrible place on which to attempt to live, "stupefying to the mind and poisonous to the temper," what with the ceaseless motion, "the lack of space, the cruel publicity, the villainous tinned goods, the sailors, the captain, the passengers—but you are amply repaid when you sight an island, and drop anchor in a new world."

They bathed in the warm lagoon, like swimming in warm milk, and cooked breakfast on a battered American stove that had been dumped on the beach. Fanny had pounced on it and put it to use: she had a knack for improvising. In his skimpy white shirt and loose white trousers Louis looked as if he were in pajamas. "I am in the water for hours wading over the knees for shells," he told Colvin like a happy child.

After the heavy heat of the day the gentle breezes of sunset were doubly welcome. Fanny, who could write imaginatively when the mood took her, described the shadows that fell from the coconut leaves in the light of the moon as "so sharply defined that one involuntarily stepped over them." They would have a last dip in the lagoon after dinner, which would be a simple affair, and then loll on mattresses on the veranda. As on other islands, the islanders had been converted to the Catholic faith, but one underpinned by paganism. The sister of one chief, Louis discovered, was an ardent churchgoer who secretly worshiped a shark.

Their one chair was kept vacant for "our invariable visitor." This was often the only European on the island, Mr. Donat, a half-caste. They sat entranced at his feet, thrilled by the stories he had to tell of Tahiti and the Tuamotans. They were often occult, which delighted Fanny. She remembered that one of the stories was of the return of the soul of a dead child, "the soul being wrapped in a leaf and dropped in at the door of the sorrowing parents." Louis recalled some of those tales told by moonlight when he came to write *Island Nights' Entertainments.*

Suddenly Louis's marvelous run of luck ended. The past he had evoked in his memory of Drummond Street came back in the form of one of his ominous colds. It led to a hemorrhage. Fanny turned into a demon of urgency, ordering Otis to sail at once for Tahiti and the nearest doctor. The weather was uncertain and he refused. She raged at him but he was adamant. Did she want to risk grounding them all on a coral reef? The next morning dawned bright and clear, and they got under way.

THE *Casco* reached Tahiti after several days heading southwest and anchored off Papeete, the main town of the Society Islands. Louis was now very ill. The French doctor there predicted death if Louis suffered another flow of blood. The patient nodded stoically, still smoking his hand-rolled cigarettes. He sent for Otis and gave him precise orders about how to proceed if the worst happened. The sardonic captain was impressed, not for the first time, by the composure of this strange, normally excitable writer. He admired his courage, as he did that of his wife. Louis gave Lloyd a sealed letter to be opened if the doctor were right.

Once again he gave death the slip. They moved into a small rented house, scarcely furnished, surrounded by mangoes and situated near the old prison where Melville had once been incarcerated. Louis rarely stirred from it. It was left to his mother to say what they thought of the shantytown of Papeete, and indeed of Tahiti itself. In a letter to her sister she wrote bluntly, "I don't much like Tahiti. It seems to me a sort of halfway house between savage life and civilization, with the drawbacks of both and the advantages of neither." Three years later Gauguin, arriving from France, expressed the same disenchantment. To his jaundiced eye it displayed the worst features of a Europe he had come here to escape—made worse by colonial snobbery and by puerile and grotesque imitation "to the point of caricature." A French judge at the time, reports Gavin Bell in his book following Stevenson's Pacific tracks, observed that "This race is dancing gently into oblivion. Our presence is killing them. So far we have found no way of civilizing the natives other than to make them disappear." The humidity and the squalid beachcombing atmosphere later went into Louis's *The Ebb Tide*. Hearing that the other side of the island was unspoiled and wild, they sailed to Taravo on the south shore. Mosquitoes and more humidity plagued them. Fanny heard good reports of Tautira, a village in the opposite direction from Papeete. It was left to Fanny, setting her "firm Vandegrift chin," to persuade a reluctant Chinese to hire out his wagon and horses for their transport. Captain Otis, who had detected problems with the jibboom of the *Casco*, stayed at Taravo to have it repaired.

The family began a nightmarish journey over sixteen miles in a jolting wagon that weakened Louis even more. The so-called road was crossed by twenty-one streams. Once there at the village the sick man collapsed. A fever raged through him and his lungs were congested. Fanny rented one of the "bird-cage" houses—walls were slithers of bamboo—clustered under coconut palms beside the lagoon. The French gendarme and a Dutch priest were the only white people. As Louis's condition worsened, Fanny wondered if this was the maddest decision she had ever taken. How could she reach a doctor from this place? Could she ever justify her action if he died? What must his mother think of her? There came a knock on the door and a graceful native woman called Moe, speaking excellent English, stood with a plate in her hand. She had heard about the sick foreigner and came with a concoction of her own—white mullet cut in strips, soaked in brine with a sauce of coconut milk, lime juice, and wild red pepper. Moe kept returning with her dish. Several times a day Louis was fed with this remedy. In less than a week he was up and walking again. Fanny fervently believed that Moe had saved her husband's life: it was the kind of magic she was always eager to embrace.

Captain Otis had discovered defects in his yacht calling for urgent repairs. The spars were hollowed out with dry rot. He had no option but to sail around to Papeete for extensive work, probably involving a new mainmast. Meanwhile Louis had recovered well enough to continue *The Master of Ballantrae*. Money was running low, but if desperate he could always contact McClure, who had offered ten thousand dollars for a series of letters from the Pacific. Purely by chance they had landed in a beautiful spot, cradled by the lagoon, behind them a group of mountains rising out of a deep valley and looking uncannily like the Scottish Highlands, the dark crags sometimes half lost in cloud. When they came to explore these highlands, up a narrow road ending on a plateau, they were startled to find green meadows filled with buttercups and daisies. The air was freshened by soft rain, a mist shrouding the island below, and they realized they had escaped the sultry heat down on the shore. Water gushed down, hidden in deep gullies. The smell of grass and trees reminded them of Britain. Louis, gazing up from the lagoon to these heights wrapped mysteriously in cloud, would think of this heaven as "Hans Christian Andersenville."

TAHITI HAS CAUGHT the imagination of so many artists and writers, among them Gauguin, Somerset Maugham, and Rupert Brooke. Melville came hoping to find Chateaubriand's Noble Savage at home, laughing and naked with his golden limbs and his ignorance of original sin. The English writer Robert Keable arrived in the early twentieth century, when the rot had well and truly set in. Like Stevenson he was a martyr to his lungs. Disillusioned or not, he stayed there, because like Stevenson he found Polynesia good for his health. He built a splendid villa of white wood overlooking the lagoon. He wrote bestsellers, notably a religious novel, *Simon and Peter*, a sequel, *Recompense*, and a number of charming Tahitian works, among them *Tahiti, Isle of Dreams*, perhaps his best-known book. He put on record a recollection of Stevenson by a very old man who held his hand when he said he admired the man he called "Master." The old man said, "We shall never see his like again in Tahiti. He is dead and we are dying. None of the Europeans are as he was, whose body, soul and spirit were white as the moon and pure as the stars."

Louis's party, settling in to wait for the return of Otis, were treated royally by the subchief, Ori. The *Casco* had again given them status, with Louis called Ona. Fanny, who liked to boast of her claimed descent from Captain Cook, became known by transliteration as Tapena Tutu. Ori insisted that they move into the chief's house, where Moe was in residence. They were told she was a princess. In her diary Maggie wrote approvingly that "Ori is the finest specimen of the native we have yet seen . . . more like a Roman emperor in bronze," and to cap it all he was a Christian, speaking good French and passable English.

Louis, still treating himself gingerly, took sea baths and sat about quietly, playing his flageolet. He taught himself Tahitian, read Virgil, and wrote down the native songs and legends. Lloyd went around clicking away with his new camera. The villagers swam in the river, children shinning up to the high trees, from where they "threw themselves down into the water like ripe fruit dropping." Louis, saved by a princess, was truly in "Fairyland." The nursery world of his childhood, like other key aspects of his past, could always be recovered.

He took up *The Master of Ballantrae* and worked steadily on it. Anxiety about the need to earn nagged away in his mind, so he took up work to combat it. Several weeks passed like a dream. Was the *Casco* a dream too? Their money, in a sack containing half-dollars and quarters, was dribbling away. A letter arrived from Otis in Papeete:

there was yet more work to be done on the *Casco*. They were literally stranded, their funds virtually gone. Fanny burst into tears. Their host, Ori, said in a solemn speech of great dignity, "You are my brother; all that I have is yours. I know that your food is done, but I can give you plenty of fish and taro. We like you and wish to have you here. Stay where you are till the *Casco* comes. Be happy—*et ne pleurez pas*." Then it was Louis's turn to weep. He had often disconcerted his friends by weeping at emotional moments.

For the next few weeks the family lived on native food. Their staple diet was poi, cooked taro root, pounded and mixed with coconut milk into a sort of porridge. Stormy weather at sea and flooding streams cut them off from any communication with Otis at Papeete. Louis was happy enough eating fish and poi and pig, but the others dreamed of European fare.

The novel that now absorbed him would be his finest complete achievement. At Tautira he reached chapter seven. Frank McLynn's comments on this blackest of all his books are pertinent. The ambiguity runs deep and has multiple layers. James is a Jacobite, his brother Henry a Calvinist. Their clashes are representative of the struggle for the Scottish soul. James would seem to be wholly evil and Henry good, but Louis as we have seen always believed that good and evil were mingled one with the other. "Good and evil braided be," wrote Melville in *Benito Cerena*. *Jekyll and Hyde*, that study of the divided self, is here given over to the influence of Melville, whose book *Pierre, or the Ambiguities*, emphasizes the very point in its title. Overshadowing the writing of Louis's novel was his loss of contact with his cousin Bob, ever a brother to him, because of the estrangement from Bob's sister Katherine. He was turning more and more to Lloyd, who like Louis had lost his father, as if wanting to make a younger brother of him. The writing in *The Master* takes on a power and beauty that he had never achieved before, as in his account of the duel between Henry and James:

> There was no breath stirring; a windless stricture of frost had bound the air; and as he went forth in the shine of the candles, the

blackness was like a roof over our heads. Never a word was said, there was never a sound but the creaking of our steps along the frozen path. The cold of the night fell about me like a bucket of water; I shook as I went with more than terror; but my companions, bare-headed like myself, and fresh from the warm hall, appeared not even conscious of the change.

Still no word came from Otis about the *Casco*. Ori took it on himself to sail around to Papeete with a crew of three to assess the situation. He set off in a raging sea and a storming wind. A week later he was back with provisions and a letter from Otis. The captain was employing a beachcomber who had been a ship's carpenter. The spars he needed could be utilized from those of a wrecked bark, but repairs took forever in the South Seas, and another five weeks passed before he sailed back to collect his passengers. As they prepared to leave, Ori provided a farewell feast. Fanny took over the cooking, stuffing and roasting a pair of fowls and making a pudding. Her mother-in-law recorded the event in her meticulous diary.

Louis had come here as a tourist, but the eight weeks had almost made him into a native. These generous people were his friends, and by "exchanging names" with Ori he became his brother. This man who had fed and cared for them was his first real friend in the South Seas. He would not be forgotten. The party sailed on Christmas Day, with everyone in tears except the captain, who no doubt looked suitably uncomfortable. He was certainly affected, lowering the ensign and firing off a volley of shots with his rifle.

The journey to Hawaii was a horrendous one. It took them thirty exhausting days and they were hit by everything, by "calms, squalls, head sea, waterspouts of rain, hurricane weather all about." By the end they were nearly out of food. Half a month of calms had brought them to a menu of bully beef and hardtack. They crossed the equator on January 13, 1889, and by then the wind was working up to a gale. Because of the shortage of food they had no choice: with the *Casco* double-reefed they ran before the wind. The family were flung to and fro in their cabins "like eggs in a tin." The sky thundered;

there were flashes of lightning. Fanny was seasick most of the way, and Louis maddeningly exhilarated. Nothing was more astonishing than his vivid delight in storms, regardless of danger. This more than anything won Otis's respect. When a hurricane came up astern he had to decide between riding it out or running with it, which could have meant being overwhelmed by a following sea. He put it to the Scotsman, who said without hesitating, "Run for it." Seamen were lashed to their posts, the passengers battened down in their cabins. At one point the pumps gave up the struggle, then started again.

Hawaii was in sight when they were becalmed once more, wallowing for twelve hours off Honolulu, living off the last of the moldy beef and stale biscuits and tormented by visions of hotel meals. At night they saw the lights of Honolulu tantalizingly close, then went to bed hungry, "to rise again in the morning and find ourselves, not nearer, but farther off. . . ." At last a strong breeze filled the *Casco*'s sails and they came in triumphantly past Waikiki as if finishing a race.

If Louis was now seduced by the Pacific, Fanny made her position clear in a graphic and eloquent letter to Mrs. Sitwell. She was no sailor, she admitted, and never would be. Freedom and the mania of sea-wandering that afflicted her husband meant acute discomfort for her. "I hate the sea," she declared, "and am afraid of it, but I love the tropic weather, and the wild people, and to see my two boys so happy. . . . When Louis and I broke loose from the ship and lived alone among the natives I got on very well. It was when I was deathly sea-sick, and the question was put to me by the cook, 'What shall we have for the cabin dinner, what for tomorrow's breakfast, what for lunch? and what about the sailors' food' etc etc. In the midst of heavy and dangerous weather, when I was lying on the floor clutching a basin, down comes the mate with a cracked head, and I must needs cut off the hair matted with blood, wash and dress the wound, and administer restoratives. I do not like being the lady of the yacht, but ashore! O then I felt I was repaid for all."

CHAPTER FOURTEEN

To See These
Dread Creatures Smile

Rumors flying round Honolulu had led Belle to fear that her mother and all hands had gone down in the *Casco*. Then the yacht came around Diamond Head at a fine speed with all sails set. Belle and her boy Austin went out in an open boat for the reunion. "Scooped up out of our boat" they were nearly sent sprawling on the deck. Fanny scolded her daughter for such recklessness, and Louis and Lloyd stood by laughing. It was a happy moment.

The family's arrival at Hawaii was a turning point in more ways than one. Even before disembarking Louis had given in to Fanny's pleas for a respite from life under sail. And time spent in Hawaii would enable him to finish his novel. The problem of the ending remained unsolved, but in a swift burst he rounded off the book anyway. "*The Master* is finished," he wrote, "and I am quite a wreck and do not care for literature." The truth was that he would rather have been at sea. He got down to writing his travel pieces for McClure and drafting yet another version of *The Wrong Box*.

He was considering a book about the ocean, its moods, its iconography, and then Henley came in suddenly on the tide of his

251

thoughts. Not that he had ever been really banished. The loss of a friend was the worst possible outcome for Stevenson, who hated to feel himself alone, though in reality he would always be an internal exile, since exile was his fate. Clearly, from the letter he wrote to Baxter from Honolulu, he longed for a reconciliation: but not with Katherine. Somehow she had become the prime suspect. Of Henley he wrote: "He little understands the harm he did me; but I am sure, upon all our cruise, the number of times we—all of us—longed for his presence would show it was no change of liking for him that we feel. For all that, time has not diminished my fear of him, and I doubt if I ever desire to correspond again. As for Katherine, I had an answer to my appeal, which settled the matter. I do not wish to see her." The idea of Fanny longing with him for Henley's presence is enough to make one blink, but this was perhaps intended as a peace offering for Baxter to hold out.

Captain Otis was paid up and thanked. Valentine also left them. "The usual tale of the maid on board the yacht," Louis commented laconically. She had fallen for one of the seamen. She collected her wages and said farewell to her employers. In the time she had been with them she had become devoted to Louis but was glad to be free of Fanny. She went off to California and eventually married a Mr. A. Brown. Her only son would be named Louis. Years later she was still in touch with Louis by correspondence.

Belle's several years in Honolulu had been a mixture of good and bad. Socially she was a great success, popular with the "royal set" as the vivacious wife of an artist who had secured commissions from King Kalakaua himself. Honolulu, a bustling modern city of twenty thousand inhabitants, already had a telephone system and electric streetlights, installed a year before the Stevensons arrived. The Strongs attended the king's coronation and were soon on friendly terms with the island's aristocracy, a mixture of brown, white, Asian, and half-caste, all splendidly arrayed in bustles, jewels, and feathers.

Joe Strong seemed to go from strength to strength, as did his wife, who taught art in the government school and was commissioned by the king himself to design the Hawaiian flag. Her patron was an imposing figure, tall, well educated, who favored white suits and straw hats decorated with peacock feathers. On state occasions he looked magnificent, if a little extravagant, as if he had stepped out of an opera. His round-the-world trip, which included a visit to Queen Victoria at her Jubilee, had inspired him to model his court on those he had seen in Europe.

It all started to go terribly wrong for Belle after her second child was born. It was surely tempting fate to give it the name of Hervey. One morning on a visit to the island of Maui to stay with friends, she was frightened by her eleven-month-old baby's "drooping head and languid eyes." A doctor came after a ride of forty miles and told Belle to let her child sleep. "My baby slept, but he never woke again."

Catastrophes rarely come singly. Joe Strong, always a worry with his hard drinking and partying, became bored with his painting one fine day and took himself off for a day's fishing off Waikiki Beach. His bare right arm, badly sunburned as he lay asleep, led to complications. He declined physically and emotionally, depressed by the constant pain and unable to work. Before long he broke down completely and was bundled off to a sanatorium. Belle, opening Joe's pistol box one day, discovered a mass of unpaid bills. They had always lived fecklessly: now she found herself faced with the rent and the grocer, in debt as well for carriage hire, artist's materials, and meals at restaurants.

Louis stepped in to help as soon as he heard. He would be dipping into his pockets for some time to come. Belle, obliged to cut down drastically on her spending, started dancing classes for children and obtained commissions from kindly friends to draw place cards and novelties. Enterprising as her mother, she even tried her hand at journalism, writing the society news column and occasional articles for the *Honolulu Advertiser*. Someone gave her the loan of a carriage and she drove out to visit her husband. He grew worse, then slowly better. At last the phoenixlike Joe rose up, "completely recovered and his mind at peace."

This recovery had taken place when the Stevensons were still at sea. Just before Fanny and her entourage arrived in port, King

Kalakaua had sent the rejuvenated Joe Strong on a journey to Samoa as the official artist with a royal delegation. Their mission was to lay the foundations for a federation of the various Pacific islands. "The *opéra bouffe* embassy was a bibulous farce," writes Fanny's biographer, but the episode undoubtedly played a part in reviving Louis's interest in Samoa. Kalakaua, the "merry monarch," had taken it upon himself to be a Hawaiian revivalist. He was a delightful character, and the Stevensons would be much involved with him. He composed the national anthem and revived the hula, banned by successive waves of missionaries who saw it as suggestive.

Lloyd, the beloved acolyte egged on by his mother to build on his small talent, was soon bashing away at his typewriter to express his distaste for the gossip denigrating the much maligned king: "From the stories told of him one would picture a grotesque savage who was constantly drunk; a sort of Sambo in ridiculous uniforms, whose antics and vices became so intolerable that finally a long-suffering community had to sweep him away. He was, on the contrary, a highly educated man, with an air of extreme distinction and a most winning graciousness and charm, who would have been at ease in any court in Europe. . . . He was the greatest gentleman I have ever known." This was so much in the spirit of Louis that his stepfather might have mistaken it for his own. And indeed Lloyd never managed to find a distinctive voice.

Introduced by Belle to the imposing monarch, Louis and Kalakaua took to each other at once. The king quickly reached for champagne, a taste for which he had acquired in Europe, and told the famous writer how he had read and enjoyed *Treasure Island* and *Dr. Jekyll*. Through their talks, accompanied by convivial boozing, Louis began to familiarize himself with the tangled web of Pacific politics. Samoa cropped up again as the fulcrum around which the king's struggles for nationalism turned, with a predatory America waiting in the wings.

Accumulated mail had been waiting for them at Honolulu. Now they would find out if they were broke or not. "No money, and not one word as to money," Louis wrote in despair to Baxter, "which leaves me in a fine uncertainty and quite penniless on these isles. . . ." There was no need for alarm: *The Master of Ballantrae* was being serialized in its unfinished state by McClure, and his other books were selling well. Communication was the only problem.

Honolulu with its electricity, commercialization, and "awful whites" was not for him. Like many Victorians he had come to think of his century as one of the wickedest ever, and was prepared to speak up for embattled traditional values. He had stumbled onto something else, and turned away from that blight of nineteenth-century capitalism called civilized society. "Our cities," wrote Ruskin in *Unto This Last*, "are a wilderness of spinning wheels . . . yet the people have not clothes. We have blackened every leaf of English greenwood with ashes, and the people die of cold; our harbors are a forest of merchant ships, and the people die of hunger."

It must have been Fanny who took action, finding them a house to rent at the eastern end of Waikiki Beach. Four miles out of the city, it was a quiet settlement of twenty or so people, no more than a rural hamlet by a coral sand beach. To reach the house one went over a causeway and through a garden with oleander, scarlet hibiscus, and a huge *hau* tree. The king who had befriended them was a frequent guest. The Strongs came out on weekends. They were still being bailed out by Louis, but Joe, never embarrassed by financial dependence, would go into his act as an artist, setting up his easel and doing his best to compete creatively. Louis and Fanny were quickly besieged by callers who wanted to meet the author. Before long they were being informed by Fanny that they had a day when they "received." Belle noticed how proficient her mother was at breaking up the party with an announcement that her husband was fatigued. Her habit of riding roughshod over situations of which she disapproved often ran counter to Louis's instinctive courtesy and his almost feminine gentleness. Eventually he took evasive action by installing himself in a shack nearby that was papered with old newspapers. "It is a grim little shanty," he reported in a letter. "Cobwebs bedeck it; friendly mice inhabit its recesses; the mailed cockroach walks upon the wall. . . ." At least these residents did not ask anything of him or disturb him, gregarious though he was when he was sick of writing.

His plan to write a book about their Pacific experiences led to arguments with Fanny, who wrote to Colvin expressing her dismay. Dealing with "Lou-us" was, she said, like managing an overbred horse; and went on to say with her usual lack of modesty that she could write a book herself "that the whole world would jump at. . . ." Colvin, though he may well have wrinkled his nose at this, would, she knew, lend a sympathetic ear to her complaint. He still considered the whole Pacific adventure foolhardy in the extreme, the "drinking with dusky majesties" and the "isolation from anything like equals." Louis, she wrote, "has the most enchanting material that any one ever had in the whole world for his book, and I am afraid he is going to spoil it all. He has taken into his Scotch-Stevenson head that a stern duty lies before him, and that his book must be a sort of scientific and historical, impersonal thing, comparing the different languages (of which he knows nothing really) and the different peoples. I am going to ask you to throw the weight of your influence as heavily as possible in the scales with me. . . ."

None of this would wash with Louis, who went on stubbornly to write it with no encouragement from anyone. He was revising it when he died. *In the South Seas* was published posthumously in 1896.

One happy outcome of his stay in Hawaii was his friendship with Princess Kaiulani, a sweet creature of thirteen who was the half-caste daughter of Archibald Cleghorn—a former merchant from Edinburgh—and a sister of Kalakaua. This sister had died the year before Louis arrived. The two Scots with Edinburgh in common became friends. The writer far from home would walk over to Cleghorn's estate on the edge of Waikiki and talk by the hour to the princess and her father. Gavin Bell came across a booklet in a Honolulu bookshop when he was there in 1993: it was called *Stevenson: Poet in Paradise*. Inside were photographs of Kaiulani as a flowerlike child and as a young woman in Victorian dress and feathered hat, with long black hair and large dark eyes, one squinting slightly. Louis was enchanted by her. He wrote a poem in her autograph album which she discovered when she sailed to England for a boarding school education:

> Forth from her land to mine she goes,
> The island maid, the island rose,
> Light of heart and bright of face:
> The daughter of a double race.
> Her islands here, in Southern sun
> Shall mourn their Kaiulani gone,
> And I, in her dear banyan shade
> Look vainly for my little maid.
>
> But our Scots islands far away
> Shall glitter with unwonted day
> And cast for once their tempests by
> To smile in Kaiulani's eye.

He didn't see her again. She died tragically of pneumonia at the age of twenty-three. The monarchy was overthrown in 1893 in a republican *coup* staged by white businessmen. Louis came on a visit to Hawaii from Samoa a few months after the *coup*. He shook Cleghorn's hand on leaving and said, "Now, Cleghorn, if I can be of any service to the royalist cause, just drop me a line and I will come right back here." But the cause was lost and Louis had only a year to live. His quixotic gesture was simply that. More than one writer has had dreams of breaking out of literature into a life of action, and in a small way, unforeseen but entirely honorable, Louis would find himself doing so in Samoa. In 1898 the Hawaiian Islands were annexed by the United States.

THE STEVENSON FAMILY had been six months at Waikiki, and though it was agreed that they should move on, their plans were confused. Louis told one friend that he would be in England soon, then proposed a meeting with Baxter in Madeira. Maggie Stevenson left in

May to visit a sick sister in Scotland, under the impression that her son would follow the next year. Finally Louis, Fanny, Lloyd, and Ah Fu knew where they were bound. There had been much heated discussion, Louis even talking wildly of buying an island of their own. One day he came back in high excitement from Honolulu, shouting out before he had even jumped down from his horse, "I've chartered a schooner: I arranged the details and signed the charter as she was casting off. . . ."

The *Equator*, a schooner of sixty-four tons, was due back from San Francisco in a month to pick up the Stevensons. Her first port of call would be the Gilbert Islands, and she would be under the command of Captain Reid, a Scotsman. She would ply for trade in Micronesia, and while the crew loaded copra the party could go ashore and explore. Louis had put down his lump sum for a cruise lasting four months with the option to renew, and with additional stops if required. How Fanny responded initially to the prospect is unclear, but she wrote with admirable fortitude to Mrs. Sitwell that it was a pity to return to England before Louis's health was on a firm footing, "and also a pity not to see all that we can see quite easily. . . ." Nevertheless there was that hateful sea to contend with. As for the rest, she had no trouble coping with rough surroundings, and she could shoot pretty well if necessary. There was no doubting her spirit. When it came to it she could rise to an occasion.

Before they left, with a month of waiting on his hands, Louis, who had a journalist's nose for copy, decided he would visit the leper colony on the island of Molokai. He also wanted to set foot on Big Island, confusingly also named Hawaii. This was where Captain Cook had been murdered more than a century before. If Louis needed an excuse, it would have been that he was gathering material for the McClure "Letters."

He was impelled by more than journalistic curiosity and the desire to net a newsworthy story. He had heard stories, some of them defamatory, of the priest there, Father Damien, and wanted to establish the truth for himself. Fanny, in her preface to *Lay Morals*, recalled something that happened while they were at Anaho. A native man stepped out from under some coconut trees and was

> regarding us hesitatingly, as though fearful of intruding. My husband waved an invitation to the stranger to join us, offering his cigarette to the man in the island fashion. The cigarette was accepted, and, after a puff or two, courteously passed back again. . . . The hand that held it was the maimed hand of a leper. To my consternation my husband took the cigarette and smoked it out.

After another incident with a leprous girl, and after seeing leprosy in other places, he said more than once, Fanny remembered, that he must see Molokai for himself. He had to obtain permission, but after tedious delays and difficulties he was on his way at last to the place on Big Island marked on the map as "collecting point." He saw a little girl in a red dress waiting for shipment to Molokai, around her a small group of weeping relatives. He was deeply upset. "The thought of the girl so early separated from her fellows—the look of her lying there covered from eyesight, like an untimely birth—perhaps most of all the penetrating note of the lament—subdued my courage utterly."

He wanted to turn back, but this was not something he ever did. As he approached the cliffs on the steamship *Kilauea Hau* with only a group of Franciscan sisters for company, he tried to hold on to his resolve. His dispatch to the *New York Sun* could hardly have been more graphic: "In the chronicle of man, there is perhaps no more melancholy landing than this of the leper immigrants among the ruined houses and dead harvests of Molokai . . . when we drew near the landing-stairs and saw them thronged with the disordered images of God, horror and cowardice worked in the marrow of my bones."

The first victims had been dumped on this grim shore in January 1866. Medical assistance in those days was nonexistent, and there was no adequate shelter. It became a hellhole and remained one until the coming of a young Belgian priest in 1873. Working tirelessly he created an orderly colony and gave its unfortunates a measure of dignity. Louis arrived there only three weeks after Father Damien died of the disease. He was forty-nine.

The lonely writer wandered for an hour and calmed down. Typically he was ashamed of his uselessness and grateful for the experience. "All horror was quite gone from me," his dispatch continued. "To see these dread creatures smile and look happy was beautiful. On my way through Kalaupapa I was exchanging cheerful alohas with the patients coming galloping over on their horses; I was stopping to gossip at house-doors; I was happy, only ashamed of myself that I was here for no good." Jack London would visit the place years later: he saw lepers taking part in horse and donkey races in what seemed to him a "happy colony." True, there were horrors, but then the disease itself was horrible. In his book *The Cruise of the Snark*, London concluded that lepers in the settlement were far better off than lepers having to live like criminals outside.

Louis, as well as investigating conditions in the colony, was eager to hear about Damien firsthand and form a picture of him. He talked freely to the lepers and put up with the Catholicism, as he had done long ago at the monastery in the Cévennes. He soon came to the conclusion that if Damien had been a hero, he was a very human one. He presented Colvin with a figure stripped of his own illusions: "He was a European peasant, dirty, bigoted, untruthful, unwise, tricky, but superb with generosity, residual candor and fundamental good humor." In other words he was an ordinary fallible human being, "with all the grime and paltriness of mankind, but a saint and hero all the more for that."

His authenticity was clearly not in doubt as far as Louis was concerned. A Protestant, the Reverend C. M. Hyde of Honolulu, thought differently. Catholics had proposed erecting a monument to Damien's heroism, and Hyde had written a letter to the press objecting to the idea, vilifying Damien as a man riddled with vice, though without saying so directly. The implication was that the priest took leprous women into his bed. Louis had heard such stories but couldn't believe they would appear in print. He was in Samoa when the attack was made public. Catholic and Protestant missionaries had always been in conflict, and this affair was sectarian in origin. Louis, incensed, found the letter "too damnable for belief," but there it was. His passionate "An Open Letter to the Reverend Dr. Hyde of Honolulu" pulled no punches. He waded into Hyde's mealymouthed allegations for their hypocrisy, without taking issue on their accuracy or otherwise. He was back on his old theme of ambivalence and duality, his old conviction that "bad men can do good things, and vice versa." All ready to rush into print, he consulted his family first on a step which might well land them in trouble legally. Fanny, who always relished a fight, cried, "Print it! Publish it!" A lawyer by the name of Moses advised against publication in its present form, presumably because it was actionable. This was wise counsel, and the advocate in Louis recognized the fact. Instead he had his "Open Letter" privately printed. A native newspaper in Honolulu printed a translation, and the proceeds of its sale as a pamphlet went to the lepers of Molokai. Fanny in her preface to *Lay Morals* had the last word: "Father Damien was vindicated by a stranger, a man of another country and another religion from his own."

What had brought on his invective even more than his hatred of religious cant and false piety was the plight of the lepers and his memory of his first night in the settlement. Nothing he had written or would write is more moving than his account of it in his dispatch to the *New York Sun*. The feeling of isolation had bitten deeply into him as he returned at night to a vacant house, near a hospital and an old store. He sat by his lamp and stared at solitary walls, unable to shake off the sights of pain "in a land of disease and disfigurement, bright examples of fortitude and kindness, moral beauty, physical horrors, intimately knit. He must be a man very little impressionable if he recall not these hours with an especial poignancy; he must be a man either very virtuous or very dull, if they were not hours of self-review and vain aspiration after good."

He kept reliving the eight days he had spent there, as if unable to shake off a haunting, recurring dream. While there he had taken no precautions. How could he, when the nuns took none? He refused to wear gloves, sitting with the men and living as they did, playing cards with them. He attended little concerts at the Bishop home for the girls, applauded the plays they put on in the evenings, and instructed them in the use of a croquet set someone had donated. On the day of his departure he was suddenly seized with panic. He had been issued an entry pass, but the captain of the steamer became officious, insisting on one he did not have, one that allowed him to leave the settlement. His mouth full of fear, Louis persuaded the captain to relent. He had not known till then how he had longed for deliverance. Back in Honolulu he bought a piano and had it shipped to the girls' home. How magnanimous! In his heart he knew the truth. He was cravenly saying thank you to the gods for letting him go, for not condemning him to be one of them.

AS THEY WAITED for the return of the *Equator*, due in June, it looked as if their party would include Joe Strong as well as Ah Fu. A pantomime of indecision on all sides developed. Was he coming with them or wasn't he? The idea it appears was to get him away from his "weaknesses," especially since Belle had more or less washed her hands of him. "After his illness," she wrote, "he was never the same again. . . . He and I began to get on each other's nerves more and more, till it was positive relief to see him sail away. . . . I felt that I didn't have to worry about him any more."

That sounds straightforward enough. The truth was that Fanny had begun having second thoughts. Were they being taken for a ride by this man yet again? She distrusted him instinctively, confiding to Mrs. Sitwell that she and her husband had had an "unpleasantness" with Joe. Clearly he wanted to come with them, but he was his own worst enemy, "using carriages while Louis walked." She advised brutal frankness, which her husband was to administer. Joe was told that if he came he would be spending no money without permission, that "abject obedience was to be expected of him," and so forth. Insulted, he walked away from them and their orders. Being Joe, he was soon back, having thought better of the alternatives. He put on his best performance to date, employing a degree of restraint and submission cleverly aimed at a side of Louis he knew only too well. They had given him the chance of a lifetime and he had thrown it back in their faces, they said. He hung his head and agreed. They had never seen him so contrite, never heard him so grateful for their kindness and generosity. He had sunk pretty low in his time, and now he sank lower, kissing them both and walking away in a fine imitation of a man accepting his fate. "Had he been maudlin and wept . . . or tried to defend himself, I should have still held out against him," declared Fanny. But he didn't, and the strategy worked. He had studied his benefactors at close quarters for three months. They went after him and offered him another chance.

Next they had a lawyer draw up a paper for him to sign, placing him and his affairs absolutely in their hands. He signed it gladly. What was one more piece of paper? As for Belle, it was her intention to carry on living in Honolulu with Austin, her son, who was too young in any case to cruise the Pacific, and if she had gone she would have had to leave him in a boarding school. Discussions went round and round. One afternoon she was asked to Louis's cottage, where he put forward a plan agreed to by her mother. Leaving her alone and at the mercy of friends who were a dubious influence was out of the question. They had bought tickets on the *Mariposa* for her and Austin to sail to Sydney, Australia, all expenses paid. They had even chosen her accommodations. Every month she would be able to draw on the bankers Towne and Company for a fixed sum. Belle put up a wavering resistance: she was beginning to realize how thoroughly her future had been organized. "What happens then?" she asked. What was she supposed to do in Australia? "Wait till called for," her stepfather said.

So it was settled, in so far as anything to do with the Stevenson ménage was ever settled. They took forty-eight hours to pack up their possessions: a barrel of sauerkraut, another of salt onions, a bag of coconuts, their native attire, tobacco, fishhooks, and items for trading purposes such as red combs, trinkets, and Turkey red calicoes. They also stowed a hand organ, photograph and painting materials, and their magic lantern. All this was loaded onto a whaleboat and taken out to the *Equator*, together with assorted musical instruments belonging to each of them. Lloyd had a taro-patch fiddle, a kind of native banjo. Louis was never parted from his flageolet, and Joe carried his accordion. Fanny had no ear for music, but not to be outdone, lugged along a guitar.

They left on June 24, 1889. The *Honolulu Advertiser* duly announced the event to its readers, wishing the party well and adding wryly: "It is to be hoped that Mr. Stevenson will not fall victim to native spears; but in his present state of bodily health, perhaps the temptation to kill him may not be very strong." Their first destination was the Gilbert Islands. Only days before they sailed they made the acquaintance of two Belgians who asked if they could join the company. Something told Louis to turn them down, or perhaps it was Fanny with her second sight. A year or two later he heard that the two were brigands who specialized in signing on as hands on schooners, then poisoning everyone and selling the vessel. It was a tale straight out of *Treasure Island*.

CHAPTER FIFTEEN

It Does Make You Feel Well

*I*N HER MEMOIRS Fanny intimated that after ten days at sea on the *Equator* her husband talked of making his home "for ever" in the islands. He may well have talked about it, but his immediate plan or dream was a freebooting life as an island trader on a schooner of his own. He would buy the vessel with money generated by *The Wrecker*, another of his dubious collaborations with Lloyd. He dreamed of making a fortune by trading, giving up the endless grind of churning out books. He'd call his dream schooner the *Northern Light*, and Captain Denny Reid would be his skipper. Reid, astonishingly youthful but a fine sailor, whose great exploit was sailing the *Equator* through the terrible hurricane in March of that year, was described by Fanny as "a small fiery Scots-Irishman." Louis's grand plan was to sell everything from sewing machines, revolvers, and calico to cheap trinkets, and also trade in copra.

Lloyd was all for the idea. Fanny pulled a disbelieving face. Anyone less like a trader than Louis would be hard to imagine. He was between novels, and, if he was honest, vastly enjoying himself. The madcap venture remained a fantasy, like many of his wilder schemes. The $15,000 needed for the schooner soon accumulated, but by then he had other uses for it. His own words, written so long ago in his "Apology for Idlers," were coming home to roost: "There is no duty we so much underrate as the duty of being happy. By being happy, we sow anonymous benefits upon the world, which remain unknown even to ourselves. . . ."

He was answering once more the call of the nomad within him. The literary world represented by Henley and Colvin had never seemed more paltry. Like Chekhov a year later, about to turn his back on literature and travel across Siberia, Louis wanted to engage in serious work unconnected with art, namely his projected volume of anthropology *In the South Seas*. Collecting material for it fulfilled his desire for adventure "such as befell the great explorers." He would not have spoken explicitly like Chekhov of "the strange disease of modern life," but by wanting to live with a good conscience among unspoiled happy peoples he was making his own solitary protest.

The Wrecker had its origin in the predicament of sailors who had been dumped penniless on the wharf at Honolulu after being picked up by a passing vessel. Their wrecked ship, the *Wandering Minstrel*, was meant to be fishing for sharks, but there must have been another reason for the wages of the seamen being so high, as they apparently were. During the voyage out on the *Equator* he and Lloyd put their heads together with the aim of making fiction of the tale. It was never meant to be anything other than a good yarn. It meandered all over the place, made use of autobiographical recollections of Paris and Edinburgh, and though it had fine stuff in certain passages, the story as a whole fails to convince. All the same Scribner's gave him fifteen thousand dollars for the novel.

At sea on the *Equator* they were lucky with a long spell of fine weather, of bright days and clear moonlit nights. The trading schooner was cramped but new and clean. Fanny was grateful to be free of seasickness, not in any sense enamored of the ocean as Louis always was but feeling "that the sea belonged to us and we to the sea." Drawing near to the equator in the Gilberts, still the days were idyllic. They were among low flat islands looking rather featureless, inhabited by Micronesians, who were shorter in stature than the Polynesians, darker too, and with different languages. The travelers were as remote here as Louis could have wished, with no communication with the outside world and no mail delivery. At Nutaritari they waded ashore while the *Equator* went off to barter for copra.

Their timing was unfortunate. American influence being strong, the whole island was on a ten-day binge drunkenly celebrating the Fourth of July. In the primitive little town of thatched huts, two American traders were about to barricade their bars. King Tebureimoa had been persuaded by them to lift the taboo on alcohol, and was now as drunk as his wives, his court, and his subjects. Fanny's account rings with contempt for this "besotted, dull, obese man." Louis went even further: this brutish despot was grotesque, wearing pajamas "which sorrowfully misbecame his bulk; his nose was hooked and cruel . . . he seemed at once oppressed with drowsiness and held awake by apprehension."

The Stevensons retreated to the bungalow of the Hawaiian missionary and his wife, who happened to be away. Renting the place, they decided to sit it out. It was a dangerous situation, and indeed they had no choice: it would be a month before the *Equator* returned to take them on their way. They had brought revolvers ashore with them, and to bolster their shaky confidence and at the same time discourage ugly-looking tottering marauders they had shooting practice sessions on the beach, with Fanny taking her turn. Her prowess impressed everyone, and there were plenty of empty bottles to aim at. At last things calmed down as the villagers nursed their almighty hangovers.

For the first and only time they had been in real danger. It had been a degrading spectacle, and for the searcher after paradise a sobering one. His imagination could come to terms with crime, pestilence, and death, "but it instinctively rejects . . . whatever shall call up the image of our race upon its lowest terms, as the partner of beasts, beastly itself, dwelling pell-mell and hugger-mugger, hairy man with hairy woman in the caves of old. And yet to be just to the barbarous islanders we must not forget the slums and dens of our own cities; I must not forget that I have passed dinnerward through Soho and seen that which cured me of my dinner."

He now felt free to wander about and see what he had come to see. Coming on a silent village half buried in trees he had the experience of being in that dream of immemorial centuries evoked by Lawrence in his essay on Melville: "It must once have been a vast basin of soft, lotus-warm civilization, the Pacific," Lawrence mused, a traveler himself over this same ocean. "And now the waters are blue and ghostly with the end of immemorial peoples. And phantom-like the islands rise out of it, illusions of the glamorous Stone Age."

Before he left, Louis was subjected to an excruciating Sunday service. He sat on a hard chair in unbearable heat listening to the worst singing he had ever heard. The penitent natives groaned happily on the green, they moaned and yawned "upon a singing note, as you may sometimes hear when a dog has reached the tragic bitterest of boredom." He had to admit he felt sympathy with the preacher at his weekly task of "flogging a dead horse and blowing a cold fire. . . ."

They did however chalk up one undoubted success with Louis's magic lantern, an early version of the slide projector. The church was packed for the white wizard's picture show. Ah Fu ground out a strange music on the hand organ for accompaniment, the pictures shone and vanished on the screen. Each time a new image appeared there would be a hush, a whisper, a shuddering rustle, "and a chorus of small cries among the crowd."

At last the visitors were lifted off the island by the returned *Equator*, delayed by three weeks, and headed for their next port of call, Apemama. They were curious to meet King Tembinoka, a tyrant who held sway over a triple-island kingdom in the Gilberts. Gruesome legends attached to his name. They moored in the lagoon and waited with a mixture of fascination and trepidation their inspection by this "Napoleon of the Gilberts." There had been feverish activity below deck to make their cabins presentable before the sovereign came aboard. Louis was to describe him vividly in *The South Seas*. Tembinoka's idea of fashionable attire was extraordinary. His voice, shrill and powerful, had a note like a seabird's. He favored naval uniforms, alternating these with women's frocks, in which he looked "ominous and weird beyond belief." He also wore costumes of his own design, sometimes of green velvet, sometimes cardinal red silk. Now and then he appeared decked out in a frock coat, red flannel drawers, a top hat, or a sunbonnet. Nevertheless, he somehow managed to avoid looking ridiculous. His interests ranged over politics, history, and the Western world. He wrote poetry, he told Louis, all about "sweethearts, and trees, and the sea—and no true, all-the-same lie."

Boarding the *Equator* he went on a majestic tour of inspection. He spotted Fanny's dressing-case and said he must buy it. They told him no, it was not for sale, and finally presented it to him as a gift. Discomforted, he admitted, "I shamed." This little incident raised the white chief's status immensely. Tembinoka was impressed too by the photograph he saw of Louis with King Kalakaua of Hawaii. All the same he held off stubbornly for two days before granting them permission to stay.

Once they were ashore he allocated a place for them to live and provided for houses to be erected. Lloyd's account of this operation, as he studied the art of writing in his desultory fashion, is one of the funniest things he ever wrote. An Apemama house, he explained, was a sort of giant clothes basket with a peaked roof, standing on stilts about a yard high. The king directed his laborers by firing his Winchester over the heads of anyone who seemed backward. With a dozen pairs of legs under this "house" you could steer it to any spot you liked. "We started with four such houses and forty-eight pairs of legs. . . . We settled near a grove of palms. . . . Then a large shed came staggering in that was to serve as our dining room, and a smaller shed by way of a kitchen. . . ." The king added a final touch by walking a circle of taboo around the settlement to ward off theft and curiosity.

If the king was bizarre, so was his thatched palace. It overflowed with old clocks, weapons, clothing, and heaps of rusting and mildewed gadgets, including dozens of sewing machines—so many that he used them as anchors for his fleet of fishing boats. Commenting on this mania for material goods, Louis wrote, "He is possessed by the seven devils of the collector. He hears a thing spoken of, and a shadow comes on his face. 'I think I no got him,' he will say, and the treasures he has seem worthless in comparison."

The Stevensons called their cluster of houses Equator Town. Every evening an old man they named Uncle Barker, because his speech reminded them of a barking dog, brought them fresh coconuts for drinking. They were given several slaves, three of them playful young girls who spent most of their time frolicking in the pool. A kind of peace descended: alas, so did a plague of flies and mosquitoes. Fanny, ever resourceful, made an enormous net of mesh, under which they took their meals in the dining shed and did their writing. When Louis developed a cold, the king sent a shaman to cure him. "The effect was marred by the levity of the magician, entertaining his patient with small talk like an affable dentist, and by the incongruous presence of Mr. Osbourne with a camera. As for my cold, it was neither better nor worse." The flummery might work in fiction, he added skeptically, but they managed these things better in "the desert place" where Aladdin lived.

Tembinoka had a fearsome reputation, but Louis came to see him as a benevolent dictator. He never saw him angry and was impressed by a man he regarded as a gentleman and a scholar. For all his comic opera appearance he was no fool and made sure he learned as much as he could from Stevenson. His interests covered etiquette, government, law, the police, money, and medicine. He admired Fanny, telling Louis, "She good; look pretty; plenty chench [sense]." Flattered by his regard, she designed a flag for his kingdom.

By the time the *Equator* came to take them on to Samoa, Louis and the king were enjoying a relationship of affection and mutual respect. The tough old king descended into melancholy at the thought of saying farewell. Losing Louis was like losing his brother, he told Fanny. After Louis and Fanny retired to bed he said he wanted to talk to Lloyd, patting the mat beside him. Overcome with emotion he managed to say:

I very sorry you go. Miss Stlevens he good man, woman he good man, boy he good man; all good man. Woman he smart all the same man. My woman (glancing towards his wives) he good woman, no very smart. I think Miss Stlevens he big chiep all same cap'n man-o'-wa'. I think Miss Stlevens he rich man all the same me. All go schoona. I very sorry. . . . You no see King cry before. King all the same man: feel bad, he cry. I very sorry.

UNDER WAY AGAIN, the vague plan was to sail to Samoa and transfer to the mail steamer bound for Sydney. They would then return by fits and starts to Britain for the visit Louis had been promising himself. None of them were in great shape physically—the depleted diet on Butaritari had seen to that. In a nostalgic mood Louis would speak rapturously of being back in London again: "I can hear the rattle of the hansom up Endell Street and see the gates swing back, and feel myself out upon the Monument steps—Hosanna home again." His cheerful good faith would not have been shared by his wife, whose mistrust of literary London and the "Shepherd's Bush gang" remained unchanged.

The voyage of twenty-six days to Samoa was anything but comfortable. The boiling heat made the floor of their cabins almost impossible to stand on in bare feet, and proper sleep was virtually hopeless. The *Equator* stank with the reek of fermented copra, which gave off a disgusting steam. Lice were everywhere, and huge cockroaches. The decks had buckled in the heat, and when the rain descended Fanny's berth was directly under a leak. Ah Fu, devoted to her, shifted her bedding into the little galley, where she tried to sleep in her clothes beneath an umbrella he had rigged up. The boat ran aground once, and once narrowly missed a reef. A sudden violent squall that sprang at them out of nowhere caught the *Equator* fully rigged, sent it leaping and reeling like a wild thing, and snapped the fore topmast. It was Ah Fu who climbed heroically to the top of the galley and sawed through the rope that freed the rigging. Louis was cured, if temporarily, of his sea fever: the voyage had put a stop to his writing. His bad temper was vented on Ah Fu when the signal hal-yard was missing and Louis learned that the cook had presented it to Fanny, who had taken a liking to it.

As they approached Samoa in early December he wrote to tell his mother that Fanny had withstood the rigors of what would be his final cruise wonderfully well. He would find it very hard to impose another on her. His own general health had stood up well, "though I am now done for lack of green food. Joe is, I fear, really ill, and Lloyd has had bad sores on his leg." He paid tribute to Fanny's gutsy char-acter in a poem which would go into his *Songs of Travel*:

> To My Wife
> Trusty, dusky, vivid, true,
> With eyes of gold and bramble-dew,
> Steel-true and blade-straight
> The great artificer
> Made my mate.
>
> Honor, anger, valor, fire;
> A love that life could never tire,
> Death quench or evil stir,
> The mighty master gave to her.
>
> Teacher, tender, comrade, wife,
> A fellow-farer true through life,
> Heart-whole and soul-free
> The August Father
> Gave to me.

Heartfelt though this surely was, the mate he honored could seem and sound like an enemy when his ambitions for a "prose-epic" came up, a work that would confront the "unjust (yet I can see the in-evitable) extinction of the Polynesian islanders by our shabby civi-lization," as he outlined it to a Honolulu editor a year before his death. Earlier he was telling a skeptical Colvin that "nobody has had such stuff, such wild stories, such beautiful scenes, such singular intimacies, such manners and traditions, so incredible a mixture of the beautiful and horrible, the savage and the civilized." This was how he envisaged *In the South Seas*. Though he never abandoned his grand scheme for it, he reined in his ambition in the face of Fanny's adamant objections, "and I prefer her peace of mind to my ideas." It would lie unpublished in its truncated form until after his death.

Fanny had an ally in McClure when it came to this vexed issue, not to mention Colvin. The copy sent to McClure and the *New York Sun* was edited harshly. It was not what they had been expecting, even though Louis had warned them that he would be sending book extracts, not letters as such. Fanny and her husband clashed repeatedly on the subject. She confided to Mrs. Sitwell that "He says I do not take the broad view of the artist, but hold the cheap opinions of the general public that a book must be interesting. How I do long for a little wholesome monumental correction to be applied to the Scotch side of Louis's artistic temperament." She should have learned by now that he was never going to change.

On December 7, 1889, they reached Samoa, landing at Apia on the island of Upolu. Though of course he was not to know it, he had come to his final destination, a place he called "beautiful beyond dreams." By an extraordinary fluke he had arrived at the island he had heard his father's New Zealand visitor talking about in that other existence at Heriot Row. The American trader who boarded the schooner was a man named Harry J. Moors, and the man who confronted him was a strange fellow who looked thirty but was nine years older. His skin was sallow, his moustache scraggly, and his hair falling around his neck gave him the appearance of an artist. He was barefoot and wore a thin calico shirt, baggy trousers, and a white yachting cap with a sharp peak. As so many others had been, Moors was struck by his brown, strangely bright eyes that seemed to dive into you. He didn't need to be told that the stranger was in poor health but was puzzled by his manner: he seemed intensely nervous, restless, excitable. Moors brought him ashore, and Louis began to walk in so lively a fashion that it was almost eccentric. "He could not stand still."

On the front at Apia the party was noticed by the Reverend W. E. Clarke of the London Missionary Society. He spotted a woman in a print gown, large gold crescent earrings, a Gilbert Islands hat of plaited straw decorated with a wreath of small shells, a scarlet silk scarf round her neck, and a plaid shawl over her shoulders. Her bare feet were in canvas shoes, and she carried a guitar slung on her back. The younger male wore a striped pajamas suit, a native slouch hat, dark blue spectacles, and outsized gold earrings—he had had his ears pierced in San Francisco. In his hand was a taro-patch fiddle. The other man was really shabby, in white flannels and white shirt that looked slept in. He was smoking a straggle of cigarette. Trailing along behind was a piratical-looking character who needed only a green parrot on his shoulder, and sometimes affected one. The Reverend Clarke took them for wandering players on their way to New Zealand, perhaps "compelled by their poverty to take the cheap conveyance of a trading vessel."

Part of Louis's agitation was due to the effect of the arduous trip and the relief—together with the strange sensation—at being on dry land again. Fanny and Lloyd were just as edgy in their different ways. Joe Strong had been causing them concern for weeks, refusing to eat anything he suspected of being shark meat and making himself generally obnoxious: no one knew for certain what could be ailing him. It was decided he should see doctors, and by the next steamer from Apia he went on to join Belle in Sydney.

The energetic Moors and his Samoan wife put up the Stevensons at their home on the outskirts of the seedy little town. The Samoan natives, tall and handsome in their "kilts," as Louis called the *lavalava*, their brown skin glossy with perfumed coconut oil, made an agreeable impression. By contrast the white and half-caste population, about three hundred in number, were a disreputable mixture of beachcombers, fugitives, and castaways, washed up there at some time or other. There were wooden houses with verandas belonging to the traders, several churches, stores, and bars, and a long pier and warehouse used by the trading and planting company of the islands.

*

LOUIS, like Lawrence on his travels, was forever vacillating. Did he want to go west or east? How badly did he need to return to England? What did his instincts, or his soul, tell him? He had not intended to stay long in Samoa, though he was under pressure from Fanny to drop anchor somewhere. He began to wonder if they should settle here. Apia had good communications, very necessary if he were to maintain contact with publishers and newspapers. Mail steamers went regularly to Sydney and San Francisco. He was having yet another change of heart. He gave his reasons in a letter to his friend Henry James. "I was never fond of towns, houses, society, or (it seems) civilization . . . the sea, islanders, the island life and climate, make and keep me truly happier." Was he saying he had made a decision? Not quite, not yet. He wandered around for six weeks, exploring. Samoa was politically unstable, with Germany, Britain, and the United States hovering, maneuvering for rights, though at the moment it was still independent. He talked at length to Moors, a persuasive and efficient salesman, who had his own reasons for wanting Louis to stay. Fanny for her part was only too eager to put down roots. And after all, they could return to England whenever they liked: she felt robust enough to withstand the glare of the publicity they would meet there, and could imagine a key role for herself in it. Moors, giving them his full attention, soon came up with a property he thought they would find suitable.

Vailima was the name they chose for the 400 acres of land on a high plateau two miles inland from Apia which Louis found himself buying for $4,000. The mountainside air, after muggy Apia, was perhaps the deciding factor. A little wooden shack was built for them as a temporary shelter in the few acres of dense jungle that had been cleared. This would be their abode while a substantial house was under construction. The name Vailima meant Five Waters, or so they understood. These were the five streams he described in his report to

Baxter, crisscrossing a property that included waterfalls, precipices, "profound ravines, rich tablelands . . . a great view of the forest, sea, mountains, the warships in the haven. . . ." He sounded ecstatic, and he was. Great trees stood around them in their clearing, and there was endless birdsong. "I have never lived in such a heaven."

But it was a distinctly uncomfortable one. After camping out for a month or so in their rudimentary shack they decided to leave things to the builders and take a steamer to Australia. Belle had been sending them alarming messages, though by the time they reached her she was sorting out her problems and beginning to enjoy life. Louis and Fanny left Samoa on the SS *Lübeck* in February 1890.

For Belle it had been a testing time. Waiting in Sydney to hear from her family she had been shocked to discover that the bank at which she expected to draw Louis's weekly allowance had not heard of her, or indeed of the arrangement. Out in the street, "more frightened than I had ever been in my life," she tried the American consul. He was no more interested than the bank. She didn't know a soul in Australia. Unable to pay for the expensive guest house arranged by the Stevensons, she transferred to a cheap theatrical boardinghouse run by a warm Irishwoman in the sleazy Wooloomooloo district of the city. At long last her funds arrived from Honolulu.

The jolly theatrical residents at Mrs. Leaney's were good company, and Belle made friends and wrote pieces for the *Sydney Bulletin*. Then in late February she heard someone charging upstairs to her top-floor room. It was her brother Lloyd. Her mother and stepfather were at the Victoria Hotel. Arriving in a horse cab, she burst into the lobby and was astonished to see her stepfather raging like a fiend at the reception clerk. As had happened in France and elsewhere, the hotel staff were being offhand to the odd-looking couple with their battered luggage. The woman, dressed in a Mother Hubbard and as brown as a gypsy, stood beside a man whose suit had been shoved for weeks in the hold of a schooner, and looked it. Belle was not the only witness to be startled by this suddenly metamorphosed Louis. "When in a rage," Harry Moors recalled, "he was a study. Once excite him and you had another Stevenson. I have seen him in all moods.

I have seen him sitting on my table, dangling his bony legs in the air, chatting away in the calmest manner possible; and I have seen him become suddenly agitated, jump from that table and stalk to and fro across the floor like some wild forest animal. . . . His face would glow and his eyes would flash, darkening, lighting, scintillating, hypnotizing you with their brilliance and the burning fires within. . . ."

Belle was able to guide them to the less salubrious but pleasant Oxford Hotel. The next morning the press had the story of the famous author's arrival. The manager of the Victoria came personally and in haste to apologize and offer special rates. Louis declined: he was now enjoying himself. The bigger hotel was now obliged to send his flooding correspondence over to him in market baskets.

Hounded by newspapermen, invited to social gatherings, enjoying the restaurants and bookshops, it was the razzle-dazzle of New York all over again. Not lacking in a certain vanity, nevertheless for Stevenson a little fame went a long way. He was not fully aware that he had become a world figure, his personal appearance known everywhere. His own myth had begun to exact its price, part of which was the assault on his privacy. The lionizing soon wore him to rags, and he picked up a dreadful cold. In no time he was running a fever and spitting blood. A doctor friend of Belle's ordered his removal to the quiet Union Club and forbade callers. A retreat to the islands was the only salvation. They made urgent plans to leave. A seamen's strike made a boat hard to find. Fanny located the *Janet Nicholl*, but its Scottish owners refused point-blank to take on a passenger who seemed to be dying. It was touch and go until the owners wilted under Fanny's relentless badgering. They set sail on April 11. Belle watched "some half-naked black men" carry her stepfather on board the grimy steamer wrapped in a blanket. He looked ghastly. She wondered if she would ever see him again.

Slowly he recovered, resting in his berth, as they made first for Auckland. If his precarious health had held up he would have liked to have seen something of Australia. Fanny had no such desire, glad to get away from what she called the "criminal stamp" of the faces in

Sydney—once asking an Australian to tell her what "Sydney ducks" (convicts) were. Louis, stewing as ever in worries about his adopted family, wrote to Baxter that Joe Strong, the "loveable" charlatan, had been taken back by Belle and was behaving himself. He would soon learn from her that Joe was back to his old habits, money from Louis running through his fingers in the bars among his shiftless friends. His reluctant benefactor and Fanny would decide before long that the only solution, for Belle's sake, was to bring them both to join them at Samoa where they could keep an eye on them.

The *Nicholl* reached Apia on April 30. The Stevensons disembarked and went out to inspect progress on Vailima, the only real home they would ever have. There had been some movement but it was nowhere near complete. It was Louis's excuse for them to rejoin the iron steamship and sail to and fro for several months, including another trip to Australia, calling at more than thirty atolls in all. This seems inexplicable when one recalls him leaving Sydney helplessly rolled in a blanket, until one realizes that he could never resist expeditions. Was it simply the lure of the sea? "Once a sailor, always a sailor," wrote Jack London. "The savor of the salt never goes away." Deep inside he was always unwilling to put down a permanent anchor anywhere.

From Samoa they cruised through the Tokelaus and Line Islands to the northeast, turning due west for the Ellice Islands, then north for a return visit to the Gilberts. They arrived at Arorai on June 9 and eventually came to Apemama where they had stayed so contentedly. Tembinoka was absent but they enjoyed a reunion with him on another island. They met him again later on yet another of his islands, Aranuka, the king embracing them sorrowfully in floods of tears when they parted. They would not see him again.

Cast down suddenly at what he saw as the loss of his friends in Britain by attrition—even Bob responded only in halting embarrassment—Louis wrote to tell Baxter that only he and Colvin had stayed loyal to him. "You do not know what you become to me, how big you bulk; you must not measure it by my mean letters . . . you remain alone of my early past, truer now than ever, and I cling to the thought of you. . . . I prefer to think of two that have stood by me, you and Colvin, with a warmth that grows ever greater. When we talk you shall tell me, and I will try to learn, where I have been at fault with the others. . . ."

The *Nicholl*'s next destination was New Caledonia. On Noumea was a French penal colony that Louis thought he might inspect, leaving Fanny and Lloyd to return to Sydney for more time with Belle. Alone on Noumea he put himself under a doctor's supervision and prepared himself for the convict system by reading Zola's *La Bête Humaine*, which he was bound to loathe. "Nervous maladies: the homicidal ward" would be a better title for it, he pronounced. It was August before he retraced his journey and got back to Sydney, where he inevitably caught a cold and was confined to the male-only Union Club, while Fanny and Lloyd stayed where they were in the Strongs' boarding house. More plans were hatched. Maggie Stevenson was missing her son and longed to be back with them. Lloyd was given the task of traveling to England, selling Fanny's house in Bournemouth, and then escorting Maggie back from Scotland.

More disquieting revelations as to Joe's character filtered through to Louis, though he would hardly have been surprised. Some time ago he had sent money to enable Joe to give his wife a holiday. Instead the cash had been squandered on himself, with Belle and Austin seeing nothing of it. Even the money for having his child's tooth stopped had disappeared. "O Christ Jesus! it is sometimes too much to have to support this creature. And yet withal he's kind of innocent. . . ." It was the innocence of a child who made a mess on the hearth rug and "I wish somebody would mop it up. . . ." That somebody would always be him. What could he do? You couldn't disown your dependents, even if they did cheat and deceive you. "But we'll keep our hearts up."

With Lloyd gone to sell Skerryvore, ship out furniture from Scotland, and accompany the senior Mrs. Stevenson, Fanny and Louis left for Apia in the German steamer *Lübeck* on one of its regular passages. When they landed, a man called Paul Einfürer who had jumped ship asked them to take him on in some capacity. He spoke little English. In the event he worked hard at whatever they gave him to do. He asked them not to let him go to town or he would get drunk.

Moors had cleared a dozen or so acres and erected a temporary cottage, but they were still roughing it in the wilderness as they had done at Silverado. Fanny responded well, proud to labor away as a pioneer, making the place as habitable as she could with next to nothing. She tacked up some yards of rich tawny cloth from her luggage, and cooked out of doors in tropic fashion. The start of the rainy season didn't help, but these survival struggles brought out the best in her. Eager to be a smallholder, she had pigs fetched from town and asked Moors to build her a chicken house. The pigs ran away and had to be rounded up: this happened so often that the Samoan helpers believed they were possessed by devils living in the woods.

All this toil and sweat out in the open began to change Louis from a writer to a Robinson Crusoe kind of character who exulted in physical activity for its own sake. He told Colvin, who would have hated to hear it,

> Nothing is so interesting as weeding, clearing and path-making; the oversight of laborers becomes a disease . . . and it does make you feel well. To come down covered with mud and drenched with sweat after some hours in the bush, change, rub down and take a chair on the veranda, is to taste a quiet conscience. And the strange thing that I mark is this: if I sit in the house and make twenty pounds, idiot conscience wails over my neglect and the day wasted.

Fanny was his "little blue bogie planter." In anticipation of all this she had bought quantities of seeds in Sydney. Working away, they uncovered evidence of some previous cultivation, now swallowed up by undergrowth. They found banana plants and a taro patch, and later on a grove of frangipani. The preliminary clearing of the ground had encouraged pawpaws to spring up, which Fanny intended to feed to her cow when she had one. Meanwhile she broadcast handfuls of seed in the bush—melons, tomatoes, and lima beans—and planted boxes with cantaloupe. The buffalo grass she had ordered from America was sowed in cuttings in an effort to cover the paddock. Pineapples sent as gifts by their nearest neighbor, a Britisher named Carruthers, were sliced up for eating and the tops saved to be planted.

In breaks from his labors Louis did more work on *The Wrecker*, on his verse, and on the rewriting of a short story based on a legend he had heard on the big island of Hawaii. The idea behind "The Bottle Imp" would have appealed to Isaac Singer. A demon living in a bottle would grant the owner anything he wished in exchange for his soul. This Faustian arrangement could only be countermanded by selling the bottle at a loss. The tale went into the *New York Herald* in 1891 and influenced the Samoans profoundly when they came upon a translation by a Samoan missionary which appeared in a native paper. If this man communed with an imp in his bottle, this was where his obvious wealth came from: he must surely have magical powers. The legend of "Tusitala," or the Teller of Tales, was born.

Sweating away daily in such primitive conditions, they were in no position to entertain visitors. Nevertheless Stevenson would always have a need for congenial company, and inconvenient or not they soon had their first guest, escorted uphill by the American consul. The snobbish Henry Adams, a distinguished historian (though Louis had not heard of him) and a Bostonian friend of Henry James, arrived with his traveling companion, a painter. Writing gleefully to describe the encounter in as diverting a manner as possible, Adams wrote that he found himself in a clearing of burned stumps, meeting two extraordinary apparitions in their "two-storey Irish shanty." The celebrated author looked like a bundle of sticks in a bag, wearing dirty striped pajamas, the baggy legs stuffed into coarse stockings which didn't match. As for the woman, she wore "the usual missionary nightgown" that was as dirty as her husband's shirt, though she was minus the stockings. Her face was dark and strong, "like a half-bred Mexican." Adams did his best to avert his eyes from the squalor and dirt while finding Louis highly entertaining.

As a gentleman, Louis felt obliged to return their call. He arrived at five and brought his wife to dine. Fanny came lagging behind, and Louis put in an appearance "looking like an insane stork. . . . Presently Mrs. Stevenson, in a reddish cotton nightgown, staggered up the steps and sank into a chair, gasping and unable to speak." Louis explained that she was overcome by the heat and the walk, and might she lie down? Later, Adams found her on the piazza, "as well and stalwart as any other Apache squaw."

On closer acquaintance Adams and his companion condescended to a sort of liking for Fanny, whom they found more human than her husband. Louis baffled them completely. There was something uncanny about him. The squalor in which he lived was, they thought, "somehow due to his education" (by which they meant his lack of it) and his association with second-rate people. Clearly he could not differentiate between one person and another. In his letter Adams pompously observed that instead of buying so much land his hosts might have purchased soap.

But Adams's sneering hypocrisy had gone undetected. Louis wrote courteously to Henry James of his pleasure in the "enlightened society" of James's friends. Adams said privately that to live as the Stevensons did was incomprehensible. "Stevenson gloats over discomforts," he wrote. In fact the simplicity of their existence, tough though it was in the extreme, gave him a new lease on life. He took pride in working with his hands, he who had been so useless, fit for nothing but scribbling and lying flat on his back in sickbeds. Now he grubbed and tore his skin, and when he got to the dinner table he "could cry for weariness of my loins and thighs." Who would have imagined he would be well enough to ride his island horse Jack, a joy in itself? At times he felt so at one with the animal that he almost became him, Jack trotting along at a fast steady pace with his head down, sometimes his nose to the ground. When he wanted to do that "he asks for his head with a little eloquent polite movement indescribable." Horse and rider threaded through the darkest of the wood. One night it was starry, "and it was singular to see the starlight drip down into the crypt of the wood, and shine in the open end of the road. . . ." He was reading Tolstoy, profoundly affected by him. Perhaps at times he was imagining himself like the reborn Levin in *Anna*

Karenina, enchanting himself with his own labors at harvest time in bursts of joy.

Native boys came up to help them, and then Henry Simile appeared, a Samoan "chiefling" with a smattering of education, who was given a job as overseer for ten dollars a month including board. He joined in the heaviest planting and clearing and rode down to the town on errands. Soon he was indispensable. Servants came and went, but another permanent addition was "a huge mutton-headed Hercules" called Lafaele. He took charge of the garden, wielded an axe with fearsome zeal, and was deeply superstitious. The thought of ghosts petrified him; they were devils in disguise. To fox them he painted his face white with lime. He knew native lore and how to find herbs for healing grazes and wounds. His wife had deserted him though he was newly married. "He says if his wife does not suit me I am just to kill her," Fanny said. He promised to "work like hell," and he did. When Fanny mentioned to a servant that the Samoans did not have proper regard for their women, the man objected vigorously that it was not so. If a man's wife ran away, "he felt bad for two or three days."

Their contests with the exuberant vitality of tropical vegetation had become silent battles with an adversary it seemed nothing could defeat, as they fought to create garden ground for planting. Lianas twisted themselves unrelentingly around everything in sight. Louis depicted the campaign at some length in his poem "The Woodman":

> That there might live, where thousands died
> All day the cruel hoe was plied;
> The ambulance barrow rolled all day,
> Your wife, the tender, kind and gay
> Donned her long gauntlets, caught the spud
> And bathed in vegetable blood. . . .

Exhausted by so much manual labor, Louis did little writing now, somehow keeping up his correspondence. He heard about a promising young writer by the name of Kipling and tried to fight off his usual anxieties about money. "Gracious, what a strain is a long book!" he told Henry James. He was referring to *In the South Seas*, which moved forward sporadically. He still had "desperate engagements" with Fanny on the subject.

There were now as many as four gangs at work, with the mistress—temporarily out of action with rheumatism, and with injuries received while chasing pigs—shouting commands from the veranda. Louis conveyed the comic aspects of her cries to Colvin:

> "Here, you boy, what do you do there? You got no work? You go find Simile, he give you work. Peni, you tell this boy he go find Simile. . . . I no want him here. That boy no good."
>
> Peni (*from the distance in reassuring tones*): "All right, sir!" "I no want him stand here all day. I no pay that boy. I see him all day. He no do nothing."

Louis reported that Fanny had become preoccupied with the pregnant black sow. Two Sundays ago he had been walking by the waterside with his wife and Moors and they saw the black sow, looking guilty. Fanny's *cri de coeur* struck him as marvelous. "G-r-r-r!" she cried with such feeling, "nobody loves you!"

Always an early riser, writing if he could in the cool of the morning, Louis penned a letter soon after dawn one day to Colvin to express his rapture with a life of sheer sensation. The morning itself seemed in a state of astonishment, so fresh, so sweet, with unimaginable color "depth upon depth," all buried in a huge silence broken only by the far-off murmur of Pacific surf. A single bird was piping in this Eden. "You can't conceive what a relief this is; it seems a new world." He had not given up on friends who had long ago given up on him.

COMIC MISUNDERSTANDINGS were tending lately to upset the balance of Fanny's mind. Her task, running the household and carving out a homestead against the odds, would become increasingly burdensome when Belle, Joe, and her mother-in-law joined them. At times it must have seemed as if she was trying to climb something as insuperable as the mountain that rose behind them. One day she asked Lafaele to plant vanilla seedlings in a cleared patch of ground. He planted them with a will, but upside down. Fanny dispatched him on an errand to get him out of the way while she replanted them the right way up. Lafaele, hurt to think he had made his mistress cross, crept back under cover of night and planted them rightly, or so he thought. They were upside down again. These failures of communication made her wonder whether she would ever bridge the gulf between her and the Samoans.

Not long after the visit by Adams, Louis, either in a choleric mood for some reason or making a tactless compliment, told Fanny that she had the soul of a peasant. Was it unacknowledged retaliation because of her opposition to his nonfiction work? The remark hurt her cruelly and she brooded over it for weeks, writing pages of self-justification in her diary and even trying to accept it as a serious judgment. His attempt to pull back from the implication of his words only made it worse. "He assures me that the peasant class is a most interesting one, and he admires it hugely." This makes his blunder sound almost as supercilious as something the Bostonian Adams might have said. She went over it again and again obsessively. "I am feeling very depressed," she wrote bitterly, "for my vanity, like a newly felled tree, lies prone and bleeding. . . . I have been brooding on my feelings and holding my head before the glass and now I am ashamed. . . . Louis says that no one can mind having it said of him that he is not an artist unless he is supporting his family by his work as an artist, in which case it is an insult. Well, I could not support a fly by my sort of work, artistic or otherwise. . . . I so hate being a peasant that I feel a positive pleasure when I fail in peasant occupations."

It was crushing not to be seen as some sort of creative artist herself, which she fondly believed she was. Now in her loss of self-esteem she regarded even the domestic animals as enemies. "My fowls won't lay eggs, and if they do, the cocks . . . eat them. The pigs, whom I loathe and fear, are continually climbing out of their sty and doing all sorts of mischief. . . . I love the growing things but the domestic beasts are not to my taste." She identified with a servant whose carpentry skills were in question, writing that "I cannot bear to be harsh with him because my own wounded vanity makes me sensible of disappointments." Louis's carelessly inflicted wound would never properly heal.

Fanny's dream of making them self-sufficient by means of their plantation had suffered a severe blow. All the same there were successes as well as failures. Refusing to give in, she managed to produce tomatoes, peppers, aubergines, oranges, celery, avocados, asparagus, pineapples, mangoes, bananas, and cabbage. Weeds in the tropics were a permanent enemy, capable of choking everything almost overnight. Proper implements were difficult to obtain. And her struggles with her Samoan workforce continued. When the new house was half complete early in 1891, Fanny ordered one of her workers to take a pail of water upstairs. Staircases were outside his experience, so he took the pail between his teeth in order to shin up a pole. Taboos on all sorts of things maddened her: certain plants shouldn't be touched, and there were trees to be avoided, otherwise spirits would be made angry.

When the disruptions of endless building and domestic crises threatening to overwhelm Fanny became too much for her husband to contemplate, he ran off—no other word will do—ostensibly for a "change of air" and to meet his mother in Sydney. Henry Simile stood guard over his mistress. In early February Lloyd appeared out of the blue, bringing with him two of Belle's cats. The ménage of Vailima was beginning to assemble. Fanny and her son were soon living through the worst hurricane of their lives. The new house was still unfinished, the cottage too flimsy to withstand the blasts, so they took refuge in the newly built stable. They were there in a state of fear for several days, fighting back water with brooms and lying in soaked beds.

The *Lübeck* arrived at last with Louis, recovering slowly after going down in Sydney as usual with some malady and being nursed by his mother. Maggie Stevenson had brought along her own sofa and also her maid, Mary Carter, "which showed plainly that she meant to stay," recorded Fanny tartly in her diary. Her assumption was premature. Maggie took one look at the impoverished accommodations and general squalor and decided they were more than she could manage. She got back on the *Lübeck* and went on to New Zealand to stay with relatives until the new house was fit to inhabit.

On reflection Louis admitted that it had been wrong of him to leave Fanny alone through the worst of the hurricane season. Their reunion after long weeks of separation brought back a state of calm and appreciation to their relationship which the hard business of rough living had begun to erode. The American biographer J. C. Furnas has called their partnership more a symbiosis than a marriage. Whatever one might call it, there had been sensuality as well as likemindedness in their first encounters in France, and in him at least it still lingered. It flamed up in his unpublished poem "Dark Women":

> . . . Dark as a wayside gypsy,
> Lithe as a hedgewood hare,
> She moves a glowing shadow
> Through the sunshine of the fair;
> And golden hue and orange,
> Bosom and hand and head
> She blooms, a tiger lily
> In the snowdrift of the bed. . . .
>
> Take, O tiger lily,
> O beautiful one—my soul.
> Love lies in your body
> As fire slumbers in coal.
> I have been young and am old,
> I have shared in love and strife
> And the touch of a dusky woman
> Is the dear reward of life.

CHAPTER SIXTEEN

Do I Look Strange?

H OW IRONIC it was that Louis's exile was now creating envy as
well as puzzlement in some circles. As Ian Bell remarks, his
famed reclusiveness could be seen as elusiveness. "Since Byron was in
Greece," wrote Edmund Gosse, "nothing has appealed to the ordinary
literary man so much as that you should be living in the South Seas."
Later he added the reservation that "the fact seems to be that it is very
nice to *live* in Samoa, but not healthy to *write* there." And few of those
envying him would have given up their comforts for the problems
Stevenson had experienced, or been capable of the simple merriment
he could conjure up out of himself at unpromising moments.

The reality in April 1891 was far from rosy. Belle and Joe
Strong, with their problematic lives and ten-year-old son Austin,
were now in residence. Maggie was due soon. Louis was already
$12,000 in debt to Harry Moors. The trader did well from commis-
sions and sales and was overcharging on materials. Louis, worrying
over the need for money, tried not to dwell on thoughts of his predecessor Walter Scott, driving himself into bankruptcy to maintain Ab-
botsford. Fanny, having thrown off a series of psychosomatic
ailments, was given fresh impetus by their move into the new house,
half empty though it was, with books and furniture still in transit on

the high seas. Nevertheless they were at last *in,* "like a family after a sale." His mother returned. In a furious burst of joint effort they had her room ready for her in time. "It was a famous victory."

The new house evolved in stages, like the "clan" he gathered around him out of a sense of responsibility. He was now the provider for five adults and a child, apart from himself. Expenditure on the house as it grew in size and filled up with imported goods of all kinds would eventually run to $6,000 a year. How did it happen? It was as if the place possessed a life and purpose of its own. In the three years left to him everything accelerated, until the velocity became part of the rhythm of his days. Was he rushing ahead or falling? And where was the heaven he had known in that simple time, threading safely through the darkest of the wood on Jack, his horse?

The mansion, as they began to call it, was soon the biggest private residence on the island. Natives saw it as a palace, but white visitors were put off by something overgrown and barnlike. Built of wood, its walls peacock blue, it had a red corrugated-iron roof. In its final state it would have four rooms on the ground floor and five upstairs. Wide verandas extended on both levels. There was an enormous hall, sixty feet in length and forty wide, walls and ceiling clad in gleaming redwood ordered from California. The library of hundreds of volumes had varnished covers—like the varnished walls—to protect them from mildew. Out of nostalgia Louis insisted on a fireplace. It made him feel at home and set him back a thousand dollars. His study, opening off the upstairs library, was as spartan as Chekhov's in Yalta, a bare room with a narrow bedstead, a shelf of books, a table, and two chairs.

In truth the new house was ugly. Critical visitors muttered that it was badly designed and inconvenient, but at least it was large and airy, and Maggie Stevenson, who had contributed five hundred pounds, liked it. Shutters had been installed against the gales, and screen windows to repel flies and mosquitoes. Instead of doors there were hanging rush mats. The cookhouse was set apart from the house but connected by a covered way.

Extensions and improvements went on year by year. A drawing

room was added later. The dining room, Fanny's pride and joy, was decorated as she wished, papered with yellowish tapa, the woodwork dull blue, windows and doors hung with Indian fabrics of yellow silk. In the wide corner stood the fireplace which was always a source of wonder to "our people." The old leather-covered chairs and the Chippendale sideboard had been shipped over from Heriot Row. On the walls were various pictures, including one of cousin Bob's. "The painting of Louis with a conceited smile and a dislocated leg is by Sargent," quipped Fanny in a letter to Will Low.

Belle was now on reasonable terms with Louis after years of hostility toward the man who had usurped her father. She astonished the islanders by walking around with her white cockatoo, Cocky, perched on her shoulder. It had one word, "Mamma, Mamma," which it croaked softly. Long afterward Belle remembered her first impression of the island, riding up the steep trail through dense jungle, great trees making a tunnel overhead, and then drawing "long breaths of pure delight" as she saw Vailima for the first time. As for Joe, he wasted no time getting acclimatized, wearing a brightly flowered lavalava or Samoan skirt instead of trousers, a bandanna knotted over his shirt, his loose white-visored cap at a rakish angle. When anyone pointed a camera at him he liked to pose with Cocky on his shoulder.

And at first all was well: he helped in the plantation work with a will, joining Lloyd to oversee a workgang of Samoans in the forest where they hacked away at underbrush to plant cacao. Belle took over the kitchen and supervision of the housework so that her mother could continue with the outdoor work she liked best. Joe, trailing his shady past, was soon reverting to type, scrounging money for drinks and sneaking off to Apia. It would get worse. Fanny fought down her boiling resentment, and Belle, changed into a peacemaker, took Louis's side in any action he felt bound to take. Everyone with the exception of Maggie smoked—she disapproved of the fashionable habit. Louis took charge of Austin's education, as he had done with Lloyd, and wrote immensely long and fascinating letters about Vailima and the island to Colvin, who didn't deserve or value them.

Both Louis and Fanny had been given native names: his of

course was Tusitala, Teller of Tales. The Samoans called Fanny Tamai-tai, which was the usual title for the mistress of the house. They had another name for her among themselves—Aolele, meaning Flying Cloud. Some said it was inspired by her dashing movements around the place, or less politely by the wagging of her bottom. Lloyd's name was readily liquefied into Lois. Belle became Teuila, "adorner of the ugly," because of her deftness at house decoration.

In Apia, Louis was coming to grips with the unstable political situation. His book *A Footnote to History* would grow out of the ensuing island war. Louis kept England informed of the complex circumstances by means of frequent letters to the *Times*, exposing what he regarded as the venal and stupid involvement of the white powers. Louis saw his own position as a simple one: Samoa belonged to the Samoans. After a miniwar in 1888, a German "President of the Council" had been appointed. Rivalry between island chiefs, which Germany, the United States, and Britain had helped to foment in 1888, was erupting again. A puppet "king" installed by the Germans was opposed by Mataafa, a chief who had Stevenson on his side because he was independent. His stand affronted the Protestant missionaries, since Mataafa was a Catholic. With the threat of war darkening the horizon Louis told Baxter, "We sit and pipe upon a volcano which is being stoked by bland, incompetent amateurs." His staff of islanders at Vailima were supporters of Chief Mataafa to a man. Down in Apia they were being dubbed "popies" or Catholics.

Louis was now no longer the freebooter who liked nothing better than to sail off into the unknown with a song in his heart. Responding to responsibility as his father would have done, he saw himself as the guardian of his Samoan workers, whether house servants or laborers on the estate. The child who had pretended to be a minister in his nursery and the student who had clashed bitterly with his parents in opposition to their bourgeois Christianity now took it upon himself to conduct family services at Vailima in which everyone was included. Hearing that his friend Adelaide in Bournemouth was going into mission work, he outlined his ideas for a religious code that anyone could understand and find acceptable: "Forget wholly and forever all small pruderies, and remember that *you cannot change ancestral feelings of right and wrong without what is practically soul-murder*. Barbarous as the customs may seem, always hear them with patience, always judge them with gentleness, always find in them some seed of good; remember that all you can do is civilize the man in the line of his own civilization, such as it is."

The Strongs now lived in the old shanty that had been taken down and completely renovated. Fanny recruited Joe to help her construct a culvert in the old jungle trail before the start of the rainy season. She went on to lay out a tennis court single-handed, and dammed a spring on the mountainside with the help of her Samoan boys in order to bring water down to the gardens by a system of pipes. Belle marveled at her mother's newfound engineering skills. Fanny came up with one scheme after another, a few of which were spectacular failures: for instance, her plan to make beer from bananas ended when the resulting brew exploded violently.

IN THE SUMMER of 1892 there was another far more damaging explosion. Joe Strong, always on probation as far as Louis was concerned, became exposed as a petty criminal, and worse still as a bigamist. Fanny, when she could bring herself to face the horrible truth, poured the sordid story into her diary: "About the time I stopped writing we found Joe Strong out in various misdeeds: robbing the cellar and store-room at night with false keys. In revenge, when he found he was discovered, he went round to all our friends in Apia and spread slanders about Belle. We turned him away and applied for a divorce for Belle, which was got with no difficulty, as he had been living with a native woman in Apia as his wife ever since he came here. . . . Also, he had been engaged in an intrigue with Faauma. He came up here late one night to beg forgiveness and ask to be taken back. I was so shocked at seeing him that I had an attack of angina, which seems to remain with me. . . ."

Faauma was a maid at Vailima, a lovely creature to whom Louis alludes several times in letters to Colvin ("dear Faauma, the unchaste, the extruded Eve of our Paradise"), homage to her beauty that would be deleted later by the anxious critic. Joe had contrived to keep his other "wife" hidden by contriving several visits to the dentist, coming home late at night with the benefit of this excuse.

Repercussions from the scandal and disgrace would affect Fanny disastrously in the next two years when she dwelt on the shameful outcome and the meal they would be sure to make of it down on the beach as the gossip circulated. It held up the Stevensons as laughing-stocks, and it made an enemy of Harry Moors, "more particularly Lloyd's and mine, we two being Joe's pet aversion. . . ." So she suspected in her anguish. In fact Moors had never really liked her. His memoirs are loaded against her with subtle touches. Louis would come down to him to be cheered up when the womenfolk smothered him, he suggested. With the decree signed and Joe on his way back to California, Belle and Austin moved into the main house, vacating the cottage for Lloyd to occupy as bachelor quarters.

One malicious piece of gossip around the beach, triggered by Belle's dark looks, alleged that she was Louis's child by a native woman. The fact that she was only eight years his junior seemed to have passed them by. Fanny, her mind seething with obscure suspicions and jealousies of her own after the Joe Strong business, had begun to resent the growing closeness between her daughter and Louis. Belle was siding with him in various ways and would soon assist him in his literary work. They were closer in age than Fanny was to her husband. This dark cloud floated away when young Graham Balfour, the tall handsome young Scot who was Louis's cousin, arrived: he was on a slow trip round the world, having read law at Oxford. Balfour would be Louis's first biographer. Belle, vulnerable after the demise of Joe, promptly fell in love with him. Clearly Fanny would have been happy to acquire such a son-in-law, but it was not to be.

The Stevenson social life had been transformed now that Vailima was occupied. Louis enjoyed entertaining, and friends included local missionaries; Bazett Haggard, the British land commissioner—

who happened to be the brother of Rider Haggard; and Haggard's counterpart from America, Henry Ide, later to be Samoa's chief justice. When Balfour arrived the Stevensons were expecting a visit from the Countess of Jersey, wife of the governor general of New South Wales. She stayed with Bazett Haggard and he brought her and her brother to meet Louis and Fanny at Vailima. Thus for the first time she came face to face with a slim, bright-eyed figure in a loose black velvet jacket over his white vest, and a scarlet sash. By his side stood the short dark woman with cropped curly hair and the strange piercing gaze she had been told about.

The countess came several times to Vailima. The ménage was it seems something quite unique in her experience. Louis's work ground to a halt, and Fanny, unhappy at facing anyone after recent events, found it hard to be civil to this woman brimming with grace and confidence who was as unusual a character as herself. More to the point, her husband danced attendance on her. Fanny, who had memories of sitting in London during the early days of her marriage smiling hypocritically at his English friends "like a Cheshire cat," had no intention of repeating the performance: too much water had gone under the bridge since then. In her diary she wrote acidly that the governor's lady was "too much like Kipling's Mrs. Hawksbee." Lady Jersey, thin and leggy, staring at her with bold black eyes, struck her as "very selfish and greedy of admiration, a touch of vulgarity, courageous as a man and reckless as a woman." Louis was certainly an admirer, finding her plucky, kind, and gracious. Her brother he thought "a nice sort of glass-in-the-eye chap."

Louis came to almost dread her visits, since Fanny gave him such a hard time afterward. On one occasion Lady Jersey came with an idea. Would Stevenson take her on a *malaga* to see the rebel Chief Mataafa? She was willing to go incognito, in fact she enthused over the prospect: it would be such fun. Fanny was conspicuous by her absence, though she would be at her husband's side later, on a more serious expedition. Lloyd and Graham Balfour went along "for the lark," with Henry Simile acting as interpreter.

It became clear that Lady Jersey had been identified when she was served first with kava, as well as being met with a fanfare of bugles and conches. Quite apart from the indiscretion of "the Queen of Sydney" involving herself, however lightheartedly, in Samoan politics, Stevenson's action ruffled feathers as far away as London. The local status quo had been flouted, and the British consul in Samoa was not amused. Stevenson had no business meddling in affairs that had nothing to do with novelists and poets. The outing may well have appealed to his sense of romance, but he was also hoping genuinely, if ineptly, to help bring about a reconciliation between rival chiefs. His efforts came to nothing, and a year later the war he had been predicting broke out. His men servants blacked their faces to show allegiance to Mataafa, who was leading a rebellion against the puppet Maletoa and his German masters. "I wish you could see my 'simple and sunny' heaven now," Louis wrote to Mark Twain. "The government have started a horrid novelty, taking women's heads." Men were dying in hospital. He was torn between wanting a suppression of the rebels to avoid further bloodshed and a feeling of solidarity with them.

The rebellion, such as it was, was put down in a matter of days and Mataafa exiled to the Marshall Islands. Many of his supporters were in jail in Apia. Louis, with Fanny, Belle, and Lloyd, visited the prisoners openly with gifts of food. For a time he was in danger of being deported. He would always maintain that the three powers should withdraw and the natives be left to settle things for themselves. When the last of the imprisoned chiefs was released in 1894 they wanted to repay Louis as a token of their gratitude, and decided on the construction of a new road from the main island track to Vailima. Twenty-two chiefs were named on the signpost at the entrance to the road, below an inscription paying tribute to "the surpassing kindness of Mr. R. L. Stevenson and his loving care during our tribulations while in prison."

*

SAMOANS on the staff at Vailima came and went, sometimes disappearing for no reason like aborigines going walkabout, but gradually a group formed around Louis which regarded him as a white *matai*, the head of a tribe. It was not of his doing but now he had a clan, like a Highland chieftain, obliged to care for those who looked to him for leadership. In return he gave them unswerving loyalty. And they were in awe of his magic, spinning out wealth with no more than a pen. Where was this Bottle Imp of his? Did it perhaps reside in his inkpot? Graham Balfour in his biography estimated that Louis had produced 400 pages a year for 20 years. Fatigue was now setting in. According to J. C. Furnas, he wrote 700,000 words of print copy while in Samoa. No wonder he felt bemused at times, at a crossroads. "The truth is, I have a little lost my way," he confessed to Edmund Gosse.

Yet during 1893, in the midst of the turmoil of rebellion and his increasing difficulties with Fanny and her "illusions," his output never faltered. He completed *The Ebb-Tide*, in which ideas for the plot were contributed by Lloyd—a South Seas story with only four characters, "but they are such a troop of swine!" Close to the book in setting is a long short story, "The Beach of Falesá," later included in his book *Island Nights' Entertainment*. He described it to Colvin as "very strange, very extravagant . . . and has a pretty love affair, and ends well." For Louis and his times it was lurid and daring, a contemporary tale told in the first person by the hero Wiltshire, a selfish trader who acts honorably. The veracity of its opening makes it one of his finest beginnings:

> I saw that island first when it was neither night nor morning. The moon was to the west, setting, but still broad and bright. To the east . . . the daystar sparkled like a diamond. The land breeze blew in our faces, and smelt strong of wild lime and vanilla: other things besides, but these were the most plain; and the chill of it set me sneezing. I should say I had been for years on a low island near the line, living for the most part solitary among natives. Here was a fresh experience; even the tongue would be quite strange to me;

and the look of these woods and mountains, and the rare smell of them, renewed my blood.

The white man, cynically imposing his culture on a more primitive one and in the process being altered by it, is the crux of this tale of double moral standards. "Golly it's good, but the story is craziness," he wrote later as he progressed with it. "Miss Uma is pretty. All my other women have been ugly as sin." Uma has been fishing when Wiltshire sees and falls for her. "All she wore was a chemise, and it was wetted through. She was young and very slender for an island maid, with a long face . . . and a shy, strange, blandish look, between a cat and a baby's." The publishers were upset by Uma and by much else besides when he submitted it. Changes were demanded. "It seems it's immoral and there's a to-do." This clash with the objections of editors to such sentences as "The want of her took and shook all through me, like the wind in the lull of a sail" put him off further attempts at realism, and he convinced himself that he was happier with "romance." Yet in his maturity he reached a new confidence in his dealing with man-woman relations, and would create two flesh-and-blood women for the first time in *Weir of Hermiston*. In *The Beach of Falesa* he set out to render plain physical sensation "plainly expressed . . . hence my perils." But in this novella the male-female relationship is not really confronted.

He had told Henry James that his sequel to *Kidnapped* was "on the stocks at last." It was published serially in *Atlanta* as *David Balfour*, though in Britain it has always been entitled *Catriona*. It is different from *Kidnapped* in that Louis is more personally involved in it, as can be seen in the dedication to Charles Baxter: "You are still . . . in the venerable city which I must always think of as my home. And I have come so far; and the sights and thought of my youth pursue me; and I see like a vision the youth of my father, and of his father, and the whole stream of lives flowing down there far in the north, with the sound of laughter and tears, to catch me out in the end, as by a sudden freshet, on these ultimate islands. And I . . . bow my head before the romance of destiny."

The emotional involvement revealed by this leads David Daiches to suggest that Stevenson appears to be retreating from something he cannot or will not resolve, so that David Balfour is seen to live in a curious brother-and-sister relationship with Catriona. As Daiches puts it, "the girls in the novel are not, as it were, telling the whole truth." The presence of Fanny in the background could, suggests more than one critic, have discouraged him from exploring his hero's dealings with women as he would have liked. This was to change dramatically when it came to his final unfinished novel.

HE WAS WRITING NOW with new assurance and a belief in his powers that seemed unshakable. Whereas in his first attempts at fiction he had faltered and failed, starting novels and abandoning them halfway, now in a flow of astonishing vitality he had several books going at the same time, breaking off one to give another its head as the mood took him. As the island war broke out he was writing *Catriona*, completing *A Footnote to History*, working on the biographical "Records of a Family of Engineers," and beginning to rough out a novel he first called *The Justice-Clerk*. This is the first we hear of his unfinished novel *Weir of Hermiston*, and from the start he had no doubt that it would be his best work. "I never felt so sure before in anything I ever wrote," he declared to Belle.

Baxter heard of it in its early manifestation. "It is pretty Scotch, the Grand premier is taken from Braxfield (Oh, by the by, send Cockburn's *Memorials*)—and some of the story is—well—queer. The heroine is seduced by one man, and finally disappears with the other man who shot him. . . . Mind you, I expect *The Justice-Clerk* to be my masterpiece." And probably, if death had not intervened, it would have been. He called it "my Braxfield" because he based Weir of Hermiston on the man whose portrait by Raeburn he had seen as a young man in the Royal Scottish Academy.

As well as all this he began a book that would be called *St. Ives*.

Belle knew it as *Anne*. It flowed along cheerfully while the war drums were beating. The book's eponymous hero is an English-speaking Frenchman. An adventure story, it seems to hark back to an earlier Stevenson. But Louis himself was being drawn back in memory to his early self in Edinburgh, and perhaps unconsciously he was casting about for a refuge. The hero is made French to indicate his bohemianism, just as Stevenson's velvet jacket and his change of name from Lewis to Louis set him apart in his own eyes from bourgeois conventions. St. Ives sees the lamplighter at work as Louis the child had, he takes part in pranks in the night streets as Louis and Bob and Baxter had done, and the girl he loves lives in the Swanston cottage Louis had known as a retreat in his student days.

The moods and tantrums he was now trying to weather in his encounters with Fanny went on throughout the summer, until he felt removed from the world. She nagged at him with immense persistence in a violent barrage, finding fault with everything he did or didn't do. She alienated her daughter, imagining in her unhappiness that Belle and Louis were hatching some sort of conspiracy against her. Belle was now Louis's secretary and amanuensis, taking dictation, handling correspondence, and telling him candidly what she thought of chapters he read aloud to her as he prowled to and fro. Fanny and her husband slept in different rooms and spent most of the day apart. She still sat unsmiling at the dining table, and the silences stretched out between them. It was like having a stranger sitting there. How could this thing be happening which had no basis in reality? But of course there are many realities and this was one, with two persons who had been through so much together now shutting themselves off.

In an attempt to distance himself from the continual strife and misery, Louis wrote a lengthy letter on April 2, 1893, to J. M. Barrie who, God forbid, was planning a visit to Vailima the following year. To prepare him for the ménage he would encounter, Louis wrote humorous and deadly sketches which are worth giving more or less in full.

Fanny V.de G. Stevenson: If you don't get on with her, it's a pity about your visit. She runs the show. Infinitely little, extraordinary wig of grey curls, handsome waxen face like Napoleon's, insane black eyes, boy's hands, tiny bare feet, a cigarette, wild blue native dress, usually spotted with garden mold. In company manners presents the appearance of a little timid and precise old maid of the days of prunes and prisms—you look for the reticule. Hellish energy; relieved by fortnights of entire hibernation. Can make anything from a house to a row, all fine and large of their kind. Doctors everybody, will doctor you, cannot be doctored herself. . . . A violent friend, a brimstone enemy. . . . Is always either loathed or slavishly adored—indifference impossible. . . . Dreams dreams and sees visions.

Belle. Runs me like a baby in a perambulator, sees I'm properly dressed, bought me silk socks and made me wear them, takes care of me when I'm well, from writing my books to trimming my nails . . . manages the house and the boys, who are very fond of her. Does all the hair-cutting of the family. Will cut yours and doubtless object to the way you part it. Mine has been re-organized twice.

Lloyd. Six foot, eye-glasses—British eye-glasses too. Address varying from an elaborate civility to a freezing haughtiness. Decidedly witty. Has seen an enormous amount of the world. Keeps nothing of youth, but some of its intolerance. . . . When he is good he is very very good, but when he is cross he is horrid. Of Dutch ancestry, and has spells known in the family as "cold blasts from Holland." . . . Rather stiff with his equals, but apt to be very kindly with his inferiors . . . and except for my purple patches the only mannered one.

Robert Louis Stevenson: Exceedingly lean, rather ruddy, black eyes, crow's-footed, beginning to be grizzled, general appearance of a blasted boy—or blighted youth. . . . Past eccentric—obscure and oh we never mention it—present industrious, respectable and fatuously contented. . . . Name in family, The Tame Celebrity. Cigarettes without intermission, except when coughing or kissing. Hopelessly entangled in apron-strings. Curses some. Temper unstable. If accused of cheating at cards, would feel obliged to blow out brains, little as he would like the job. Has been an invalid for ten years but can boldly claim you can't tell it on him. Given to explaining the Universe—Scotch, sir, Scotch.

It is poignant to think that these reflections with their eager life presented him as a man firmly in control of things, when in fact he was in the midst of darkening chaos, spinning ever farther beyond his grasp. He drafted yet another novel, *Heathercat*, a work set in the time of the Convenanters. The late run of Scottish-based books was not merely nostalgia or the awareness of an exile who would never go back. It was as if recreating his homeland gave him a secret hiding place where he was immune to the onslaught of an increasingly demonic Fanny. It would never succeed. Was his adversary a devil he had brought into being from a Jekyll inside himself? What had he done to change a passionate friend and comrade into this unrelenting enemy? As the trite song goes, nobody knows how close love and hate can be. Fanny took herself off on a short holiday to Fiji and came back unaltered. When Graham Balfour went to Honolulu, Louis seized the chance of a respite and accompanied him. He stayed on alone at the Sans Souci Hotel and wrote to the *Hololulu Advertiser* complaining of the telephone "bleating like a deserted infant from the dining room."

Inevitably he caught one of his colds. It became pneumonia. Graham Balfour had gone, so Fanny arrived by the next available steamer. Nursing him restored her to power, but in Vailima he was well again and she relapsed bitterly into a redundant woman who had lost control of everything. He was acting strangely himself during these desperate months, contemplating his own death and writing to Bob, the man who had first helped to set him free, a letter anticipating D. H. Lawrence: "If I had to begin again, I know not. . . . I know not at all—I believe I should try to honor sex more religiously. The worst of our education is that Christianity does not recognize and hallow sex. . . . It is a terrible hiatus in our modern religions that they cannot see and make venerable that which they ought to see first and hallow most. Well, it is so. I cannot be wiser than my generation." Yet in these words and in much else besides, he was.

The gaiety of his pen portraits to amuse Barrie came from that involuntary laughter which is sometimes part of despair. There were scenes with Fanny, all disorder, screaming and mad accusation, which he was too ashamed to relate to anyone. She was having hallucinations, nightmares. In a brief lull he wrote a worried letter to Colvin, wondering if there was a danger "to mind" if not life. "It is a beastly business." Fanny was terrifying everyone, eyes snapping, voice shaking with rage. At one point the family boat and all in it seemed about to smash up against a wall of terrifying blackness. Sometimes she would be derisive and begin to laugh. She had always had forebodings. Now she swore that evil was approaching. One night in a state of terror she tried to run away, run anywhere, became physically violent and had to be held down to prevent her from harming herself. One of the doctors they consulted in Apia, Dr. Funk, treated her with laudanum but had no answer as to the cause of her illness. For the rest of the time left to him Louis saw her "quite sensible" again from time to time, but never her old self.

AS HE MOVED into 1894, his last year, there were signs that his long ordeal with Fanny and the fact that he was living on credit at Vailima had combined to take their toll. He had always been a good invalid: now those days were over. Overcome at times with fatigue, he said on New Year's Day that he was too tired to work any more for six months at least. Of course he had never been able to stop for long. In September Belle expressed amazement in her diary at her stepfather's ability, with hardly more than a line or two to keep him on track, to continue dictating without once faltering for a word, giving her the sentences exactly punctuated "as clearly and steadily as though he were reading from a book." He was afflicted with writer's cramp, another reason why she was invaluable to him, and he liked to escape from his desk on peregrinations around the room. Belle put on record the reality of one day's work as his assistant: "Louis and I have been writing, working away every morning like steam engines on *Hermiston*. Louis got a set-back with *Anne*, and he has put it aside for a while. He worried terribly over it, but could not make it run smoothly. He read it aloud one evening and Lloyd criticized the love scene, so Louis threw the whole thing over for a time. Fortunately he picked up *Hermiston* all right, and is in better spirits at once."

It was not to last. A sorrow resided in him that bore down on his tired heart. In October he wrote a letter to Colvin that was all defeat and disillusion. Earlier in the year he had already confided to Baxter that he was longing for death, and wished suicide was not seen as pitiable. How long could he hang on? "I don't know, say the Bells of Old Bow." It was his built-in melancholy speaking. But he was weary beyond words. "I have unwrapped my thoughts about life so long that I have not a filament left to hold by." He had the satisfaction of knowing that *Hermiston* was easily the best thing he would do. It was not enough. He was at the climacteric, a testing time for men, and for Stevenson especially so. His boyhood, which had not only survived but seemed eternal, was now suffering its own little death, and the man who had spent so much of his life in the timeless world of his work found himself in the small age he despised, measured by grey hairs and haggard looks. "Small is the word," he wrote. "It is a small age, and I am of it."

His letter of dejection to Colvin has him wishing he had listened to his father and been an engineer. "My skill deserts me, such as it was or is. It was a very little dose of inspiration and a pretty little trick of style, long lost, improved by the most heroic industry." What did it all amount to? "I am a fictitious article, and have long known it. I am read by journalists, by my fellow novelists and by boys." He threw off this prolonged bout of self-pity in time to celebrate his forty-fourth birthday, attended by his "clan" and by guests from two ships. He wrote loyally to Ida Taylor of Fanny's fortitude with an admiration that had not deserted him. "Ill or well, rain or shine, a little blue indefatigable figure is to be observed hawking about certain patches of garden. She comes in heated and bemired up to the eyebrows, late for every meal. She has reached a sort of tragic placidity." For his birthday the household killed a fatted cow, pigs, chickens, pigeons, and consumed pineapples and bananas. Tinned salmon was a rare delicacy. Wine flowed, and champagne chilled with ice from one of the steamers lying offshore. His mother noted with touching innocence in her diary, "Dear Lou, what cause for thankfulness that he has been spared to see this birthday in so much health and comfort."

On December 3, 1894, he pushed on with *Hermiston*, rode down to lunch with Bazett Haggard, and came back in the dark. The lamps of his house shining through the foliage of trees always gave him pleasure. He changed for dinner as always. Fanny had been gloomy with one of her premonitions, a fear of some disaster which had oppressed her for days. She later told Mrs. Sitwell that she had been driven "almost insane" by a conviction that something terrible was about to happen. Louis, finding her still gloomy, fetched a bottle of his best Burgundy from the cellar. An access of well-being prompted him to talk of a lecture tour in America. To raise her spirits he played a game of cards with her, then asked her to help him make a salad for the evening meal. He stood chatting easily on the downstair veranda, then suddenly snatched at his head with thin hands and cried out, "What's that? Oh, what a pain!" He asked urgently, "Do I look strange?" Fanny lied "No," but he was already being driven to his knees beside her.

By the time Fanny and a servant had got him into a chair he had lost consciousness. Lloyd rode down frantically to Apia to fetch a doctor. Louis died at eight o'clock of the cerebral hemorrhage that had felled him.

Dr. Funk came, and the ship's surgeon from the Wallaroo. There was nothing for them to do. He had chosen his burial site years before on Mount Vaea, high above Vailima. The chiefs came to pay their last respects, and Samoans dressed in black cotton lavalavas hacked a pathway to the mountain peak. They could be heard cutting and slashing a way to the top all night.

The Reverend Clerk, a friend of the family, conducted the Anglican service, and Louis's own prayer was recited: "Suffer us a while longer to endure, and (if it may be) help us to do better. Bless us our extraordinary mercies, and if the day come when these must be taken, have us play the man of affliction. Be with our friends; be with ourselves." Henry James, who always refrained from joining in with others in attacks on Fanny, wrote a measured and elegant letter of sympathy to his fellow American which began:

> What can I say to you that will not seem cruelly irrelevant or vain? . . . To have lived in the light of that splendid life, that beautiful, bountiful being—only to see it, from one moment to the other, converted into a fable as strange and romantic as one of his own, a thing that *has* been and has ended, is an anguish into which no one can enter with you fully and of which no one can drain the cup for you. . . .

As the news rushed round the globe a note came from Hawaii, in pencil and without signature: "Mrs. Stevenson, Dear Madam, All over the world people will be sorry for the death of Robert Louis Stevenson, but none will mourn him more than the blind white leper of Molokai."

At one o'clock in the afternoon a first relay of Samoan pallbearers made the difficult ascent with the coffin on their shoulders. Half an hour later nineteen whites and sixty Samoans climbed the steep slope, some finding it too slippery and dropping out. The coffin at the top lay under the worn British flag that used to fly over the *Casco* in those adventurous days. Maggie, unable to make the climb, wrote to her sister, "None of us has realized yet what has happened, and we shall only feel it all the more as the days go by. . . . I feel desolate indeed, and don't know what I shall do."

Eventually a tomb of large cement blocks was built on the mountaintop, and in 1897 a plinth was added, with two bronze plaques. One, in Samoan, was inscribed "The Tomb of Tusitala," bearing carved images of a thistle and a hibiscus flower and carrying the words of Ruth to Naomi . . . "thy people shall be my people, and thy God my God: where thou diest, will I die. . . ." On the other side was the requiem Stevenson had written in San Francisco fifteen years before, when he believed he was about to die:

> Under the wide and starry sky,
> Dig the grave and let me lie.
> Glad did I live and gladly die,
>   And I laid me down with a will.
>
> This be the verse you grave for me;
> Here he lies where he longed to be.
> Home is the sailor, home from sea.
>   And the hunter home from the hill.

Postcript

HENRY JAMES, asked to take on the job of literary executor, delicately excused himself. He had stood up loyally for Fanny but was realist enough to know what he would be letting himself in for with her. As for the authorized biography, he steered clear of it with his distaste for biographers. He left that minefield to Colvin.

Fanny battled on for another twenty years, a vision of the afterlife always before her. If anyone believed she would, with her combative nature, contest aspects of her husband's will, they were mistaken. He had left an estate in Britain worth 15,525 pounds, accumulated from his earnings and held by Baxter. Half was to provide an income for his mother until her death, and a third went to Bob, Katherine, and Dora, the children of Alan, his father's brother. There was a legacy to Austin. The rest, including manuscripts, furniture, and other effects, was for Lloyd. To Fanny went the royalties and a pension of sixty pounds per annum, due to her as the widow of a Scottish advocate.

She saw her task as the honorable one of giving to the world the picture of Stevenson she thought it should have. Who else was so qualified? She worked tirelessly at introductions and prefaces, preparing papers and sifting through huge accumulations of letters. She quarreled bitterly with anyone who questioned her version of the truth. No one was going to sully his name while she stood guard over his work and exploits.

Maggie Stevenson returned to Edinburgh after her son's death to live with her sister and begin a postmortem life. Twice, she said to friends, she had been torn up by the roots. In the family Bible she recorded her son's death and added, "I am left alone and desolate." In her mid-sixties she learned to ride a bicycle. As sometimes happens, she saw her beloved child in the room just before she died, and felt bound to join him. In May 1897 she died of pneumonia, aged sixty-eight.

Fanny, Belle, and Lloyd retreated to California after Louis's death. After Maggie's death they went back to Vailima, but only to sell it. The place fell into the hands of a German merchant. Why it realized only 1,750 pounds is a mystery. In a succession of owners it became in turn Imperial Germany's when it annexed Samoa and installed its governor there; the property of the British government after World War I; and the home of the U.S. administrator when America exerted its mandate. Fanny retained the land around the tomb on the mountaintop at Vaea. A few years ago, after long negotiations, Mormon missionaries purchased a lease on the crumbling Vailima with the aim of establishing a museum and foundation.

In 1896 Lloyd married a missionary teacher, Katherine Durham, and they had two sons. They had met in Honolulu. Their first boy, Alan, was with them when they returned to London two years later. Colvin and his future wife, Mrs. Sitwell, met the train. Later Henry James was given the baby to hold, observing that Stevenson's widow looked like "an old grizzled lioness." A visit was made to Scotland, and then Lloyd and his family lived temporarily in a rented house in Surrey.

Fanny was soon clashing with Colvin, wanting to know why his biography of the man whose life she was determined to oversee was making such slow progress. (Finally Graham Balfour took over: his two-volume *Life* appeared in 1901.) She was at odds too with her daughter-in-law, despite the fact that they both felt in touch with Louis through the séances they favored. Lloyd wavered weakly between the two strong women—a wife who made no mistakes and a mother notoriously short-tempered. Katherine named her second son Louis. By this time amicable relations between the women had broken down. When they met, Fanny refused to call the baby anything. The stage was set for Katherine to feed slander to willing ears from within the camp. Fanny had not only thought she was marrying a corpse, alleged Katherine, hoping to profit as Louis's widow, but she had told her so. Many were eager to gobble up her stories, but as many were skeptical. Ellen Shaffer maintains that Katherine was totally unreliable: "Katherine was real cooky. She even accused Belle and Lloyd of poisoning Fanny." This, needless to say, was after she and Lloyd had split up. Lloyd, by now something of a womanizer, had a child by a Frenchwoman and returned to California. He wrote a number of light novels and developed a passion for fast cars. He died in 1947.

Fanny traveled through Europe, fell ill with gallstones, and moved on again, eventually back to California, where she could see the Pacific. Often melancholy, she wrote to Belle that the years ahead "seem like large empty rooms." Out of the blue she suddenly announced a friendship with a Hearst journalist known as Ned. His name was Salisbury Field. Gossip bubbled and spat because he was twenty-five to her sixty-five. He became her traveling companion and secretary. Fanny survived the 1906 San Francisco earthquake and was in Palm Springs for her health in 1914 when a sudden stroke killed her, as it had killed her husband. Her ashes were taken to Samoa, where she had lived for so long in her thoughts, a reluctant survivor. Most of her large estate, valued at 120,000 pounds, went to Belle. Later in the same year a rich Belle married Ned Field, then in his mid-thirties. Though twenty years his senior she outlived both him and her son Austin. She died in 1953 at the age of ninety-five, the last member of the Vailima clan.

*

STEVENSON LIVED ON, in great quantities of letters and in edition after edition: the Edinburgh, the Pentland, the Vailima. Bewildered letters of self-examination in his final months show that he was at a crisis, "like all men who lived by their wits." An emptiness told him what he had long been denying, that his days of vagabondage were over. He found it hard to take himself seriously as an artist. There were intimations of death, temptations to lie down and give up the struggle, but his fiery will to live and his sense of humor, those vital ingredients for survival, had not deserted him. He quoted Job: Man is born to trouble as the sparks fly upward. He spoke bleakly, as if beleaguered, aware of his "so obvious limitations," of being stripped of his few illusions. He had given up trying to make others see that these islanders whose cause he championed had won his heart. How could he leave them now?

An imp of devilment prompted him to worry Colvin with an unsettling question. Could it be that literature "is a morbid secretion, and abhors health?" He was more than half serious. He sensed the coming of something new in the world wind, which he called anarchism. At times he thought he might like to retire into a communistic retreat, if such a place existed. As for what civilization and Christianity had become, "Go and reason with monkeys!" He still marveled at memories of a youthful Bob, the winged one, who "wouldn't imitate, hence you kept free—and came damn near to starving for your pains."

"The mind runs ever in a thousand eddies," he wrote to Bob, "like a river between cliffs."

Acknowledgments

THE COMPLETE EDITION of Stevenson's letters issued by Yale University Press (1994–1995) is exemplary and constitutes a biography in itself, with its annotations and linking commentary. Yale has also (1997) boiled this down into a *Selected Letters*, edited by Ernest Mehew, which has proved invaluable. The definitive biography is now surely the splendid book by Frank McLynn, published in 1994 to mark the centenary of Stevenson's death. One cannot imagine it being surpassed in the foreseeable future. Behind it lies the work of scholars such as J. C. Furnas and David Daiches, to which this biography also owes a debt. The former's *Voyage to Windward* must have inspired many writers approaching Stevenson and the nature of his appeal for the first time, as it has me. Ian Bell's *Dreams of Exile* (1992), a biography with a slant all its own, has been a real stimulus. As for G. K. Chesterton, Stevenson's great champion, I find his criticism as pertinent as anyone's.

Since Stevenson's death, enthusiasts have followed his trail and will no doubt continue to do so. One of the earliest of these books visiting his sites is Clayton Hamilton's *On the Trail of Stevenson* (1915); the latest is *The Teller of Tales* by Hunter Davies (1994). *Footsteps* (1985) by Richard Holmes, a blend of biography and autobiography, has fascinating chapters on Stevenson. Then there are those stalkers who embark on pilgrimages to the South Seas, such as Gavin Bell, whose excellent book *In Search of Tusitala* (1994) is part travelogue, part biography. These have all shed light in their different ways and have helped sustain my journey through the complexities of Stevenson's character. Finally, a compilation of interviews and recollections edited by R. C. Terry (1996) presents Stevenson through the eyes of fifty witnesses—relatives, friends, and strangers. This was a lucky find, enabling me to see the artist more clearly.

My editors, Ivan R. Dee in Chicago and Carol O'Brien in London, have urged me on to good effect, and my agent Elizabeth Fairbairn has been her usual invaluable self. My thanks to them for their support.

Chronology

1850   November 13: Stevenson born in Edinburgh.

1867   November: enters Edinburgh University.

1868   July–September: visits Anstruther and Wick as trainee-engineer.

1869   Elected to the Speculative Society.

1871   April: changes from engineering to law studies.

1873   July: meets Mrs. Sitwell and Sidney Colvin after clash with father.

1874   April: in Menton, France, for his health. Elected to Savile Club in June. Resumes law studies in November.

1875   February: meets W. E. Henley at Edinburgh Infirmary. Admitted to Scottish bar in July. Summer in France with Bob Stevenson. Meets Mrs. Fanny Vandegrift Osbourne.

1876   Autumn canoe trip with Walter Simpson in Europe.

1877   At Grez in summer. Paris in September with Fanny Osbourne.

1878   August: Fanny returns to America. Walking tour in the Cévennes, September–October. Edinburgh: *Picturesque Notes* published in December.

1879   Writes *Deacon Brodie*. Publishes *Travels with a Donkey* in June. Sails for America in August. Reunion in California with Fanny and family.

1880   May: Married to Fanny in San Francisco. Returns to England with wife and stepson. Reconciled with parents. Winter of 1880–1881 in Davos, Switzerland.

1881   April: publishes *Virginibus Puerisque*. In Scotland begins *Treasure Island*. To Davos again in October until following April.

1882   March: publishes *Familiar Studies*. In Scotland June–August. Retreats to South of France for his health, settles near Marseilles with Fanny.

1883   Moves in March to chalet "La Solitude," Hyères. *Treasure Island* published in December.

1884   Fears of cholera cause Stevenson and Fanny to return to England. They set up home in Bournemouth.

1885   *A Child's Garden of Verses* published in March. Fanny acquires the house Skerryvore.

1886   *Dr. Jekyll and Mr. Hyde* published in January. July: publication of *Kidnapped*.

1887   Thomas Stevenson dies. Louis, his mother, Fanny, and Lloyd sail for New York. *Memories and Portraits* and *The Merry Men* published.

1888   Sails from San Francisco on first South Seas voyage. Quarrel with Henley.

1889   *Master of Ballantrae* published in September. Buys Vailima in Samoa.

1890   To Sydney, Australia, in February. Cruise to Gilberts, Marshalls, and other islands. Return to Australia. Settles in Samoa, October.

1893   Outbreak of war in Samoa. *Catriona* (sequel to *Kidnapped*) published.

1894   *The Ebb-Tide* published in September. Dies on December 3, at Vailima, leaving *Weir of Hermiston* unfinished.

Works by
Robert Louis Stevenson

An Inland Voyage, 1878
Edinburgh: Picturesque Notes, 1879
Travels with a Donkey, 1879
Deacon Brodie, with W. E. Henley, 1880, revised edition, 1888
Virginibus Puerisque, 1881
Familiar Studies of Men and Books, 1882
New Arabian Nights, 1882
The Silverado Squatters, 1883
Treasure Island, 1883
Admiral Guinea, with W. E. Henley, 1884
Beau Austin, with W. E. Henley, 1884
Prince Otto, 1885
A Child's Garden of Verses, 1885
More New Arabian Nights: The Dynamiter, with Fanny Vandegrift Stevenson,
    1885
Macaire, with W. E. Henley, 1885
The Strange Case of Dr. Jekyll and Mr. Hyde, 1886
Kidnapped, 1886
The Merry Men, and other tales and fables, 1887
Memories and Portraits, 1887
Underwoods, 1887

Memoir of Fleeming Jenkin, 1887
The Black Arrow, 1888
The Misadventures of John Nicholson, 1888
The Wrong Box, with Lloyd Osbourne, 1889
Ballads, 1890
Across the Plains, 1892
The Wrecker, 1892
A Footnote to History, 1892
Island Nights' Entertainments, 1893
Catriona, 1893
The Ebb-Tide, 1894
Vailima Letters, 1895
The Amateur Emigrant, 1895
Weir of Hermiston, 1896
In the South Seas, 1896
St. Ives, 1897
Letters to His Family and Friends, edited by Sidney Colvin, 1899

Selected Bibliography

BOOKS ABOUT R.L.S. AND STUDIES OF HIS WORK

Richard Aldington, *Portrait of a Rebel: Robert Louis Stevenson*. London, 1957.
Graham Balfour, *The Life of Robert Louis Stevenson*. London, 1901.
Bella Bathurst, *The Lighthouse Stevensons*. London, 1999.
Ian Bell, *Robert Louis Stevenson: Dreams of Exile*. Edinburgh, 1992.
Gavin Bell, *In Search of Tusitala*. London, 1994.
Adelaide Boodle, *R.L.S. and His Sine Qua Non*. London, 1926.
Jenni Calder, *R.L.S.: A Life Study*. London, 1980.
G. K. Chesterton, *Robert Louis Stevenson*. London, 1947.
Lettice Cooper, *Robert Louis Stevenson*. London, 1947.
David Daiches, *Robert Louis Stevenson*. London, 1947.
Malcolm Elwin, *The Strange Case of Robert Louis Stevenson*. London, 1950.
Isobel Osbourne Strong Field, *Memories of Vailima*. New York, 1902.
J. C. Furnass, *Voyage to Windward*. London, 1952.
Clayton Hamilton, *On the Trail of Stevenson*. London, 1915.
George Hellman, *The True Stevenson*. Boston, 1925.
Frank McLynn, *Robert Louis Stevenson*, London, 1993.
Margaret Mackay, *The Violent Friend*. New York, 1968.
Harry J. Moors, *With Stevenson in Samoa*. London, 1910.
Lloyd Osbourne, *An Intimate Portrait of RLS*. New York, 1924.
James Pope-Hennessy, *Robert Louis Stevenson*. London, 1974.
Nellie Vandegrift Sanchez, *The Life of Mrs. Robert Louis Stevenson*. London,
    1920.

Janet Adam Smith, *Henry James and Robert Louis Stevenson*. London, 1948.

Mrs. Robert Louis Stevenson, *The Cruise of the "Janet Nichol."* London, 1915.

Roger G. Swearingen, ed., *The Prose Writings of Robert Louis Stevenson*. London, 1980.

Frank Swinnerton, *Robert Louis Stevenson: A Critical Study*. London, 1914.

R. C. Terry, ed., *Robert Louis Stevenson: Interviews and Recollections*. London, 1996.

BOOKS OF GENERAL REFERENCE

Marcus Aurelius, *Meditations,* trans. Robin Hard. London, 1997.

Horatio F. Brown, *John Addington Symonds*. London, 1903.

Horatio F. Brown, *Letters and Papers of John Addington Symonds*. London, 1923.

G. K. Chesterton, *The Victorian Age in Literature*. London, 1925.

John Connell, *W. E. Henley*. London, 1949.

Alison Cunningham, *Cummy's Diary*, ed. Robert T. Skinner. London, 1926.

Alex de Jonge, *Dostoevsky and the Age of Intensity*. London, 1975.

Leon Edel, ed., *Selected Letters of Henry James*. London, 1988.

Leon Edel, ed., *Complete Notebooks of Henry James*. London, 1987.

Malcolm Elwin, *Old Gods Falling*. London, 1939.

L. Fiedler, *No! In Thunder*. London, 1963.

Martin Green, *Dreams of Adventure, Dreams of Empire*. London, 1980.

John Herdman, *The Double in Nineteenth Century Fiction*. Edinburgh and London, 1990.

Richard Holmes, *Footsteps: Adventures of a Romantic Biographer*. London, 1985.

R. D. S. Jack, *The Road to Never Land*. Aberdeen, 1991.

Andrew Lang, *Adventures Among Books*. London, 1905.

Alexandra Lapierre, *Fanny Stevenson*. London, 1996.

D. H. Lawrence, *Studies in Classic American Literature*. London, 1924.

Jack London, *The Cruise of the Snark*. London, 1911.

E. V. Lucas, *The Colvins and Their Friends*. London, 1928.

Moray McLaren, *Stevenson and Edinburgh*. London, 1950.

Craig Mair, *A Star for Seamen: The Stevenson Family of Engineers*. London, 1978.

Herman Melville, *Typee*. Northwestern-Newberry Edition, 1968.

Karl Miller, *Doubles*. London, 1985.

John Pemble, *The Mediterranean Passion*. Oxford, 1987.

Llewllyn Powyes, *Swiss Essays*. London, 1947.

Nicholas Rankin, *Dead Man's Chest*. London, 1987.

G. B. Stern, *He Wrote Treasure Island*. London, 1954.

Irving Stone, *Sailor on Horseback: The Story of Jack London*. London, 1938.

John Addington Symonds, *Recollections of a Happy Life*. London, 1892.

John Addington Symonds, *Our Life in the Swiss Highlands*. London, 1907.

Index

A NOTE ON THE AUTHOR

Philip Callow was born in Birmingham, England, and studied engineering and the teaching of English before he turned to writing. He has since published fourteen novels, several collections of short stories and poems, a volume of autobiography, and five biographies—*Chekhov: The Hidden Ground*; *Lost Earth: A Life of Cézanne*; *From Noon to Starry Night: A Life of Walt Whitman*; *Vincent Van Gogh: A Life*; and *Son and Lover: The Young D. H. Lawrence*—all of which have received critical acclaim. He lives and writes in Evesham, England.